Abraham

Called by God

WITNESS LEE

Living Stream Ministry
Anaheim, California

June 1998

ISBN 0-7363-0359-6

Published by

Living Stream Ministry
1853 W. Ball Road, Anaheim, CA 92804 U.S.A.
P. O. Box 2121, Anaheim, CA 92814 U.S.A.

Printed in the United States of America

98 99 00 01 02 03 / 9 8 7 6 5 4 3 2 1

CONTENTS

PREFACE

Abraham—Called by God is composed of messages taken from *Life-study of Genesis,* a detailed study of the book of Genesis that emphasizes the experience of Christ as life for the fulfillment of the eternal purpose of God to have a corporate expression of Himself. The messages in this volume are devoted primarily to the experience of Abraham, the one called by God to become the father of the called race. Having been called by God, Abraham was trained to live by faith in God as the unique source. Living the life of an altar and a tent, Abraham eventually came to know grace for the fulfillment of God's purpose and to live in fellowship with God. Because the experience of Isaac is, to a great extent, interwoven with that of Abraham and because many of the aspects of Isaac's life are covered in the messages on Abraham, this volume includes messages that concentrate on the spiritual significance of Isaac, who rested in and enjoyed the riches bestowed on him by Abraham. May all the children of God, all the called ones, walk in the steps of the faith of our father Abraham (Rom. 4:12).

1

THE SIGNIFICANCE OF
GOD'S CALLING

Now the Lord had said unto Abram, Get thee out of thy country,
and from thy kindred, and from thy father's house,
unto a land that I will show thee: and I will make of thee
a great nation, and I will bless thee,
and make thy name great; and thou shalt be a blessing: and
I will bless them that bless thee, and curse him that curseth thee:
and in thee shall all families of the earth be blessed.
Genesis 12:1-3

The Scripture, foreseeing that God would justify the Gentiles
out of faith, announced the gospel beforehand to Abraham:
"In you shall all the nations be blessed."
Galatians 3:8

INTRODUCTION

In this chapter we come to the most wonderful section of the book
of Genesis, the section on God's calling (11:10—50:26). Genesis, a
book of fifty chapters, is divided into three sections. The first section
(1:1—2:25) covers God's creation, the second (3:1—11:9) covers
the serpent's corruption of mankind, and the third covers Jehovah's
calling. Each of these sections begins with a special phrase. The

first section begins with the words, "In the beginning God." The second section begins with the phrase, "Now the serpent." The third section begins with the words, "Now Jehovah" (12:1, Heb.). In these three sections we see three titles—God, the serpent, and Jehovah. These titles mean a great deal to us. After God created, the serpent crept in to corrupt, and then Jehovah came in to call. So the book of Genesis mainly relates these three major things.

According to the revelation of the Bible, Elohim, the Hebrew word for God in 1:1, is a title that mainly relates to God's creation. The title of Jehovah, however, is especially concerned with God's relationship to man in the matter of life. Jehovah is part, a main element, of the wonderful name of Jesus, for Jesus means "Jehovah the Saviour." Since the name Jesus includes Jehovah, we may say that Jesus is the New Testament Jehovah and that Jehovah was the Old Testament Jesus.

In these three sections of Genesis we see that God created, the serpent, Satan, corrupted, and Jehovah called. Thus, in these sections we have creation, corruption, and calling. Which of these do you love the most? I love God's calling. We are not only the created ones but also the called ones.

GOD'S CREATION, REVEALING GOD'S PURPOSE AND PROCEDURE   ✦
God's creation unveils His eternal purpose. God's eternal purpose is that man express Him with His image and represent Him with His dominion. We, the human race, are destined to express and represent God. This is clearly revealed in the first chapter of Genesis. In the second chapter we see God's procedure to fulfill this divine purpose. His procedure is by the divine life. God must work Himself into us as our life that we might be able to fulfill His eternal purpose. Thus, in chapter one we see God's purpose and in chapter two God's procedure for the fulfillment of this purpose.

THE SERPENT'S CORRUPTION, CAUSING MAN'S FALL   ✦   In the second section (3:1—11:9) we see that the serpent, Satan, crept in to cause man's fall. The serpent corrupted man and caused him to fall to the uttermost. Man fell lower and lower until it was impossible for him to fall any further. At that time Satan was happy and could celebrate his success. The whole human race was in rebellion against God. In a sense, God had been driven out from the earth.

THE LORD'S (JEHOVAH'S) CALLING, FULFILLING GOD'S PURPOSE BY GOD'S PROCEDURE   ✦   Although Satan, working through fallen man, had apparently driven God out from the earth, God is sovereign and cannot be defeated or frustrated by any kind of attack. All of Satan's work simply affords Him an excellent opportunity to display His wisdom. Although sometimes I was sorry that I was a fallen person, most of the time I rejoiced, because I had been redeemed, regenerated, and regained. Because of the fall, our relationship with God the Father is sweeter and more meaningful than it would have been without the fall. If you will spend some time to review your life, I believe you will weep, not in sorrow, but in sweet remembrance of God's wise and gracious work. When we enter into eternity, we shall exercise our spirit and recall our time on earth, and the memory of that time will be sweet, tasteful, and meaningful. God is wise. He allowed the serpent to come in. God watched the serpent and seemed to say, "Little serpent, what are you doing? Go ahead and do more. The more you do, the more opportunity I have to manifest My wisdom. Little serpent, do your best. Go on until you are satisfied and can do nothing more." Eventually, Satan had to say, "I have done all that I can do. I have exhausted myself in causing mankind to fall lower and lower. I cannot make him fall any further. This is all I can do. I am finished." When this point was reached, God came in, not as Elohim, but as Jehovah, the seed that was promised in 3:15. Nothing can frustrate God, defeat Him, or force Him to forsake His eternal purpose. He will complete what He has determined to perform. Nothing can change Him. Any interruption simply affords Him the opportunity to express more of His wise counsel.

If God had not been so wise, the book of Genesis would have been very short. But for God to display His wisdom, it has fifty chapters. The last thirty-nine and a half chapters are an abstract of the whole New Testament. Do you know how the New Testament begins? It begins with the words, "The book of the generation of Jesus Christ Son of David, Son of Abraham" (Matt. 1:1). According to the genealogy in Matthew, the gospel begins with Abraham. The New Testament begins with the genealogy of Abraham. This corresponds with Genesis 12. Nearly everything found in the New Testament is sown as a seed in Genesis. So the thirty-nine and a half chapters that compose the third section of Genesis are a brief of the entire New Testament.

As we have pointed out on other occasions, the New Testament begins with the preaching of the gospel of the kingdom. When Jehovah came in to call Abraham in Genesis 12, He gave him a promise, and that promise was the preaching of the gospel. Galatians 3:8 proves this: "The Scripture, foreseeing that God would justify the nations by faith, preached the gospel beforehand to Abraham: In you all the nations shall be blessed." The first preaching of the gospel is not in Matthew but in Genesis 12. In the preaching of the gospel to Abraham, the main item is the nation. The nation is the kingdom. In the next message we shall see that God promised to make Abraham a great nation and that this nation is the kingdom of God including Israel as God's kingdom in the Old Testament, the church as God's kingdom in the New Testament, the millennial kingdom in the coming age, and also the new heaven and the new earth. This is the kingdom and this is the gospel of the kingdom.

Galatians 3:14 speaks of the blessing of Abraham: "That the blessing of Abraham might come to the nations in Jesus Christ, that we might receive the promise of the Spirit through faith." What is the blessing? It is the Spirit. Who is the Spirit? The Spirit is Jesus (2 Cor. 3:17). The Spirit is Jesus, Jesus is Jehovah, and Jehovah is God. Therefore, this blessing is just God Himself. In God's preaching of His gospel to Abraham, He promised the called ones that He would give Himself to them as a blessing. This blessing is Jehovah Himself. Jehovah is Jesus, and Jesus is the Spirit whom we have received through faith in Christ. This is the gospel. Remember, Genesis is a book giving us an abstract of the whole New Testament. How we must worship God for His sovereign wisdom!

This long section of Genesis covers the lives of only three persons—Abraham, Isaac, and Jacob. When God revealed Himself to Moses, He said, "I am the God of thy father, the God of Abraham, the God of Isaac, and the God of Jacob" (Exo. 3:6). As we shall see later on, this is clearly related to the Triune God. The New Testament is simply an autobiography of the Triune God—of the Father in Abraham, the Son in Isaac, and the Spirit in Jacob. Perhaps some will wonder about Joseph. As we shall see, Joseph does not stand alone; he is a part of Jacob. The entire story of the called ones in the book of Genesis is a story of these three persons, and the whole New Testament is a record of the divine Trinity, the Father, the Son, and the Spirit, experienced by all the New Testament believers.

THE SIGNIFICANCE OF GOD'S CALLING

THE NEW BEGINNING OF GOD   ✦   Now we need to consider the significance, the meaning, of God's calling. Firstly, God's calling was a new beginning. When God created man, there was a beginning. But that man was corrupted and spoiled. The man whom God created for Himself fell and forsook Him. So God came in to call man that He might have a new beginning with the fallen man. Even with us, God's calling was a new beginning. We all have had a new beginning. I thank God that after living over nineteen years in the old creation, I received a new beginning before I was twenty. God's calling is a new beginning made by God Himself. God would not give up man. Rather, He came in to call man that He might have a new beginning.

The man whom God called was Abraham. When God created Adam, He did not create a single man but a corporate man. When God called Abraham, in a sense He called a corporate man, but, in another sense, He called a single person. Although all of the descendants of Adam were created in Adam, we cannot say that all the descendants of Abraham were called in Abraham. Although it appears so outwardly, actually this is not the case, for Romans 9:7-8 says that not all the seed of Abraham are the children of God. Simply because a person is a Jew by birth does not mean that he has had a new beginning with God. Even those who are Jews by birth need a new beginning. Whether we are Jews or Gentiles, as long as we have had a new beginning by faith in Christ, we are Abraham's seed (Gal. 3:7). Most of us are not Jewish, but we are all the seed of Abraham through faith in Christ. We are the seed of Abraham because we have had a new beginning. At the time of His calling of Abraham, God began to have a new beginning, and now we all have entered into this new beginning through faith. Whenever you speak about God's calling, you must realize that His calling means a new beginning. I can never forget that afternoon in 1925 when I was called by God. Immediately I had a new beginning and my whole life, being, and concepts were changed. This is God's calling.

THE TRANSFER OF RACE   ✦   In His calling, God's new beginning with man is a transfer of race. God's calling of Abraham meant that He had given up the race of Adam and had chosen Abraham with his descendants as the new race to be His people for the fulfilling of His eternal purpose. This was a transfer of race, a transfer from the created Adamic race to the called Abrahamic race (12:2-3; Gal. 3:7-9, 14; Rom. 4:16-17). When we say that God's calling is a new beginning, we must understand that this new beginning is a transfer of race. We all have been transferred from the old created race to the new called race. Although we were born in a particular race, at the time of our calling we were transferred into another race, the new race of the called ones.

THE TRANSFER OF LIFE   ✦   The transfer of race in God's calling is actually the transfer of life. Although you can boldly declare that you have undergone the transfer of race, can you say that you have experienced the transfer of life? Although we have had the transfer of race, we are still in the process of the transfer of life. I dare not say that I have had a full transfer of life. Neither can I say that I have had no transfer of life. I have had some transfer of life, but this process has not yet been completed. We all are in the process of the transfer of life.

We need an inner transfer of life. Even though we have had the transfer of race, the life within us must be transferred. If we do not have this inner transfer of life, we shall remain the same as the fallen race. If we are simply removed from one position to another, we actually remain the same in life. The mere transfer of position cannot fulfill God's purpose in His calling of us. There must also be a transfer of life.

Since the transfer of life is from the life of Adam to the life of Christ, it is a transfer from the life of the old creation to the life of the new creation. Due to the fall of man, all of God's original creation became old and is no longer able to fulfill God's purpose. So God needs a new creation, a creation with a life stronger and much better than the created life of Adam. This stronger life is the uncreated life of God, the life of Christ. The transfer of life in God's calling is from the fallen life of the old creation to this stronger and better life of the new creation.

AS SEEN IN THE CALLED ONES   ✦   The significance of God's calling is clearly seen in God's called ones. In Abraham, in Isaac, in Jacob, and in the New Testament believers we can see the new beginning of God, the transfer of race, and the transfer of life. Their lives can be considered as clear pictures of the significance of God's calling.

IN ABRAHAM

The picture that is portrayed in Abraham is very clear. He had the new beginning, the transfer of race, and the transfer of life, which was a great problem to both him and God. Although the new beginning and the transfer of race in him transpired immediately at the time that he was called, the transfer of life in him took many years. It took several decades for him to have the transfer of life, and even then it was not fully completed.

FIRSTLY RELYING UPON ELIEZER   ✦   When God called Abraham out of the corrupted land, Abraham had no sons, no successors. God was sovereign. Before Abraham had undergone the transfer of race, God did not allow him to have a son. Because Abraham was childless, he relied upon Eliezer, his household servant, to be the possessor of his house, saying to the Lord, "Lord God, what wilt thou give me, seeing I go childless, and the son of possession of my house is this Eliezer of Damascus? And Abram said, Behold, to me thou hast given no seed: and, lo, a son of my house is mine heir" (15:2-3, Heb.). Abraham called Eliezer the son of possession of his house and thought that he would be his heir. Abraham was very natural, just as we are today. Although he received the promise, he interpreted it in a natural way. God rejected Eliezer, saying to Abraham, "This shall not be thine heir; but he that shall come forth out of thine own bowels shall be thine heir" (15:4). God was telling Abraham that Eliezer would not be the one to inherit the promise that He had given to him. A seed out of Abraham himself, born of Sarah, would be Abraham's heir.

THEN BEGETTING ISHMAEL BY THE STRENGTH OF HIS FLESH   ✦
After God had rejected Eliezer as the heir, Abraham, at the suggestion of Sarah that he have a son by Hagar, exercised the strength of his flesh to fulfill God's promise. He brought forth Ishmael. The wife was the one who made the proposal and eventually she was the one who was troubled by the result of her proposal. It was sovereign that Sarah was troubled in this way. On the one hand, Sarah's proposal that Abraham have a son by Hagar was of the flesh. On the other hand, her command that Ishmael be driven out was according to God's sovereignty. She told Abraham that he had to drive out Ishmael, the one who was born of the bondwoman (21:9-10). This command was very grievous to Abraham; he was deeply troubled by it. Then God

intervened and said to Abraham, "Let it not be grievous in thy sight because of the lad, and because of thy bondwoman; in all that Sarah has said unto thee, hearken unto her voice; for in Isaac shall thy seed be called" (21:12). This meant that God told Abraham to let Ishmael go, for he was not the one who was to inherit the promise that God had given Abraham. Isaac was to be his heir. We all must realize that in God's calling nothing of our natural life can be prevailing. To only have the transfer of race is not adequate. We need a complete transfer of life.

HIS NAME BEING CHANGED AND HIS FLESH BEING CIRCUMCISED   ◆
Firstly, God promised Abraham that he would have seed to inherit the promised land (12:7; 13:15-16). Later, when God told Abraham that Eliezer would not be his heir and that only the one born of himself would be his heir, God strongly confirmed His promise that Abraham would have seed of himself (15:2-5). After this, Abraham attempted to fulfill God's promise by using his fleshly strength to produce Ishmael. As a result, God came in, saying, "I am the Almighty God; walk before me, and be thou perfect" (17:1). God seemed to be saying to Abraham, "What you have done in begetting Ishmael is not perfect before Me. Now I must transform you. Your name shall be changed from Abram, which means an exalted father, to Abraham, which means the father of a great multitude (17:5). For this, you must be circumcised (17:10-14) that your fleshly strength may be cut off, that I may come to fulfill My promise, and that you may be exceeding fruitful." Here God promised Abraham to make him a great father, the father of a great multitude. This indicated that Abraham would be the father not only of his descendants according to the flesh, but also of the New Testament believers according to faith (Rom. 4:16-17). We Christians have all become Abraham's seed by faith in Christ. Although we were born of the Adamic race, we have been reborn into the Abrahamic race.

BRINGING FORTH ISAAC BY THE STRENGTH OF GOD'S GRACE   ◆   At the time when God changed Abraham's name and commanded him to be circumcised, God said to him in 17:21,...Isaac, which Sarah shall bare unto thee at this set time in the next year." Here we see that God made an appointment, setting up a time when Isaac would be born. This is referred to in 18:14 when the Lord said, "At the time appointed I will return unto thee, at the time of life, and Sarah shall

have a son" (Heb.). The appointed time, the time set for the birth of
Isaac was "the time of life." This term, "the time of life," is very
meaningful. The word life in this phrase is the same Hebrew word
that is used for the tree of life in 2:9. The time when Isaac would be
born was "the time of life." This happened after Abraham was circumcised. This indicates that "the time of life" when Christ will be
life to us will come after our natural strength has been dealt with.

After the death of the strength of his flesh   ✦   Before Isaac
was born, Abraham and Sarah were completely deadened. Sarah's
womb was deadened, and Abraham's body was considered dead
(Rom. 4:18-19). What he had—Eliezer—and what he intended to
keep—Ishmael—were all rejected, and his natural ability was terminated. Then what could he do? Perhaps Abraham and Sarah had some
unhappy fellowship. Abraham might have said to his wife, "Dear,
look at yourself. Your function has been deadened." Sarah might have
said to Abraham, "Dear, look at yourself. How old!" Both of them
were in a deadened condition. Sarah might have said, "Eliezer is
good, but God has rejected him." Abraham might have replied, "Ishmael is better, but God would not accept him either. Since Eliezer has
been eliminated and Ishmael has been rejected, that leaves you and
me in such a poor situation. What shall we do?" But when "the time
of life" came, Isaac was born of these two dead ones, as if it was by
the power of resurrection. The time of that birth was "the time of
life." Spiritually speaking, the birth of Isaac was a birth of life.

By Jehovah's visitation   ✦   The birth of Isaac was by Jehovah's
visitation, by the Lord's coming (18:14). Isaac's birth was not merely
a human birth. In that birth there was the coming of Jehovah, for the
Lord had said that at the appointed time, He would return and Isaac
would be born and that that time would be "the time of life." When
Abraham's natural strength was ended, Jehovah came to bring in
Isaac's birth at "the time of life." That was the transfer of life. Everything of the natural life must go. Even the ability to beget a son must
be terminated. Nothing of our natural life or of our self has any share
in God's economy. Everything natural must be terminated until we
are finished, dead, and have become nothing. Then, when we have
come to the end, Jehovah will come in. This coming in of Jehovah
means life. This is "Isaac." Hence, the birth of Isaac is the coming of

Jehovah. This is life, this is the new beginning, and this is the transfer of life. This is the significance of God's calling.

It is very good to realize that we all have been called and have had a new beginning and the transfer of race. But we should all agree that we are still in the process of the transfer of life. Probably, some of us still cling to Eliezer, some want to hold on to Ishmael, and some have been fully disappointed. However, others among us have come to "the time of life." In their case, "Isaac" has been born. Jehovah's coming, Jehovah's visit, has transpired with some of us. This is the transfer of life. We all need such a transfer.

We need to forget the superficial and natural teachings, such as improving and behaving ourselves. It is not a matter of behavior but of a life transfer. We all must be transferred not only in race but also in life.

When Abraham was called out of the corrupted land, he had no son. He became old and still did not have a son. Therefore, he put his trust in Eliezer, the son of possession. God rejected Eliezer. Then Abraham exercised the strength of his flesh to produce Ishmael. Abraham loved Ishmael and wanted to keep him, but God would not accept him. The promised son had to be born of Jehovah's coming in, of the strength of God's grace at the appointed time. When the appointed time arrived, Jehovah came to Sarah and Isaac came forth. In a sense, Jehovah came into Sarah and Isaac came out of her. That was "the time of life." It was altogether a transfer of life.

IN ISAAC

In a sense, in Isaac the transfer of life was accomplished but it was not fully completed. We know this by the fact that Isaac still begat Esau whom God hated (Rom. 9:13). This means that within Isaac the natural life still remained. Thus, we may say that in Isaac the transfer of life was not completed thoroughly. It was completed in Jacob.

IN JACOB

FIRSTLY BEING THE SUPPLANTER JACOB   ✦   At first, Jacob was a supplanter. His name means a supplanter. To supplant means to take the place of another, or to get something, through subtle means. Jacob was one who stole in a secret way. For instance, he stole from his uncle, Laban. Laban thought that Jacob was helping him with his flocks, but while Jacob was helping Laban, he made a flock for himself. This is an example of Jacob's supplanting. At the first, Jacob certainly did not have the transfer of life.

TRANSFORMED INTO ISRAEL, THE PRINCE OF GOD ✦ God had a way to deal with Jacob. He transformed Jacob, the supplanter, into a prince of God. Although it took God a long time to accomplish this, at a certain time He told Jacob that his name was being changed from Jacob to Israel (32:27-28). Thereafter, he was called Israel. God did the same thing to Jacob that He had done to Abraham: He changed his name and his strength. When God came in to deal with Jacob, Jacob was truly a supplanter. He even wrestled with God. He was so strong in a natural way that even God found it difficult to subdue him. We should not laugh at Jacob. We are the same as he was. We are so strong that even God finds it difficult to subdue us. When God comes to deal with us, we wrestle with Him. Although it is difficult for God to subdue us, eventually we shall be subdued by Him. Jacob's wrestling forced God to touch his thigh, to touch the strongest part of his being. After that happened, he was lame. From that day onward, his supplanting was over. The supplanter had become a prince of God. Throughout the remainder of his days he did not steal again. His supplanting hands became blessing hands. He no longer supplanted; he only blessed. He stretched out his hands to bless whomever came to him. He even blessed Pharaoh, the greatest king on earth at that time (47:7, 10). The supplanter became a blesser. This is the prince of God. Here we have the full transfer of race with the complete transfer of life. This is God's calling. God's calling began at Genesis 12:1 and will continue until the coming of the New Jerusalem. All the supplanters will be terminated and become the princes of God. The New Jerusalem will come in, not only as a transfer of race, but also as a transfer of life.

IN THE BELIEVERS

BEGINNING WITH REGENERATION ✦ In principle, the experience is the same with the believers today. With the believers, this transfer of life begins with regeneration (John 3:3, 5). After being regenerated, we are in the process of the transfer of life.

ACCOMPLISHED BY THE EXPERIENCE OF SPIRITUAL CIRCUMCISION   ✦
With the believers, the transfer of life is accomplished by the experience of circumcision, by the putting off of the flesh (Col. 2:11; Gal.
5:24). Today God is circumcising us, and this circumcision lasts
quite a long time. I believe that many among us are still under God's
circumcising hand. You may still cling to your fleshly strength or to
your natural man. This requires God to come in and cut, or circumcise, that part of you. Hence, we all are in the process of being
circumcised. In other words, we are in the process of transformation.

COMPLETED AT THE REDEMPTION AND TRANSFIGURATION OF OUR
BODY   ✦   The transfer of life will be fully completed at the time
of the Lord's coming back. At that time our body will be fully
redeemed and transfigured (Rom. 8:23; Phil. 3:21). Then we shall be
the called ones, not only in the transfer of race, but also in the complete transfer of life. At that time we shall enjoy all of the blessings
that God promised to our father Abraham. This is God's calling.
God's calling is not for Abraham's natural descendants. God's calling
is for the people who follow Abraham to exercise the obtained faith,
to live by and in God, and to experience the transfer of life by the
working of God. As a result of this process, we shall be altogether
another people, a people of God's calling. Then we shall enjoy all the
blessings of God's promise. All that God promised to Abraham will
be the blessings of the New Testament gospel in which we all shall
participate through faith in Christ.   ✖

2

THE BACKGROUND AND ORIGIN OF GOD'S CALLING AND THE EXPERIENCE OF THE CALLED

And Joshua said to all the people, Thus says Jehovah, the God of Israel,
Your fathers dwelt across the River long ago,
Terah, the father of Abraham and the father of Nahor;
and they served other gods.

Joshua 24:2

Moreover he said,
I am the God of thy father, the God of Abraham,
the God of Isaac, and the God of Jacob.

Exodus 3:6

Although Genesis is a long book, it has only three sections: God's creation (1:1—2:25), the serpent's corruption (3:1—11:9), and Jehovah's calling (11:10—50:26). In the last message we saw the significance of God's calling. God's calling means the new beginning of God, the transfer of race, and the transfer of life. On our side,

God's calling is a transfer of race and life, but on God's side it is a new beginning. God had a new beginning in His creation of man, but that man became corrupted. So God came in to have another beginning when He called Abraham. This new beginning is actually the transfer from the race of Adam to the race of Abraham, a transfer from the created race to the called race. God's calling means that we are called out of the original, created race into the present, called race. This transfer of race is not merely positional but also dispositional, for it is actually a transfer of life.

Abraham experienced both a positional and dispositional transfer. He was transferred from the old land of Chaldea to the good land of Canaan. That was a positional transfer. However, God worked upon him inwardly as well as outwardly. At a certain time, God came in and told him that his name had to be changed (17:5). According to the Bible, the changing of name always indicates the changing in life. When Abraham's name was changed, it meant that his disposition, his life, was being changed. It seems that God was telling Abraham, "You are still in your old man. You are too much in your natural life. Although you have been called out of the old race, the nature and life of the old race still remain in you, and you still live by that life. It is necessary for Me to deal with you. I must cut off that life." This cutting off of the old life was signified by circumcision. Abraham's circumcision transpired at the same time that God changed his name. Outwardly, his name was changed, and inwardly, his disposition, his nature, and his life were dealt with. After the strength of Abraham's natural life had been cut off, Isaac was born at "the time of life." In a very real sense, Isaac was not born of Abraham's natural strength; he was born of God's coming, for God had said, "At the time appointed I will return unto thee, at the time of life, and Sarah shall have a son" (18:14, Heb.). The coming of the Lord was the birth of Isaac. This means that Isaac was not produced out of Abraham's natural strength but out of a life dealt with by God. We see by this that Abraham was not only transferred positionally but also dispositionally.

Apparently Isaac did not need a transfer of life. Nevertheless, Esau, the first of the twins born to Isaac and Rebekah, was very natural. God will never accept anything that is natural. Since the first of Isaac's sons was so natural, God chose the second. The firstborn signifies the natural life. For this reason, God destroyed the lives of all the firstborn in Egypt during the night of the Passover. The second, on the contrary, signifies the transferred life. Because Jacob was the second, he was chosen.

Although Jacob had been chosen, his nature was not transferred. So, at a certain time, God came in and touched Jacob's natural strength. At that time his name was changed from Jacob, a supplanter, to Israel, a prince of God. From then on, Jacob was lame. His lameness was a sign that he had been touched by God, that his natural strength had been dealt with, and that he had become a prince of God. This is the true meaning of God's calling.

Have you been called? If you say that you have been called, then you must come out of Chaldea, Babel, the old race, and your natural life. You must get out of your natural life and get your natural life out of you. In God's calling there is the need of the new beginning, the transfer of race, and the transfer of life. We all need to be transferred. In all the years that I have been here with the saints, I have been watching the process of this transfer. I have been happy to see so many saints undergoing the transfer of life. Although at times the process of this transfer is not pleasant, after a while you can see in the saints the real transfer of life. This is the meaning of God's calling.

THE BACKGROUND OF GOD'S CALLING—BABEL

FORSAKING GOD   ✦   Now in this message we need to see the experience of the called ones. But before we come to this, we need to consider the background and origin of God's calling.

When God appeared to Abraham, he was in the darkest background. His background was exceedingly strong. The first aspect of this background was that man had forsaken God. Man's forsaking of God was signified by his building a city. We saw this in the case of Cain in chapter four. Man built a city because he had lost God as his protection. Since man no longer had God as his safeguard, he built a city to protect himself. So the building of the city was the sign that man had forsaken God. Man seemed to be saying, "Let God go. I will build a city to protect myself." The building of the city was the declaration that man had forsaken God.

EXALTING MAN   ✦   Not only did man forsake God, but he built a tower to exalt himself. The tower was a sign of man's self-exaltation.

When man forsakes God, automatically he exalts himself. Whenever man builds a city he will also build a tower to make a name for himself.

DENYING THE RIGHT OF GOD   ✦   Furthermore, at Babel man also denied God's right over His creation. Both man and the earth were God's creation. Nevertheless, man would not recognize God's right but instead established the nations. The establishing of nations signified that man had denied God's right and authority. As we have seen, after the flood God gave man the authority to rule others, but Satan caused man to abuse this God-given authority to form nations that man may have his own dominion, denying God's right and authority over man.

SERVING IDOLS   ✦   Finally, Joshua 24:2 shows us that at Babel man turned from God to idols, to other gods. Behind all the idols are demons. Whenever a man worships an idol, he worships demons. Apparently he is worshipping idols; actually he is worshipping demons.

   As the background of God's calling we have the city, the tower, the nations, and the demons. Man had forsaken God, had exalted himself, had denied God's right and authority, and had turned from God to serve idols. Do you believe that the situation is any better today? I do not believe it. It is as bad today as it was then. The situation is exactly the same.

THE ORIGIN OF GOD'S CALLING—GOD

   Who originated this calling? Abraham did not originate it. Although he was the father of the called race, the calling was not initiated by him. I believe that Abraham was the same as we are today. He never dreamed of being called by God. Suddenly, while he and his relatives were there in Chaldea worshipping other gods (Josh. 24:2), God appeared to him. God was the originator of this calling.

THE APPEARING OF GOD   ✦   Although God's calling is carried out in time, something prior to that—God's selection—took place in eternity past. God selected Abraham in eternity past. After that, also in eternity past, God predestinated, premarked, Abraham. Before Abraham was born, even before the foundation of the world when nothing but God Himself was in existence, God chose Abraham and predestinated him. One day, in time, while Abraham was worshipping other gods, having no forethought that he was to be called by God, God visited him. God just came in as the very God of glory. Abraham was surprised. The God of glory not only came to Abraham, but He appeared to him.

Because Abraham's background was so dark, God had to appear to him in a strong way. Many of us have also experienced such a strong calling of God. I can testify that one day, when I was an ambitious young man, God came to me in a strong way. That was God's visitation to me. I cannot deny it. Many of us have experienced the same thing. We were deeply fallen, and light and loose preaching would never have worked in our case. We needed the living God, the God of glory, to pay us a visit. I have heard many testimonies regarding this.

God appeared to Abraham twice. The first time was in Ur of the Chaldees (Acts 7:2; Gen. 11:31). If we study the Bible carefully, we shall see that, in Ur of the Chaldees, God did not appear to Abraham's father but to Abraham. Abraham, however, did not accept that calling immediately, and God sovereignly caused his father, Terah, to bring the family from Ur to Haran. They stayed there until Terah died. Abraham's staggering in answering God's calling brought about his father's death. God took his father away. Then, at Haran, God appeared to Abraham the second time (12:1). We can see by this that God has a specific purpose in dealing with people. I do not believe that any of you reading this message would respond immediately if God were to visit you. We all are the children of Abraham, and children are always like their fathers. Because Abraham hesitated in following God, God had to appear to him the second time.

THE CALLING OF GOD   ✦   God not only appeared to Abraham twice, but He called him twice. The first calling of God was when Abraham was at Ur (Acts 7:2-4). According to Acts 7, God called Abraham out of his country and out of his kindred. But, in the second calling at Haran, God called Abraham out of his country, his kindred, and also out of his father's house (12:1). So God appeared to Abraham twice and called him twice. The first time God called him out of his country and kindred, mentioning nothing of the father's house. So the father's family also came out of Ur. At the time of God's second calling, however, He told him not only to leave his country and kindred but also his father's house. Abraham had two appearings of God and two callings of God. These appearings and callings of God show that God was the origin of God's calling.

THE EXPERIENCE OF THE CALLED

THREE BEING ONE ✦ As you read the book of Genesis, you will notice that the records of Adam, Abel, Enoch, and Noah are quite distinct one from another. The records of Abraham, Isaac, and Jacob, however, overlap. Genesis, speaking of them, considers them as one corporate man. Isaac's life story began in chapter twenty-one, and Abraham's life story ended in chapter twenty-five. Jacob's life story began in chapter twenty-five, and Isaac's life story ended in chapter thirty-five. Jacob's life story, supplemented by that of Joseph, ended in chapter fifty. The significance of this overlapping is that, according to the experience of life, these three persons are one man, a corporate man. When God created mankind, He created man in a corporate way, for Adam was a corporate man (5:2). It is not a small thing to see this. Do not think that, as a called one, you are complete as an individual. None of us is a complete individual unit. We all need one another. You need me and I need you. In like manner, Abraham needed Isaac and Jacob, Isaac needed Abraham and Jacob, and Jacob needed Abraham, Isaac, and Joseph. All of them needed the others in order to have the completion of God's calling.

When some read this, they may ask, "Don't you believe that Abraham was an individual person?" Of course I believe it, just as I believe that you are an individual person. But the Bible tells us that we are members (Rom. 12:5; 1 Cor. 12:27). A member can never be a separate and complete individual unit. When a member becomes individually complete, that means death. My thumb, for example, is a member of my body. It is not separately complete or individual, for, if it were, that would mean death.

The God of Abraham, the God of Isaac, and the God of Jacob being one God ✦ The God who came to call this corporate person and who dealt with this corporate man was the Triune God—the Father, the Son, and the Spirit. When God spoke to Moses out of the burning bush, He said, "I am the God of thy father, the God of Abraham, the God of Isaac, and the God of Jacob" (Exo. 3:6).

In Exodus 3 we see that Moses was called by the angel of the Lord, that the angel of the Lord was the Lord Himself, and that the Lord Himself was the God of Abraham, the God of Isaac, and the God of Jacob (vv. 2, 4, 6). God did not say, "I am the God of Abraham, Isaac, Jacob, Joseph, and Moses." No, He said that He was the God of Abraham, the God of Isaac, and the God of Jacob. This God, who is the Lord, is also the angel of the Lord. Can you figure this out? If you read Exodus 3, you will find that verse 2 speaks of the angel of the Lord and verse 4 of the Lord. Then in verse 6, this angel of the Lord, who is the Lord Himself, told Moses, "I am the God of thy father, the God of Abraham, the God of Isaac, and the God of Jacob." Do you believe that these are three gods? Here there are three plus two others, the angel of the Lord and the Lord. Are these five individuals, five gods? The angel of the Lord and the Lord surely are two. Can we say that the angel of the Lord is just the Lord Himself? We can, because the Bible tells us so. No one can exhaust the study of Exodus 3. Eventually, in Exodus 3:14, God said to Moses, "I am that I am." God seemed to be saying, "I am the angel of the Lord. I am the Lord. I am the God of Abraham. I am the God of Isaac. I am the God of Jacob. I am that I am. I don't care whether you understand this or not—I am that I am. I don't care whether you agree with this or not—I am that I am." This is our God, the God who worked upon the corporate man. This God was the angel of the Lord, the Lord Himself, the God of Abraham, Isaac, and Jacob, and the great I Am.

The God of Abraham—the Father   ✦   God's calling to Abraham was the work of God the Father. Abraham's original name was Abram which means "an exalted father," and the name Abraham, that replaced this name, means "the father of a great multitude." Both of these names have the basic thought of the father. The first in the Triune God is the Father, and Abraham was the first of the called ones. Abraham was the father of the called ones, and the first of the Triune God is also the Father. The Father is the source of life. He is also the source of plan and purpose. God the Father had a plan, a purpose. Because He had a purpose, He selected and predestinated in eternity past. Eventually, in time, the Father came in to call, justify, accept, and care for the called ones. God the Father's work is to select, predestinate, call, justify, accept, and take care of the called ones. Both selection and predestination precede the matter of calling.

If you read Romans 9:11, you will see that these two items are found with Jacob. Nevertheless, in Abraham we see nearly all of the experiences that are related to God the Father. This is very meaningful.

The God of Isaac—the Son   ◆   Isaac was the son. It is very interesting to see that the second of the Triune God is also the Son. What is a son? A son is one who comes out of the father, who inherits all that the father is and has, and who accomplishes all that the father desires. If you look at Isaac's history, you will find that he was just like this. He was out of the father, he inherited everything of the father, and he worked to accomplish his father's purpose. This is the experience of Isaac, the experience which fits the second of the Triune God, God the Son. The Lord Jesus, as the Son of God, came out of the Father (John 16:28), inherited all that the Father is and has (John 16:15), and accomplished all the Father's will (John 6:38). Isaac's life corresponds to His.

The God of Jacob—the Spirit   ◆   Now we come to Jacob. Jacob, a subtle supplanter, needed more than just the experience of the calling and the inheritance. He mainly needed the dealings to transform him from a man in the flesh to a man in the Spirit. So, it is very meaningful that the third of the Triune God is the Spirit who worked upon the subtle, supplanting Jacob to discipline and transform him into a prince of God. Here, in Jacob, we see regeneration, discipline, transformation, and the growth and maturity in life. All of this is the work of the Spirit. So the God of Jacob should be God the Spirit.

The respective experiences of Abraham, Isaac, and Jacob being three aspects of a complete one   ◆   As the transfer of race began with Abraham, passed through Isaac, and was completed with Jacob, so their experiences should be considered as one complete experience. It is implied that the three were one. The Triune God considered them as members of a corporate man for His dealings and for Him to be their God in this way. The last thirty-nine and a half chapters of Genesis are a biography of a corporate person composed of three plus one. If we add together all the different aspects of the experiences of Abraham, Isaac, and Jacob including Joseph, we see a clear picture of the complete experience of the called ones.

Abraham's Experience   ◆   Abraham had a good beginning with being called, but there is no record of his being chosen or of his reaching an ultimate and matured end. For his completion, Abraham had the need of Jacob's being chosen and of Jacob's matured end. Do you believe that, according to the record of Genesis, Abraham attained to the highest and consummate maturity of life? We cannot find such a record. Abraham's offering Isaac on the altar was the climax of his spiritual life (ch. 22). However, he did not reach maturity. In chapter twenty-four we see that he did something marvelous in obtaining a wife for his son, Isaac. But, after that, he took another wife (25:1). This shows us that Abraham was not matured. Where, then, is Abraham's maturity? His maturity is in Jacob's maturity.

Let us use as an illustration of this the visits that Abraham and Jacob made to Egypt. Abraham's trip to Egypt was shameful, for he told a lie about his wife (12:10-20). But Jacob had a glorious visit (47:7). He did not go to Egypt in order to take advantage of others. He went there with a blessing hand, even blessing Pharaoh, the greatest king on earth at the time (47:10). This reveals that the maturity of life is with Jacob and not with Abraham. According to the Bible, the greater always blesses the lesser (Heb. 7:7). No young one can bless an older one. In order to bless people you need the maturity of life. Does the Bible ever say that Abraham blessed someone? No. Jacob, on the contrary, was so mature in life that he could bestow blessings on others. When he blessed his grandchildren, he did it clearly, not blindly as did Isaac. When Joseph tried to change the position of his hands, Jacob refused and said, "I know it, my son, I know it" (48:19). Jacob was fully matured. Although Abraham was high in the life of faith, we do not see in him the maturity of life that we see in Jacob. For the maturity of life, Abraham had to rely upon Jacob. Although Abraham was the grandfather, he still needed his grandson for his completion. By this we can see that, according to experience, Abraham, Isaac, and Jacob are not individuals but three members of the whole Body. Likewise, we are members one of another (Rom. 12:5) and, in certain aspects of life, we need to depend on each other.

Isaac's Experience   ✦   Isaac is another illustration of this. Isaac's experience was without beginning or end. He was never called and he never matured. Although he blessed his sons, he did it blindly (27:18-29), not so clearly as Jacob did with his grandsons. Isaac needed the beginning of both Abraham's and Jacob's experiences and the end of Jacob's experience for his completion. Isaac was in the middle. He was never dealt with. Although his father and son were dealt with, he did not need any dealings. He was fully covered by the two ends in the matter of God's dealings. Many times it is good for us to stay in the midst of other members of the Body, for those ahead of us and those behind us become our completion. This is the coordination among the members of the Body.

Jacob's Experience   ✦   In his experience, Jacob had the best, highest, and most matured end. Although he began as a subtle supplanter, after being dealt with by God, he matured to the uttermost. Although there are so many good ones, such as Abel, Enoch, Noah, and Abraham, in the book of Genesis, no one is as mature as Jacob. After he matured, his supplanting hands became blessing hands. Whenever someone came under his hands, there was no condemnation, only blessing. He not only blessed the descendants of faith but even the worldly people. He was so high and so mature.

Although Jacob was matured in life, he had neither the experience of being called nor of the life of faith. Neither did he have the experience of the inheriting of grace. For his completion, Jacob needed to have Abraham's being called and Abraham's experience in the life of faith as well as Isaac's experience in the inheriting of grace. Jacob was poor in faith. He did not know how to believe; he only knew how to supplant. After Abraham had been blessed by Melchisedec following the slaughter of kings, he met the king of Sodom. The king of Sodom encouraged Abraham, who had gained the victory for him, to take the spoil for himself. But Abraham refused to take even one thread, believing in the sufficiency of the Almighty God (14:19-23). Abraham had received the blessing from Melchisedec and did not need help from the king of Sodom. That was Abraham's experience of faith. But Jacob's experience was very different. Wherever he went, he was the first to supplant. In the midst of his supplanting life, Jacob even made a deal with God. When God appeared to him in a dream at Bethel, Jacob said upon waking, "If God will be with me, and keep me in this way that I go, and will give me bread to eat, and raiment to put on... then shall the Lord be my God...and of all that thou shall give me I will surely give the tenth unto thee" (28:20-22). Jacob made a deal with God. If God would take care of his needs, Jacob would give Him ten percent in return. Jacob seemed to be saying, "O God, if You will take care of my food, clothing, and all my needs, then I will give You a ten percent commission." According to that arrangement, Jacob received ninety percent and God only ten percent. We see by this that Jacob did not have Abraham's faith.

Eventually, however, Jacob was fully matured. He reached such a high level of maturity that Joseph, a part of Jacob, was reigning over the whole world. At that time, the world was under the hand of Pharaoh, and Pharaoh's authority was altogether with Joseph. In a very real sense, Joseph did not reign for Pharaoh but for Jacob. Here we see the kingdom. The New Testament ends with the kingdom. After the called ones have completed their experiences with the Triune God, the period of reigning will come. That will be the millennium. Joseph only reigned for a period of years, but in the kingdom we shall reign for a thousand years.

If we add together the experiences of Abraham, Isaac, and Jacob, we have a clear portrait of the complete experience of the called one. As a help in doing this, let us consider the chart that is printed on page 31. As God's called ones, Abraham, Isaac, and Jacob were chosen in eternity past. Then, in time, after their birth, they were called. Many years after Abraham was called, he was circumcised and his name was changed. This is indicated by the curve. This is one line, or one aspect, of the experience of the called ones. We see from this chart that Isaac's experience is a straight line. It resembles a tasteless glass of plain water. We see another curve when we come to Jacob's experience. After this supplanting one was touched and dealt with, he became a prince of God. Eventually, all three of the called ones became a straight line. They will all be there in eternity future. We see from this chart that Jacob, or Israel, includes Joseph. The reason for this is, as we have seen, that Joseph was the reigning part of Jacob. While Jacob was a prince of God, Joseph was the one who reigned over the world, reigning over all the earth for Jacob. Joseph was the reigning son and Jacob was the reigning father.

The experiences of Abraham, Isaac, and Jacob are the complete experience of the corporate called one. If we see this, we shall bow down and say, "O God the Father, we need You. We need Your plan, purpose, selection, predestination, calling, justification, acceptance, and care. O God the Son, we need You. We need You to redeem us that we might have the inheritance. We need You to accomplish all that the Father planned, all that the Father intended to do. O God the

Spirit, we need You. We need You to regenerate us, to discipline us, to transform us, and to make us grow that we might mature in life. We need You to make us the real Israels. We need You to make all that the Father has planned and all that the Son has accomplished real to us. Our Triune God, how we bow to You, worship You, praise You, and thank You for all that You have done to us and in us!"

After seeing such a thing, we shall be humbled and realize that the whole experience of the corporate called one is too much for us to have individually. I cannot be Abraham, Isaac, and Jacob with Joseph. Since I can only be one of these three, I must learn to rely upon my brothers for the remainder. Even if I were as mature as Israel, I would still need someone to be my Abraham and my Isaac. We all must realize that, at the most, we are only a member of the Body. We need all the other members. According to our traditional background, everyone ranks Abraham at the top, thinking that he exceeds everybody else. But he did not exceed everyone. Although he exceeded others in the matter of faith, he did not surpass them in maturity. As we have seen, Jacob was the most mature.

At present we are all in the process of this experience of God's called ones. Some of us are Abrahams, some are Isaacs, and others are Jacobs. Now we are enjoying the Triune God in our experience, not in theology. We do not have Him as a doctrinal concept but as an experiential enjoyment. We are enjoying God the Father, God the Son, and God the Spirit. How good it is to enjoy the Father's calling, justifying, accepting, and caring for us. How wonderful it is to realize the Son's redeeming, saving, bringing us into the inheritance, and accomplishing of God's eternal purpose. How excellent it is to experience the Spirit's regenerating, disciplining, transforming, and causing us to grow and mature. We are not merely discussing the Triune God. We are experiencing Him; we are participating in the Father, Son, and Spirit. The Triune God is with us experientially. In the church life, we are Abrahams, Isaacs, and Jacobs including Josephs experiencing the Triune God. We are enjoying the selection, predestination, calling, justification, acceptance, care, redemption, inheritance, accomplishment of God's purpose, regeneration, discipline, transformation, growth, maturity, and eventually the reigning. Praise the Lord! This is the Triune God with the corporate called one.

A CHART OF THE EXPERIENCE OF ABRAHAM, ISAAC, AND JACOB

Eternity

Chosen

Called

ABRAM

ISAAC

JACOB

Circumcised

ABRAHAM

ISRAEL
(including
JOSEPH)

Thigh touched

Eternity

3

THE MOTIVE AND STRENGTH OF BEING CALLED

Now the Lord had said unto Abram,
Get thee out of thy country, and from thy kindred,
and from thy father's house,
unto a land that I will show thee.

Genesis 12:1

And he said, Men, brothers and fathers, listen.
The God of glory appeared to our father Abraham
while he was in Mesopotamia, before he dwelt in Haran,
and said to him, "Come out from your land and from your relatives,
and come into the land which I will show you."
Then he came forth from the land of the Chaldeans and dwelt in Haran.
And from there, after his father died,
He removed him into this land, in which you now dwell.

Acts 7:2-4

In the last message we saw that the Triune God dealt with Abraham, Isaac, and Jacob as one complete corporate man. If we are going to get into the last section of the book of Genesis, the section on God's calling, we need to remember that Abraham, Isaac, and Jacob are not three separate and complete units but, under God's dispensation, are one complete corporate man. God dealt with each of them as a part of a complete unit. Their experiences are not three separate individual experiences but the aspects of one complete experience.

In this message we need to see the first aspect of the complete experience of God's called ones. This aspect is fully shown in Abraham's life (11:10—25:18). This is quite basic. Abraham's life is an illustration of the first aspect of the complete experience of God's called ones. His experience goes from being called, through the living by faith in fellowship, to the knowing of grace.

In his experience Abraham firstly was called by God. As we have seen, God's calling was not originated or initiated by the called one. It was initiated by the God who called. God was the originator of His calling.

As God's calling did not originate with the called one but with the God who calls, so the motive and strength to receive God's calling did not originate from the side of the called one but from the side of the calling One. The motive and the strength whereby Abraham could answer God's calling came from God Himself. What was this motive and strength? If we look into the situation in a detailed way, we can see three things that motivated Abraham to accept God's calling: God's appearing, God's calling, and God's promise. Now we need to consider each of these items.

GOD'S APPEARING

The first aspect of the motive and strength to accept God's calling was God's appearing. If I were to come to you, it would mean nothing because I am nothing. If the president of the United States were to pay you a personal visit, you would be very excited. Probably you would be unable to sleep for a whole night. But who came to visit Abraham? The God of glory (Acts 7:2). Outside of Stephen's word in Acts 7:2, where Stephen told his persecutors that the God of glory appeared to their father Abraham, there is no other verse in the Bible that says that the God of glory appeared to Abraham. While Stephen was speaking, the Jesus of glory appeared to him (Acts 7:55-56). The heavens were opened and he saw Jesus in glory standing on the right hand of God. Stephen was bold to die for Jesus because, while they were opposing him, he saw the Lord Jesus. The people stoned him, but Jesus smiled at him. Because the Lord appeared to him, it was easy, even a great joy, for him to undergo persecution. There was no comparison between that persecution and the appearing of Jesus in glory. Because Stephen was in such a situation, the Jesus in glory appeared to him. Without such an appearing, his environment would have been too difficult for a human being to take.

In the same principle, the God of glory appeared to Abraham, paying him a visit with His personal appearance, because, at that time, Abraham was under the influence of a strong background in Chaldea. As we shall see in the next message, Chaldea in Hebrew means demonic. Chaldea was a demonic place, a place full of demons. Joshua 24:2 says that Abraham and his family served other gods. They worshipped idols, and behind the idols were demons.

Chaldea was in a land called Mesopotamia. The word Mesopotamia means "between rivers." According to geography, the region of Mesopotamia was bound by two great rivers, the Euphrates (Perath in Hebrew) and the Tigris (Hiddekel in Hebrew). Between these two rivers was a great plain, the land of Mesopotamia. Chaldea was a part of Mesopotamia. This means that Abraham's dwelling place was not only in a place full of demons but also in a place that was enclosed by two great rivers. It was very difficult for him or any other person to leave such a place, for the demons held him and the great rivers enclosed him. Since there was no modern transportation, the people had to walk. How was Abraham able to get out of Chaldea? Since his background was so strong, God appeared to him in order that he might come out of it.

This is a picture, an illustration, of our situation before we were saved. We all were in a Chaldea. All the young people need to realize that every junior high school is a Chaldea, a place filled with demons. So many of the students are little demons selling drugs and trying to hold you back, saying, "How can you be different from us? If you want to be different from us, where shall you go? There are two great rivers that keep you here. You must stay with us!" Sometimes the husbands are demons to the wives and the wives are demons to the husbands. As far as the worldly people are concerned, whenever a young man gets married he enters into a demonic region. The same is true for every young woman who marries. Consider the example of a young man who falls in love with a certain young lady. This young woman has a tremendous background composed of a great many relatives and friends, all of whom are demonic. If this young man were to marry her, he would fall into a demonic region. If he came to me, I would say, "Don't think that this young lady is so pretty, nice, and kind. You must look into her background. You are not only marrying her—you are marrying her with her whole background. After you marry a girl with such a demonic background, you will find yourself in Chaldea. The demons there will hold you." But God has chosen this young man. Do not think that it will be easy for him to believe in the Lord Jesus and be saved. It is not a matter of being saved and waiting to go to heaven. No, in the Bible, to be saved is to be called out of your background, region, and environment. You need to get yourself out.

As we have seen, God's promise to Abraham was a preaching of the gospel (Gal. 3:8). As part of this preaching, God told Abraham to get out of his country. What would you have done if you had been Abraham? Behind Sarah there might have been many demons, and these demons would not agree with Abraham's getting out of Chaldea. This was the reason that the God of glory appeared to Abraham. It was neither an angel nor a dignified person who appeared to Abraham but the God of glory Himself who appeared to him. That appearing was a great attraction, inciting Abraham to take God's calling.

In Matthew we are told that as Jesus walked by the sea of Galilee He called Peter, Andrew, James, and John (Matt. 4:18-22). The Lord Jesus simply said to them, "Follow Me," and they followed Him. For many years I was unable to understand this. The little Jesus of Nazareth spoke the words, "Follow Me," and they followed Him. I did not understand this until one day I noticed that the Jesus who walked by the sea of Galilee was a great light (Matt. 4:16). Peter, Andrew, James, and John were all attracted by that great light. When Jesus looked at them and called them, they were attracted to Him. Apparently, the One who called them was a poor Nazarene; actually, He was the God of glory. Likewise, the God of glory appeared to Abraham in the land of demons, a land enclosed by great waters. I believe that, in principle, we all have experienced such an appearing. To be saved is not merely a matter of hearing the preaching of the gospel, nodding your head, and then confessing that you are a sinner and that you believe in the Lord Jesus. Although this is correct, I must say that a true saved one is one who has had the appearing of Jesus.

In our conversion many seemed to see "the glory of God in the face of Christ" (2 Cor. 4:6). This became a great stimulation to so many of us.

We, the saved ones, have all had the appearing of Jesus. This did not occur in an outward way, but in our spirit deep within. Although we might forget the day or even the year when we were saved, we can never forget the time that, deep within, we saw Jesus. Jesus appeared to us and we met with Him. This is the real experience of being saved. To be saved is simply to be called. Before the Lord Jesus appeared to you, you found it difficult to be a genuine Christian. Your background and surroundings did not allow you to be different from others. One day, however, He appeared to you. Oh, the living Jesus in glory appeared to you. That was your calling. It was also His separating and His saving. By appearing to you in this way, He called you, saved you, and separated you. Abraham had the same kind of experience. That appearing of God strongly attracted Abraham. This appearing was Abraham's motive and strength to accept God's calling. If you consider Abraham's background and situation you will realize that without such an attraction and stimulation, it would have been impossible for him to accept God's calling.

GOD'S CALLING

The second factor of the motive and strength was God's calling (Acts 7:3-4; Gen. 12:1). God did not appear to Abraham without speaking to him. When He came to Abraham, He called him. God spoke to Abraham. Calling means speaking. It is not a small thing to hear God's speaking. At the time we were saved, we all experienced the appearing of Jesus. At the same time that He appeared to us, He spoke to us. There was a divine speaking, a kind of speaking in the spirit.

Many of us can testify that at the time we were saved, deep within us we had the consciousness that Jesus was speaking to us. Perhaps the Lord Jesus came to you when you were a student and said, "What are you doing here?" You answered, "I am studying to get my degree." Then the Lord asked, "For what?" You replied, "To make a good living in the future." After this, the Lord asked, "Then what? What about your future?" With others, the Lord Jesus has spoken in a different way, saying, "Look at how sinful you are, at how bad and poor you are!" In response to this, some have said to the Lord,

"Don't bother me." Then the Lord said, "I love you. I want to save you. Don't you know that I'm Jesus. I want to rescue you from your poor situation. Aren't you willing to take Me?" To others of us the Lord Jesus said, "Don't you know that I am the living One. I am the only One who can give you eternal life." Many of us have heard words such as these, not out of the mouth of a preacher but out of the mouth of the living Jesus. Do you recall the kind of speaking you heard from the living Jesus when He appeared to you at the time you were called and saved? The non-Christians, including the professing Christians, have not had this kind of experience and they consider it as superstition. But it is not superstition! The God of glory has come to us and spoken to us. Abraham could say, "Don't tell me that this is a superstition. I heard Him speak. He said, 'Get thee out of thy country!' This word did not come from my father or from my wife. It was spoken by the God of glory." Tell me honestly, have you not heard the speaking of Jesus? I do not believe that any saved person will ever be lost again. Although a saved one may backslide, he can never forget the appearing and the speaking of Jesus. He might even say, "I don't believe in Jesus anymore," but deep within the Lord says, "How can you say that you don't believe in Me anymore?" You can never forget His appearing and His speaking to you.

A good number of young people have asked me what is the difference between a true Christian and a false Christian. All of them profess to believe in Jesus. The best answer that I can give is this: a true Christian has had the speaking of Jesus, but the professing Christian only has the preaching of a doctrine. A genuine Christian has, at least once, heard the speaking of Jesus by the living Spirit directly in the depths of his being. That speaking was the strength that enabled all of us to accept God's calling.

GOD'S PROMISE

The third aspect of the motive and strength to accept God's calling is God's promise (12:2-3). Most of God's speaking to us is His promise. If God says, "I don't want to bother you; I want to save you," that is a promise. If He says, "I love you," that also is a promise. Most of what He speaks to us is a promise.

What did the God of glory say to Abraham? Firstly, the God of glory said, "Get thee out of thy country and from thy kindred"

(12:1). You may think that this was not a promise. But it implied a promise. When God told Abraham to get out of his country, it implied that God was promising Abraham a place. Otherwise, Abraham would have said, "If I get out of my country, where should I go?" God had a place for Abraham. Even the command to get out of the country implied a promise, the promise of the good land. Abraham could say, "Since God commands me to get out of my country, this must surely mean that He has a place for me." God told Abraham to get out of his country, from his kindred, and from his father's house, unto a land that He would show him. That certainly was a promise. God's promise was an incentive for him to leave his country.

TO MAKE THE CALLED "A GREAT NATION"   ✦   In 12:2 God said to Abraham, "I will make of thee a great nation." This word was a contrast to Abraham's background. At Babel, there were many nations formed with families. Abraham lived in such an atmosphere. When God came to Abraham, telling him to get out of his country, Abraham might have said within himself, "What about the matter of being a nation?" Then God promised that He would make of him a great nation. God also said, "I will bless thee, and make thy name great." This also was in contrast with Babel. When the people built a tower at Babel, they were trying to make a name for themselves. But God, in His promise, seemed to be telling Abraham, "You don't need to make a name for yourself. I will make your name great. You don't need to form a nation. I will make a nation out of you."

God promised Abraham that He would make of him "a great nation." This "great nation" is the kingdom of God, composed of the nation of Israel in the Old Testament, the church in the New Testament, the millennial kingdom in the coming age, and the new heaven and the new earth in eternity. (In the millennial kingdom there will be two parts—the heavenly part and the earthly part. The heavenly part will be the kingdom of heaven. The overcomers of the past and present ages will be in the heavenly part of the millennium as co-kings with Christ. The earthly part is the Messianic kingdom, the kingdom of the Messiah, composed of the future Jewish nation.) The nation of Israel in the Old Testament age, the church in the New Testament age, the coming kingdom in the millennium, and the new heaven and the new earth in eternity—all are included in this "great nation" which God promised to make of Abraham. In this way

Abraham's name became great. Other than the name of the Lord Jesus, no name on earth is greater than that of Abraham. He is the father of "a great nation." He is the father of the nation of Israel, the father of the church, and he will be the father of the millennial kingdom and of all the redeemed ones in eternity. What a "great nation" with a great name this is!

TO BLESS THE CALLED ✦ God promised to bless Abraham (12:2). What is this blessing? It is the blessings of God's creation and redemption, including all that God wants to give man—God Himself and all that He has in this age and in the age to come. Galatians 3:14 shows us that this blessing eventually is the promise of the Spirit: "That the blessing of Abraham might come to the nations in Jesus Christ, that we might receive the promise of the Spirit through faith." Since the Spirit is God Himself, this means that God promised that He would give Himself to Abraham as the blessing.

TO MAKE THE CALLED A BLESSING TO ALL FAMILIES OF THE EARTH ✦ God not only promised that He Himself would be a blessing to Abraham, but that Abraham would be a blessing to all the families, all the nations, of the earth (12:3). In His calling, God turned from Adam to Abraham. This meant that He had given up the Adamic race. But, in His promise, God made another turn from Abraham back to all the families of the Adamic race through Christ, the seed of Abraham (Gal. 3:14). This is very meaningful. Firstly, God turned from Adam to Abraham and, eventually, He turned from Abraham through Christ back to the created race. By this new turn we all were captured. It appeared that God had left us and had turned to Abraham. Then God seemed to say to Abraham, "I will not only give Myself to you as a blessing, but I will make you a blessing to all those pitiful people of the Adamic race. Abraham, let us go back." We may say that God made a U-turn. By this U-turn all of the called ones from the nations have been gathered in.

Let me say a word about our attitude toward the Jews. Never mistreat the Jewish people. God said, "I will bless them that bless thee, and curse him that curseth thee." (In this word, "them" and "him" indicates people in both plural and singular number.) If you read history, you will find that during the past twenty-five centuries, from the time that Nebuchadnezzar destroyed the city of Jerusalem until now, every country, people, race, or individual that has cursed the Jewish people has received a curse. However, whoever blesses the Jewish people receives a blessing. No leader in history died in such a pitiful way as Hitler did. Hitler died in that way because he was cursed for his cursing of the Jewish people. Since the United States is helping the nation of Israel today, surely the United States is under God's blessing. This is not my opinion. This is according to God's promise in Genesis 12:3.

GOD'S PROMISE BEING THE GOSPEL PREACHED TO ABRAHAM   ✦
When I read 12:2-3 as a young man, I was not inspired by it. These verses seemed to be dry bones. I did not understand what God was talking about when He told Abraham that He would make of him a great nation, and that He would bless him, and make him a blessing. Eventually, after many years, I came back to these verses with the help of Galatians 3. I came to realize that God's promise to Abraham in 12:2-3 was the preaching of the gospel. The three items of God's promise—to make of Abraham a great nation, to bless him, and to make him a blessing to all the families of the earth—were the gospel preached to Abraham (Gal. 3:8). The contents of God's promise are exactly the same as the contents of the gospel. Firstly, the preaching of the gospel opens with the words, "Repent, for the kingdom of the heavens has drawn near" (Matt. 3:2). As we have seen, the "great nation" refers to the kingdom. Secondly, the blessing that God promised Abraham was the Spirit, that is, God Himself. In the gospel, after we repent for the kingdom, we need to believe that we may have eternal life, which is in the Spirit. The blessing promised to Abraham, which, according to Galatians 3:14, is the promise of the Spirit, is the very blessing of the gospel. This blessing, as the third item, is for all the nations, for it is said, "In thee shall all families of the earth be blessed."

IMPLYING GOD'S ETERNAL PURPOSE   ✦   God's promise to Abraham implied His eternal purpose. God's eternal purpose is that man express and represent Him. God said that He would make of Abraham "a great nation" and that He would bless him. A nation is a matter of dominion to represent God, and blessing is a matter of image in the Spirit to express God. We all shall be transformed into His image by the Lord Spirit (2 Cor. 3:18). This requires that we have a regenerated spirit. Some may ask why 1:26, 28 mention expressing God with His image first and representing Him with His dominion second. The reason for this is that there we see God's original purpose. But because man has fallen, in the gospel man has to repent in order to come back to the beginning. Therefore, in the gospel, dominion is first and image follows. In God's original purpose, it was image and dominion, but, due to the fall, in the gospel the order is reversed.

THE CONTENTS IN GOD'S ETERNAL PURPOSE, PROMISE, GOSPEL, AND FULFILLMENT BEING THE SAME ✦ In God's eternal purpose, promise, gospel, and fulfillment, the contents are the same. It is very interesting to see this.

In God's eternal purpose—with Adam ✦ In God's eternal purpose we have two items: image to express God and dominion to represent God.

In God's promise—to Abraham ✦ As we have seen, in God's promise to Abraham, the nation, which is for dominion to represent God, is mentioned first and the blessing, which is for the image to express God, is mentioned second.

In the gospel—with the believers ✦ In the gospel (salvation) with the believers we firstly have repentance for the kingdom (Matt. 3:2). This repentance is for the dominion to represent God. Secondly, we have the matter of receiving eternal life (John 3:16). This receiving of eternal life is for the image to express God.

In the fulfillment—in the New Jerusalem ✦ We also see the same contents in the fulfillment, in the New Jerusalem. The entire New Jerusalem will bear God's appearance. God's appearance resembles jasper. Revelation 4:3 says that God, the One sitting on the throne, has the appearance of jasper. In Revelation 21:11, 18b, we see that the whole New Jerusalem shines like jasper. The appearance of the wall and of the entire city of New Jerusalem will be the same as God's appearance—jasper. This means that in eternity the whole New Jerusalem will express God. Furthermore, in eternity all the saved ones in the New Jerusalem will reign as kings with God (Rev. 22:5). This will be the dominion to represent God.

Although we did not care about God's dominion and image at the time we were called and saved, deep within, in God's calling and speaking, we realized that these matters were implied. After being saved, we had the realization that we needed to be under God's ruling. This is the kingdom, the dominion. Also, deep within us, we had the sensation that, after being saved, we had to glorify God. This is the matter of image to express God. However, after we were saved, most of us met some mistaken preachers who told us many wrong things that distracted us from God's purpose. Praise the Lord that in God's recovery He has recovered us to His original purpose and He has brought us back to the beginning. We the real called ones, the sons of Abraham receiving God's calling with His speaking and promise, are now in His kingdom to represent Him and have His image to express Him.

4

THE PROGRESS IN ANSWERING GOD'S CALLING

And Terah took Abram his son, and Lot the son of Haran
his son's son, and Sarai his daughter-in-law, his son Abram's wife;
and they went forth with them from Ur of the Chaldees,
to go into the land of Canaan; and
they came unto Haran, and dwelt there.
And the days of Terah were two hundred and five years: and
Terah died in Haran.

Genesis 11:31-32

The God of glory appeared
to our father Abraham while he was in Mesopotamia,
before he dwelt in Haran.

Acts 7:2b

Then he came forth from the land of the Chaldeans and dwelt in Haran.
And from there, after his father died,
He removed him into this land...

Acts 7:4

As we have pointed out many times, nearly every item in the book of Genesis is a seed. In this message we come to the seed of river crossing, to the experience of the first river crosser. What is river crossing? It is the real and actual following of the Lord. Following the Lord is a matter of crossing the river. Although it is easy to talk about river crossing, it is not easy to have the real river crossing according to the experience of Abraham. In this message we need to see how Abraham crossed the river. His experience, an example for us all, is another of the seeds sown in Genesis. This seed is now growing in so many of us. How we need the growth of this seed!

CALLED THE FIRST TIME
AT UR OF CHALDEA IN MESOPOTAMIA

The best way to study the Word is to compare one portion of it with another. We may do this with respect to the calling of Abraham, for his calling is mentioned in both Genesis 12 and Acts 7. By the help of the Lord, it is easy for us to see the comparison in these two passages. We can see from these two portions of the Word that the God of glory appeared to Abraham twice. God did not come to him once for all. This is not our guess; it is proved by Acts 7:2 which says that the God of glory appeared to Abraham before he dwelt in Haran, while he was still in Mesopotamia. Then Genesis 12:1 indicates that after Abraham had dwelt in Haran for a time, God appeared to him again. By these two verses we see that God appeared to Abraham in two different places: at Ur of Chaldea and at Haran. It is certain that these two callings did not occur at the same time. The first call came while Abraham's father was still alive, and the second came after his father had died. This is a strong proof that God appeared to Abraham twice.

There is a very crucial difference between these two callings of God. In the first calling God told Abraham to get out of his country and his kindred (Acts 7:3). In the second calling God told him to get out of his country, his kindred, and his father's house (Gen. 12:1). When God called Abraham the second time, He not only mentioned Abraham's kindred in a general way but his father's house in a particular way. It was not sufficient for him to leave his kindred; he had to come out of his father's house. Later on we shall see the reason for this. But now we can see that Abraham experienced two different callings at two different places. In the first calling God told him to get out of his country and his kindred, and in the second calling He told him to get out of his country, his kindred, *and his father's house.*

Once we see this matter of the two callings, everything is clear.

When I was young, I was told by certain teachers that Acts 7 was a quotation of Genesis 12. These teachers never pointed out clearly that God called Abraham twice. Perhaps some of you reading this message still hold on to the concept that Acts 7 is a quotation of Genesis 12. But the call in Acts 7 occurred before Abraham was brought to Haran, and the call in Genesis 12 happened after he had lived there for a time. The call in Acts 7 preceded the call in Genesis 12.

NOT OBEYING GOD'S CALLING RIGHT AWAY

Why did God need to appear to Abraham twice and call him twice? Why did God need to repeat His calling? As far as God was concerned, there was no need for Him to repeat His calling. It was Abraham who needed the repetition. There is hardly one who has experienced God's calling just once and then immediately crossed the river. No one among us has ever answered God's calling without dragging his feet through mud and water. Hardly anyone has ever given a clean-cut answer to God's calling. You may say, "What about Peter and John when they were called by the Lord by the Sea of Galilee? The Lord called them, and they followed Him immediately." If you read other portions of the Word, you will see that even these disciples were dragging their feet. It is difficult to have a clean-cut answer to God's calling. We always drag our feet through mud and water. Our relatives might be the mud and we ourselves might be the water. Although you might have received the calling from God, you allow your relatives to be the mud through which you drag your feet. And you yourself are the water, the dirty and black water. You drag your feet through this mud and water.

While Abraham was living at Ur, the God of glory suddenly appeared to him. This appearing brought in light. (The name Ur means light.) In a demonic land, a land full of demons (Chaldea means demonic), the God of glory appeared and brought in light. This is very meaningful. Whenever God comes to call a man, there is always light. While Saul of Tarsus was on the way to Damascus to persecute the Christians there, a light from heaven shone upon him (Acts 9:1-3). At that moment, Saul was at Ur. He was under the light. When you were called, you also were under the light. You saw that your place, your environment and surroundings, was not the right place for you to stay any longer. You were called at Ur, the place of light.

TAKEN TO HARAN BY HIS FATHER
AFTER HIS BROTHER'S DEATH

I believe that Abraham received God's calling when he was young. He might have told his father, Terah, and his relatives how God had appeared to him and had told him to get out of his country and his kindred. Abraham probably did not have the boldness to do this himself. In 11:28 we are told that "Haran died before his father Terah in the land of his nativity, in Ur of the Chaldees." Haran might have been Abraham's older brother and he might have opposed God's calling to Abraham. It might have been that God waited a certain period of time. When Abraham still did not take any action, God took away Haran, the opposing one. Haran might have been Terah's eldest son. The eldest son's death might have been a warning to the father not to tarry any longer. The name Terah means to tarry, to delay, or to be laggard. Terah took the whole family, went forth with them from Ur of the Chaldees, and dwelt in Haran (11:31; Acts 7:4a). It was not Abraham who took the initiative to leave Ur; it was his father.

Terah and his family might have traveled northward along the side of the river Euphrates. Eventually, after a journey of at least five hundred miles, they came to Haran. According to the ancient method of travel, it must have taken over half a month to travel from Ur to Haran. But although they made such a long journey, they never crossed the river as God wanted them to. How many years have you been dragging along the side of the river without crossing it? You may say, "Praise the Lord that I am no longer in Ur." Right, you are not in Ur, but you are still on the other side of the river. Even in the church life you have been journeying along the riverside without crossing the river. Many of you have journeyed northward but are still on the other side. But even this journey northward was caused by God's doing.

At Ur there was a person named Haran, and now we see a city with the same name. This means that they left one Haran and came into another. In the eyes of God, both are the same. Whether Haran is a person or a place, it is still Haran. The name Haran means dry.

When the elder brother was opposing God's calling, he must have been dry. Any relative who tries to prevent you from accepting the Lord's calling is a dry one, and any place that hinders you from answering God's calling is a dry place. You can never be watered there. In such a place you have the sensation of dryness. Many of us have experienced this.

CALLED THE SECOND TIME AT HARAN
AFTER HIS FATHER'S DEATH

Christians are used to exalting Abraham. He is considered as being very high. But Abraham was not that high; he was as low as we are. When God came to Abraham, he lacked the boldness to take action. His father finally acted, taking the family to Haran where they dwelt until the father died (11:32). Then God appeared to Abraham and called him again (11:32—12:3; Acts 7:4b). Abraham's delay in answering God's calling caused two deaths, the death of his brother at Ur and the death of his father at Haran. Abraham took two steps, and each step was caused by the death of a close relative.

In His second calling God added another item, telling Abraham not only to come out of his country and his kindred but also out of his father's house (12:1). This means that he was only allowed to bring his wife with him, not any member of his father's house. God's calling was more severe the second time than it was the first time. If you look into the meaning of all the names, you will see that, apart from the name Abram, which means an exalted father, the only other name with a positive meaning is Sarai, which means my princess. The exalted father was the husband, and the princess was the wife. At Haran God called only these two. But again Abraham dragged his feet through the mud, for he took his nephew Lot with him.

In the second calling God was not only more severe, but He also gave Abraham the promise of the gospel as an incentive to encourage him to answer His calling (12:2-3). He received a more severe calling but with a great incentive.

OBEYING GOD'S CALLING IN A DRAGGING WAY

This time Abraham obeyed God's calling, but he did not do so in a clean-cut way. He was still dragging along. We know this because he did not only take his wife Sarai with him but also his nephew Lot (12:4). Lot was a member of his father's family. Did not Abraham hear when God told him to get out of his father's house? Why then did he bring with him a member of his father's house? I believe that I can tell you the reason. At that time Abraham was quite old. He was seventy-five years of age. Although he was seventy-five years old, he still did not have a son of his own. For such a long journey he surely needed a young man to help him. That was his excuse. Abraham might have said, "God called me, but should I leave my nephew? Should I not love him?" Humanly speaking, everyone would say that Abraham was right in bringing Lot.

What is the meaning of the name Lot? It means a veil, a wrapping. Your dear relatives, whom you love so much and whom you would take with you in answering God's calling, are always veils to you. Look at your situation. Many of us have answered God's calling in a way of taking a veil along with us. Lot did not help Abraham at all. Rather, he caused trouble. When we come to Genesis 13, we shall see that Lot caused a great deal of trouble to Abraham and that eventually he had to leave Abraham. If you examine your own situation you will see that probably it was exactly the same as Abraham's.

In the gospel preaching today people are mostly told that if they believe in the Lord Jesus, they will be saved from hell and will go to heaven one day. This is true, but it is shallow. From God's point of view, to be saved is to be called. God is not concerned about hell but about your country, your kindred, and your father's house. God is concerned about your environment, surroundings, and background. To be saved means to be called out of your background, to be called out of your present surroundings, environment, and situation. To be saved is not merely a matter of having your sins forgiven, of being rescued from hell, and of being qualified to go to heaven. To be saved means to be called out of your background and environment.

To be saved is also to take a journey, to walk along the way, and to run the race. *Pilgrim's Progress,* a very famous book written by John Bunyan, stresses the one point that salvation is a journey. To be saved is to be called and to be on a journey. People talk much about justification by faith, using Abraham as the example. But before Abraham was justified, he took a journey. His justification transpired in Genesis 15:6. Before Genesis 15, however, we have at least three chapters telling us that this justified one was on a journey.

I hope that all the young people will see this. The place where the young people are today is worse than Chaldea. But praise the Lord, your Ur is brighter and has more light. Today God's calling to the young people is clearer and stronger than it was to Abraham. Young people, you must get out of the land, out of the people, and away from your relatives. To be saved is to be on a journey to reach God's purpose. God came in to call Abraham with a purpose. If you are called by God according to His purpose, your salvation is guaranteed by that calling. You do not need to be concerned about your salvation. If you take care of God's purpose, He will certainly take care of your salvation.

To be saved is to be called to fulfill God's purpose. When God came in to call Abraham, it was not for the purpose that Abraham be saved from hell or filled with joy; it was for the purpose of fulfilling God's plan. God called Abraham for the fulfillment of His purpose. We all must hear this calling.

God has a plan and a purpose. He has a good land that we may enter into. Abraham went into the good land of Canaan (12:4-5). Our good land today is Christ, the church, and the kingdom. Consider the case of Saul of Tarsus who boldly persecuted the church. In the eyes of God, while Saul was persecuting the church, he was living in "Chaldea." On the road to Damascus, the Lord appeared to him, shined upon him, and called him, and Saul's Chaldea became "Ur," the place of light. The Lord did not call him in order to save him from hell to heaven, or even to justify him. Although these are included in the Lord's calling, the Lord called him out of a Judaistic Chaldea. The Lord called Saul out of that religion in order that he might enter into Christ, God's new covenant economy, the church, and the kingdom. And Paul did get into Christ, into the New Testament economy, into the church, and into God's kingdom.

If we answer God's calling, taking care of His purpose that we enter into Christ, the New Testament economy, the church, and the kingdom, He will not allow us to go to hell. Do not be concerned about hell, and do not consider that much about heaven. We have something better than heaven. Is not Christ better than heaven? Is not God's economy, the dispensation of the Triune God into man, much better than heaven? Is not the church better than heaven? Heaven is going to be shaken. Hebrews 12:26 says that God is going to shake not only the earth but also heaven. Only God Himself is unshakable.

We have received an unshakable kingdom, which is Christ with the church. Do not appreciate heaven so much. In the last two chapters of the Bible we see that the New Jerusalem will descend out of heaven. God is going to leave heaven and dwell in the New Jerusalem, which is the consummation of the church, for eternity.

We all must see that to be saved means to be called to fulfill God's purpose. To be saved is to be delivered out of many negative situations so that we may come into God's goal. Many Christians have been saved, but they have never come into God's goal. God's goal firstly is Christ. We are in Christ. We are in the enjoyment of Christ. This is God's good land. Secondly, God's goal is the church. Years ago I did not realize that, in a sense, the church is also the good land of Canaan. Furthermore, God's New Testament economy, the kingdom, and the Sabbath rest, are all the good land to us today. Are you in the good land of Canaan? If you are, it means that you are in Christ, in the riches and the enjoyment of Christ. It also means that you are in God's new covenant dispensation and in the church life. Many of us were saved for many years before we crossed the river. We were neither in God's economy nor in the church. Moreover, we were not in God's kingdom. Some of us had the concept that the kingdom had been suspended and that the millennial kingdom would come in the future, but we never entered into the reality of the kingdom life today.

Although according to what is portrayed in Genesis 12 Abraham was dragging along, Hebrews 11:8 tells us that he obeyed God's calling by faith and went out without knowing where he was going. In His calling, God told him definitely what he had to leave, but God did not tell him clearly where he had to go. Abraham obeyed God's calling and went out by faith. This was great. On the one hand, he was dragging along; on the other hand, he took a great step by faith. His not knowing where to go caused him to trust in God and to look unto the Lord all the time. We may say that the living God was a road map to him for his traveling.

REMOVED BY GOD INTO THE LAND OF CANAAN

Regardless of how long Abraham delayed in answering God's calling, he could not delay God very long. According to God's feeling, a thousand years are the same as a day. Can you delay God a thousand years? No one can do this. At the most, we might delay him for fifty years, which in God's eyes are a little more than an hour. God is sovereign and patient. God could say to Haran and Terah, "All that you are doing is in vain. After you die, I will bring My called one to My land." God is God. No one can frustrate Him. Once He has chosen and called you, He will not be stopped by anything. Sooner or later He will get through. He will come to you again and again. If one death is not sufficient to accomplish His aim, there will be another one. He has a way. He is much greater than you are. According to Acts 7:4, it was not Abraham who entered into the good land but God who removed him into the land. Although Hebrews 11:8 says that Abraham went out by faith, Acts 7:4 says that God removed him from Haran into Canaan. At most, we can delay the Lord for just a short time. Eventually we shall be gained by Him. If we delay, we shall only waste our time. God told Abraham to get out of his country. Since he did not do it in a rapid and clean-cut way, God removed him into His land.

PASSING THROUGH THE LAND
TO THE PLACE WHICH GOD CONFIRMS

At Haran, Abraham crossed the river. After crossing the river, he sojourned through the land, traveling southward until he reached a place called Shechem (12:6). The word Shechem means a shoulder which affords strength. At Shechem was Moreh where there was an oak. The name Moreh means a teacher who affords knowledge. Abraham journeyed to a place where he could get both strength and knowledge. Was that the place where God intended for Abraham to be? Yes. We know this because God did not reappear to Abraham until he had arrived at the oak of Moreh. There God reappeared to him (12:7).

God's reappearing to you confirms that you have arrived at the right place. Perhaps you experienced an appearing of God many years ago. After that time you wandered, journeyed, and traveled from place to place without having another appearing of God. One day, after arriving at the oak of Moreh, the church, the Lord appeared to you again. This appearing confirmed that you had arrived at the right place. Many of us can testify that after we were saved we traveled through Christianity without having God's reappearing. It was not until we came to today's Shechem with the oak of Moreh, that is, the church life, that the inner appearing rose up once again. Many of us can testify that after we came to the church, we had the feeling that God had appeared to us again, telling us, "This is the place."

The oak, a strong, hardy tree, signifies strength. An oak tree also affords shade from the heat of the sun. This is very meaningful. I believe that in symbol this signifies the church life which affords us the strength and shade. The church life strengthens us and shades us from the heat of the sun.

When God appeared to Abraham at Moreh, He said to him, "Unto thy seed will I give this land" (12:7). This was the first time that the promise of the land was clearly given. In 12:1 God only said to Abraham, "unto a land that I will shew thee"; God did not tell him where the land was or that He would give the land to him. But here God told him definitely where the land was and He promised to give this land to his seed. When we get to the place which God confirms by His reappearing, we also shall receive the promise of today's good land—Christ, the church, and the kingdom.

At the place where the Lord reappeared to him, Abraham built an altar. This altar was an anti-testimony to the building of the tower of Babel. At Babel, men built a tower to make a name for themselves. At Shechem, Abraham did not build anything to make himself a name; he built an altar for calling on the name of the Lord (12:8). This signifies that when we arrive at the place that God has chosen, God appears to us, and we have a deeper, fuller, richer, and more intimate fellowship with Him by calling on His name. We all can testify that we never called on the name of the Lord as much as we have since coming into the church life. Calling on the name of the Lord follows the building up of an altar to the very God who has appeared to us. In the church life, under the oak of Moreh, we have the intimate appearing of the Lord. What shall we do in response to this? We should build an altar to Him and put everything we are and have on the altar. We need to tell the Lord that everything we are and have is for Him, and then we need to call on the name of the Lord to maintain a deeper, richer, and more intimate fellowship with Him.

Now we have seen the experience of the first Hebrew, the first river crosser. Abraham was the first one to cross the river and to reach the place where God could reappear to him and where he could build an altar and call on the name of the Lord. This place is the right place.

It is not at Ur, Haran, or any place other than at the oak of Moreh. Here we have God's appearing and God's presence. Here we receive the promise of the good land. Here we can build an altar to the Lord, call on His name, and have intimate fellowship with Him.   ✖

5

LIVING BY FAITH

*By faith Abraham, being called, obeyed to go out
unto a place which he was to receive as an inheritance;
and he went out, not knowing where he was going.*

Hebrews 11:8

For we walk by faith, not by appearance.

2 Corinthians 5:7

*And the Lord appeared unto Abram, and said,
Unto thy seed will I give this land:
and there builded he an altar unto the Lord, who appeared
unto him. And he removed from thence unto a mountain
on the east of Beth-el, and pitched his tent,
having Beth-el on the west, and Hai on the east:
and there he builded an altar unto the Lord, and called
upon the name of the Lord....
Then Abram removed his tent, and came and dwelt
in the plain of Mamre, which is in Hebron, and
built there an altar unto the Lord.*

Genesis 12:7-8; 13:18

In all of human history there has never been a book as wonderful as the Bible. As the first book in the Bible, Genesis is not a book of doctrine; it is a book of history. It is not a history in a human way but in a very divine way. Genesis uses the biographies of some ancient saints to tell us something that is so divine. The divine revelation is contained in the human lives, in the human stories, of the people in Genesis. In this message we need to see the divine revelation found in Abraham's experience of living by faith.

In some of the preceding messages we have seen that the experience of the called ones has three aspects, the aspects of Abraham, Isaac, and Jacob. The first stage of the first aspect, the aspect of Abraham, was Abraham's being called by God. We have covered this point adequately in the last two messages. Now we come to the second stage of the experience of Abraham—living by faith, or we may say a life by faith. When we speak of a life by faith, we do not mean the life within but the life without, that is, the daily living, the daily walk, of the called ones. This daily walk is not by sight but by faith (2 Cor. 5:7).

Abraham's history is a seed. The entire biography of Abraham is a seed. It is not a seed of doctrine but a seed of our history. Abraham's history is the seed of our history because our history grows out of his history. In a sense, we and Abraham are one in the experience of life. We, the believers, are the true descendants of Abraham, and he is the true father of everyone who has been called by God. When we read his biography, we are also reading our own. His story is about us. As we read all of the chapters in Genesis about Abraham, we must read them in the way of realizing that his story is our story.

We need to see the steps that we must take in following the Lord. The first step is being called, and the second is living by faith. Have you been called? You must strongly say, "Amen, I have been called." Abraham was the first to be called, and, as we have seen, he did not answer God's calling in a clean-cut way but in the way of dragging his feet through mud and water. Our story is the same. Our answer to the Lord's calling was exactly the same as his. In principle, the seed is on a small scale, the growth is on a greater scale, and the harvest is on the greatest scale. We have seen that when Abraham left Haran, he took Lot with him. Did you not bring a Lot with you? If Abraham, the seed, brought one Lot, then it is probable that each one of us has brought many Lots. I am afraid that some of those reading this message have brought more than ten Lots with them. By this we see that our history is found in Abraham's biography.

Regardless of how much Abraham dragged his feet through the mud and water, God was still sovereign. God is God. Abraham was not only called; he was caught. He came out of his country, his kindred, and his father's house, and was brought to Moreh, the place where God wanted him to be and where He reappeared to him (12:6-7). God's reappearing was a seal to Abraham's answer to His calling. God's calling was clean-cut, but Abraham's answer to God's calling was not. Nevertheless, eventually God received a full answer to His calling. I do not care how much the young brothers and sisters drag their feet. Sooner or later, they will be fully caught. The Christian workers and the leading brothers must have the faith never to be disappointed with the brothers and sisters. Never feel that a particular brother is beyond hope. Rather, we must say that there is much hope with that brother. Simply wait awhile and you will see that everyone will come to Moreh.

STRENGTH—THE APPEARANCE OF GOD

At Moreh God reappeared to Abraham and he met God again (12:6). If you say that you have been called, I would ask you this question: What is the seal of your calling? The seal of our calling is God's reappearance. God's reappearance, His coming again to us, is the seal of our answer to His calling. The reappearing of God to Abraham was the strength that enabled him to live by faith.

If you read the record in Genesis, you will see that during Abraham's time mankind lived in the way of building a strong city for their protection and erecting a high tower for making themselves a name. That was the living of the humankind at Babel. But Abraham lived in an absolutely different way. His living was an anti-testimony to the way of the humankind, to the way that had been fully developed at Babel. As we saw in message thirty-six, at Babel there was a great city built by man. This city was not built with God-created stones but with man-made bricks. Those bricks were made by killing the element in the soil that grows life. But Abraham, the called one, did not live in that way. With Abraham, there was no city and no tower. After God's reappearing as the seal to Abraham's answer to God's calling, Abraham immediately built an altar, not to make a name for himself but to call upon the name of the Lord. Why did Abraham do this? Because he had the reappearing of God. How was he able to do this? Also because he had the reappearing of God. Remember that the record in Genesis concerning Abraham is a biography, not a doctrine, religion, or tradition. Abraham did not build an altar because of teaching or religious tradition. He built it because God had reappeared to him. God's reappearing meant everything to him. It not only sealed Abraham's answer to God's calling; it also strengthened him to live in a way that was absolutely different from the way of all of the humankind. It caused him to live as an anti-testimony to his generation. The altar that Abraham built was an anti-testimony to the tower of Babel.

AFTER ARRIVING AT CANAAN ✦ Now we need to find out at what time Abraham experienced God's reappearing. Our God never does anything without a purpose and He never acts in a meaningless way. Everything He does is purposeful and meaningful. After Abraham answered God's calling, believing in Him and obeying Him, he came to the oak of Moreh (12:6-7). When he came to that place, God reappeared to him because he had believed in God's calling and had obeyed it. As one who believed and obeyed God's calling, Abraham had no choice of the place where he should stay. God called Abraham a second time at Haran, and he crossed the river there, beginning a long journey. While he was on this long journey, he did not have his own choice. Hebrews 11:8 tells us that Abraham did not know where he was going. He had no road map in his hand. His road map was a living Person, the living God. While he was journeying, he had to look to God continually; he could not stop at any place he chose. As he was traveling, God's presence was his direction, his road map. He followed God in this way until he arrived at Moreh. At Moreh, God appeared to him. That appearing of God at Moreh indicated that Abraham had come to the place where God wanted him to be. There God told Abraham that He would give that land to his descendants.

God's first appearing to us does not depend upon us at all. It is God who initiates that calling. However, after the initial appearing, every other appearing depends upon our condition. Although God's first appearing is initiated by Him and does not depend upon us, the subsequent appearings depend upon our condition. If Abraham had not arrived at Moreh, he would not have had God's reappearing, the reappearing that strengthened him to go on with God. This going on with God was Abraham's living by faith in God.

AFTER THE SEPARATION OF LOT ✦ A second reappearing of God to Abraham is recorded in Genesis 13:14-17. In this chapter we see that Abraham had difficulty with Lot. In the flesh, Lot was Abraham's nephew, but before God he was Abraham's brother. Although Lot gave Abraham a difficult time, Abraham did not strive with him. Rather, he allowed Lot to have the choice. After Lot had separated from Abraham, leaving him alone, God reappeared to Abraham again. This reappearing was due to the fact that Abraham did not strive or fight for himself but left all the choices with his brother Lot. This second reappearing of God also strengthened Abraham's life by faith.

After we have been called by God, we need to live by faith. This is our need today. If you have been called by God, you have to live by faith. In the Bible, faith is in contrast to sight. If you have been called by God, you must live by faith, not by sight. Look at today's world: it is undoubtedly a harvest of the human living sown at Babel. A seed was sown at Babel, and the world today is a great harvest of that seed. People are building great cities for their living and are erecting high towers for their name. This is the situation everywhere on earth. But we have been called. What shall we do? We must live by faith. What does it mean to live by faith? It means to live by trusting in God for everything. Abraham did not declare that he lived by faith. Neither did he preach living by faith. He simply lived by faith. Now we need to see in what way Abraham lived by faith.

SIGNIFICANCE—THE ALTAR

THE FIRST ALTAR   ✦   After Abraham had arrived at Moreh and after God had reappeared to him, he built an altar (12:7). This was the first altar that Abraham built. In order to live by faith, we must first of all build an altar. In the Bible an altar means that we have all for God and serve God. Building an altar means that we offer everything we are and have to God. We need to place all that we are and all that we have on the altar. Before we do anything for God, God would say to us, "Child, don't do anything for Me. I want you. I want you to put all that you are and all that you have on the altar for Me." This is real fellowship, real worship. The real worship of the called ones is to put all that we are and have on the altar.

According to the human viewpoint, people will say that we are foolish for doing this. They will accuse us of wasting our time, of wasting our lives. If they had been with Abraham, they would have said, "Abraham, what are you doing? Are you crazy? Why do you build such a low thing as an altar, and put everything on it and burn it? Isn't that foolish?" As called ones, whatever we do will be foolish in the eyes of the worldly people. Many of our relatives will say that it is foolish for us to attend meetings so often, wondering why we do not stay at home and watch television with our family. The worldly people cannot understand why we attend meetings several times a week. They think that we are crazy. They would say, "What are you doing there in that little building? Why do you go there on Wednesday, Friday, Saturday, twice on Sunday, and even sometimes on Monday, Tuesday, and Thursday? Are you people crazy?" Yes, according to the worldly people, we are crazy. God's appearing makes us crazy.

An altar means that we do not keep anything for ourselves. An altar means that we realize that we are here on earth for God. An altar means that our life is for God, that God is our life, and that the meaning of our life is God. So we put everything on the altar. We are not here making a name for ourselves; we are putting everything on the altar for the sake of His name.

If you check with your experience, you will see that immediately after you were called, God appeared to you again, and you said, "Lord, from now on everything is Yours. All that I am, all that I have, all that I can do and am going to do is for You." I can still recall what happened on the afternoon that I was saved. As I went out of that church building and walked along the street, I lifted up my eyes to heaven and said, "God, from today on everything is for You." That was a real consecration. In a spiritual sense, it was the building of an altar. I believe that many of you reading this message have had such an experience. When we received God's calling, we were crazy, not caring about what would happen. Although we did not realize what it meant at the time, we promised the Lord that everything we had was for Him. When I said this to the Lord that day on the street, I did not realize what it involved. When after a few years I found myself in some difficulties, the Lord within me said, "Don't you remember what you said that afternoon as you walked along the street? Didn't you say, 'O God, from today on everything is for You'?" When I signed the contract, I did not know what was involved. But it was too late to repent; the contract had already been signed. To tell the Lord that everything is for Him is the real building of an altar. We all can testify how sweet is the sensation and how intimate is the fellowship whenever we tell the Lord that everything is for Him. At that time, we come deeply into the Lord Himself.

Although we may tell the Lord that everything we are and have is for Him, we may forget it a few days later. But the One who called us will never forget. He has an excellent memory. Often He will come to us and remind us of what we have said to Him. He may say, "Don't you remember what you said to Me that day?" This is not a doctrine; it is a real experience. Unless you have not been called, you are not an exception. As long as you are a called one, I have the complete assurance that you have had this kind of experience. The Lord did reappear to you, and at that reappearing you were crazy, promising to give the Lord everything, without considering the meaning of the involvement. You simply consecrated yourself to Him. You did not realize the meaning of what you promised. I thank God that we were not clear about this when we did it. We did not realize how much we became involved with God as a result of speaking one short sentence. We were bound by it. He is God. He is the calling One, and we are the called ones. It is all of Him. Even if we want to be crazy for Him, in ourselves we do not have the incentive to do it. But once He appears to us, we are crazy and say, "O Lord, everything is Yours. Take it. Lord, do what You want. I offer everything to You." Such a time of offering ourselves to the Lord is like a dream. Later we wake up and begin to realize what it involves.

In the early days of my ministry I was burdened to help people to consecrate themselves. Although I gave a lot of teaching about consecration, I did not see much result. My teaching did not work very well. Eventually, I learned that you cannot help people to consecrate themselves by teaching them. It is not teaching that causes people to consecrate themselves to the Lord; it is the Lord's appearing that motivates them to do this. If we can help people to meet the Lord and come into His presence, that will be sufficient. We do not need to tell them to consecrate themselves to God or to offer everything to the Lord on the altar. Once God appears to people, nothing can stop them from consecrating themselves. Spontaneously and automatically, they will say, "Lord, everything is Yours. From now on everything is for You." Have you not had this kind of experience? Have you not laid everything you are and have upon the altar for God and His purpose?

THE SECOND ALTAR   ✦   After Abraham built an altar to the Lord at Moreh, he traveled through the land. God did not give him just one little spot; He gave him a spacious land. In his travels, Abraham came to a place that was between Bethel and Ai. Bethel was on the west and Ai was on the east. Here, between Bethel and Ai, Abraham built another altar (12:8; 13:3-4). Bethel means the house of God, and Ai means the heap of ruins. Bethel and Ai stand in contrast one to another. What does this contrast mean? It means that in the eyes of the called ones only God's house is worthwhile. Everything else is just a heap of ruins. The principle is the same with us today. On the one hand, we have Bethel, God's house, the church life. Opposite to this is a heap of ruins. Everything that is contrary to the church life is a heap of ruins. In the eyes of God's called ones, everything other than the church life is a heap of ruins because the called ones look at the world situation from God's point of view. This point of view is absolutely different from the world's point of view. According to the worldly viewpoint, everything in the world is high, good, and wonderful, but, from the point of view of God's called ones, everything opposite to the house of God is a heap of ruins.

Firstly, we consecrate ourselves at Moreh. Then we consecrate ourselves at the place that is between the church life and the heap of ruins. As far as we are concerned, only the house of God is worthwhile. Everything other than this is a heap of ruins. Between the house of God and the heap of ruins we build an altar that we might fellowship with God, worship Him, and serve Him.

THE THIRD ALTAR   ✦   Abraham built the third altar at Mamre of Hebron (13:18). Mamre means strength, and Hebron means fellowship, communion, or friendship. According to Genesis 18:1, it was at Mamre that God came to visit Abraham. In that visit God not only appeared to him but stayed with him for quite a long time, even feasting with him. We shall see more about this when we come to that chapter. Although both Moreh and the place between Bethel and Ai were good, neither one was the place where Abraham stayed for constant fellowship with the Lord. The place where Abraham stayed for such constant fellowship with the Lord was Mamre of Hebron.

We all need to maintain a constant fellowship with the Lord. This does not happen by accident; neither should it occur occasionally. It must be constant. Perhaps some years ago you built an altar to the Lord. This is good, but what has happened since then? You may say that you built an altar two years ago, but how about today? Many of us have had the experience at Moreh but have not had the experience at Mamre. I believe that Abraham's life was mostly spent at Hebron, the place where he could have constant fellowship with the Lord. There, at Hebron, he built the third altar. We all need to build at least three altars: the first at Moreh, the second between Bethel and Ai, and the third at Mamre in Hebron. We need to build an altar at Mamre in Hebron so that we may worship God, serve Him, and have constant fellowship with Him. This is the experience of the third altar, the altar in Hebron.

EXPRESSION—THE TENT

BECAUSE ALL THE THINGS HE HAD WERE FOR GOD AND HE TRUSTED IN GOD ✦ After Abraham built an altar, he pitched a tent (12:7-8). At Babel, the people firstly built a city and then erected a tower. But Abraham firstly built an altar and then erected a tent. This means that Abraham was for God. The first thing he did was to take care of the worship of God, of his fellowship with God. Secondly, he took care of his living. The tent was for Abraham's living. Abraham did not take care of his living first. That was secondary. With Abraham, the primary matter was to consecrate everything to God, to worship and serve God, and to have fellowship with God. Only then did Abraham pitch a tent for his living. Abraham's dwelling in a tent indicated that he did not belong to the world but was a testimony to the people (Heb. 11:9).

AT THE PLACE OF TESTIMONY ✦ Abraham firstly pitched his tent at the place between Bethel and Ai (12:8; 13:3). That was the place where God's house was and where he began his testimony in expressing God by fellowshipping with Him. His altar was the beginning of his testimony for God to the world, whereas his tent was the completion of his testimony to the world for God. His tent was a miniature of the tabernacle built by his descendants in the wilderness, which was called the "tabernacle of testimony" (Exo. 38:21). Since his tent was pitched by Bethel, in a sense it may be considered as the house of God for God's testimony on earth.

AT THE PLACE OF FELLOWSHIP • Later, Abraham removed his tent to Hebron, which means fellowship (13:18). His tent firstly was a testimony for God to the world and then it became the center where he had fellowship with God. This is strongly proved by what occurred in chapter eighteen when God came to stay with him in the tent at Mamre in Hebron. By Abraham's pitching a tent God had a place on earth where He could communicate and fellowship with man. His tent brought God from heaven to earth. All of us, God's called ones, should pitch a tent. On the one hand, such a tent is a testimony of God to the world; on the other hand, it is a place of fellowship with God to bring God from heaven to earth.

Do not think that this matter of a tent is a small thing. Later, when Abraham's descendants were called out of Egypt and entered into the wilderness, God commanded them to build a tent and in front of the tent He commanded them to build an altar (Exo. 26:1; 27:1). There, in Exodus, we see an altar with a tent, a tabernacle. That tabernacle was God's house on earth. Abraham's tent was also God's house on earth. In Genesis 18 we can see that God came and stayed with Abraham in his tent. At that time, Abraham was a priest offering sacrifices to God. His building an altar and offering sacrifices to God proved that he functioned as a priest. God's intention is that all of His called ones should be priests. We are priests. We do not need others to offer sacrifices for us. We must do it ourselves. When Abraham was feasting with God in his tent, he was the high priest, and the inner part of his tent was the Holy of Holies. God was there. By this we can see that Abraham's tent was a prefigure of the tabernacle built by Abraham's descendants in the wilderness as the dwelling place for God and for the priests. Here in Genesis we see a priest named Abraham who lived with God in his tent. At the side of this tent there was an altar.

SOJOURNING BY FAITH AS IN A STRANGE COUNTRY • Do not forget that Abraham's history is yours. Do you not have a tent where you always have the Lord's presence? The worldly people do not have such a tent. They only have a great city. The only thing that the worldly people can see is their great city. They say, "Look at my corporation. Look at my education, my attainment. Look at how many things I have." But we can say to the worldly people, "You have everything, but there is one thing that you don't have—God's presence. You do not have the tent—you have the city of Babel. All that you have is a part of the great Babylon." Whether we are high-class people or low-class people does not mean very much. All that matters is that wherever we are we have a tent with God's presence. When we have a tent with God's presence, we have the deep sensation within that nothing here on earth is lasting. Everything is temporary. We are looking to eternity. The banks, the corporations, the attainments—all are temporal and mean nothing. We have nothing constant on this earth. I just like to have a tent with God's presence. I like to live in such a situation. We may say to the worldly people, "Dr. So-and-so, I don't have as much as you have, but I have the one thing that you don't have—God's presence. I don't have to wait for eternity to have God's presence. I have His presence right now in my tent. My surroundings are a tent, a miniature of the New Jerusalem. This may not be worthwhile in your eyes, but in God's eyes it means a great deal." This is what it means to pitch a tent.

Whenever we answer God's calling and God reappears to us and we build an altar for God, telling Him that everything we are and have is for Him, we shall immediately erect a tent. Spontaneously, people will see that this is an expression, a declaration, that we do not belong to this world. By pitching a tent we declare that we belong to another country. We do not belong to this country; we are looking for a better one. We do not like this country, this earth, this world. We expect to come into another country. We are sojourning by faith as in a strange country (Heb. 11:9).

WAITING WITH EXPECTATION FOR A CITY WITH FOUNDATIONS ✦ Hebrews 11:10 says that Abraham "waited for the city which has the foundations, whose Architect and Maker is God." This city which has foundations is undoubtedly the New Jerusalem, which has solid foundations laid and built by God (Rev. 21:14, 19-20). While Abraham was living in a tent without any foundations, he was looking and waiting for a city with foundations. But I do not believe that Abraham knew that he was waiting for the New Jerusalem. Even many Christians do not know that what they are waiting for is the New Jerusalem. But we have to be clear that we are living in the tent of the church life today, waiting for its ultimate consummation, which will be the New Jerusalem—the city of God with foundations.

LIVING IN A SHADOW OF THE NEW JERUSALEM ✦ Abraham's tent was a miniature of the New Jerusalem, which will be the ultimate tabernacle of God in the universe (Rev. 21:2-3). As he lived in that tent, he was living in a shadow of the New Jerusalem. While he was living there with God, he was waiting for a city, a city that eventually will be the New Jerusalem. The New Jerusalem, the eternal tabernacle, will replace that temporary tent in which Abraham lived. Abraham's tent was a seed of God's eternal dwelling place. This seed grew in the tabernacle erected by his descendants in the wilderness (Exo. 40), and its harvest will be the New Jerusalem, the tabernacle of God with man. God still needs to have such a seed in all of us. We all need to be those who live in a tent and who look forward to a better country, a country in which there will be the eternal tabernacle where God and we, we and God, will live together for eternity. Abraham's interest was altogether in a better country. Although God had told him that He would give the land to Abraham and his descendants, Abraham did not care for that. He was looking for another country and for a city with foundations. Eventually, the Bible tells us that this better country is the new heaven and the new earth and that the city with foundations is the New Jerusalem, the eternal dwelling place for God and for all His called ones.

Today we are repeating the life and history of Abraham. Once there was only one Abraham; now there are many. The church life today is the harvest of the life and history of Abraham. Abraham's life by faith is presently being repeated among us. We all are here building an altar and pitching a tent. Look at the church life: we have an altar and a real tabernacle. This is a picture of the coming New Jerusalem where we shall spend eternity with God.

The Bible ends with a tent. The New Jerusalem is the ultimate tent, the ultimate tabernacle, in the universe. Maybe one day Abraham will meet with God in the New Jerusalem, and God will say, "Abraham, don't you remember that day when we feasted together in your tent? Your tent was a miniature of this eternal tabernacle." Abraham's tent was a seed. The growth of that seed is in Exodus and its harvest is in Revelation 21. In principle, there is no difference between Abraham's tent, and the New Jerusalem, the ultimate tent. If I were Abraham meeting with God in the New Jerusalem, I would say, "Lord, I remember the day You came to my tent. Now I come to Your tent."

6

THE TRIAL
OF THE CALLED

And Abram journeyed, going on still toward
the south. And there was a famine in the land:
and Abram went down into Egypt to sojourn there;
for the famine was grievous in the land.

Genesis 12:9-10

And Abram was very rich in cattle, in silver, and in gold....And Lot also,
which went with Abram, had flocks, and herds, and tents.
And the land was not able to bear them, that they might dwell together:
for their substance was great, so that they could not dwell together.
And there was a strife between the herdmen of Abram's cattle
and the herdmen of Lot's cattle....

Genesis 13:2, 5-7

In this message we come to Abraham's experience of trials. We have seen how Abraham was called by God and how, by God's appearing, he was strengthened to answer that call. We have also seen that, by God's appearing, Abraham was brought to the very place where God intended him to be. Firstly he was brought to Shechem

(12:6) and then to the place between Bethel and Ai, the place between the house of God and the heap of ruins (12:8). That place between the house of God and the heap of ruins was the high point, and Abraham should have remained there.

However, suddenly, after such a high attainment in his experience of God, Abraham continued his journey, going toward the south (12:9). In studying this chapter, I have spent much time to find out the reason why Abraham continued his journey. Why did he journey on and not remain there between the house of God and the heap of ruins? Abraham had attained the high point, the place where God intended for him to be. By God's mercy, he should have remained there. But Abraham journeyed southward. This means that he went downward. After such a high attainment in the experience of God, any journey would be downward. This continuing of his journey was the cause of Abraham's failure.

We have seen that, at the beginning, Abraham dragged his feet through mud and water. Eventually, he was victorious, going all the way to Shechem and afterward to the place near Bethel. That was wonderful. In both of those places he built an altar and at the place between Bethel and Ai he also called upon the name of the Lord and pitched his tent as a declaration to the whole world that he was an anti-testimony to the situation at Babel. Do you not think that in doing so Abraham had arrived, attained the high point of his experience of God?

Perhaps you are thinking that if you had been Abraham, you surely would have remained there. But we should not think this way, for we are today's Abraham. The ancient Abraham was just like us. As we have pointed out elsewhere, Abraham's experience was a seed of our own experience. The record of Abraham in Genesis is his biography, but it is our autobiography. You may say, "No, it is Abraham's autobiography and my biography." But this record is your autobiography not your biography, because the biography of Abraham was written by Moses and your biography is written by yourself. Abraham's experience corresponds with ours. We and he are one. Have you not had a wonderful time with the Lord in which you reached the high point and shouted, "Hallelujah! How good it is here! No place is better than this place. This is the best place for me to be." Have you not said this? But what happened the very next day? You began to journey downward. The night before you said, "Hallelujah, this is the place for me," and the next morning you began to journey downward to the border of Egypt. This means that you journeyed to a place that was so close to the world, close to the movie theaters. One night you were on the high point in Canaan and the next morning you were moving downward to the border of the world. Has this not happened to you? I am so happy and surprised to hear the junior high young people offer such wonderful prayers in the meetings. But I need to say an honest word to them; I do not trust you. After praying such a wonderful prayer one night in the meeting, the next morning you may journey downward to the border of worldly entertainments. Today you may say, "Hallelujah, this is the best place for me," and next weekend you may move downward to the movie theater. Remember that we are today's Abraham. It is easy to reach the high point, but it is not easy to remain there. There is not much room on the high point. If you move just slightly, you will fall downhill. It is very difficult to keep the God-appointed position. The high point is surrounded by pits, and it is easy to fall into one of them. The called ones will not usually go backward, but it is easy for them to go downward into Egypt. Abraham never went back to Chaldea, but he did go down into Egypt.

In 12:9—13:18 we see Abraham's trial. The word trial is not a pleasant word. No one likes to experience trials. Do you like to have trials in your life? Although no one likes trials, they are good experiences. Not too long after Abraham was called and began to live by faith, a trial came to him. Do not pray, "Lord, You are so good to me. Don't let any trials come to me." This kind of prayer will only hasten the coming of the trials. The Lord will answer your prayer in just the opposite way. If you say, "Lord, don't send any trials," the Lord will say, "I will send a trial very quickly." I am assured that no one can say that since he was called by the Lord he has always enjoyed good times. No one can say that.

Our God is not only the God of love but also the God of sovereignty. Our God is sovereign. Our God is not only the God of love, the God of light, and the God of life, but also the God of sovereignty. Everything is under His dispensation. He manages the whole world just for us. We must all believe that God manages the entire universe for every one of us. You may say, "How small I am! How could the sovereign God manage the universe just for me?" But He does manage it just for you. You must believe this. You are not so small that God does not sovereignly arrange your environment for you. You are big enough to have God's sovereign arrangement. I have learned this from my own experience. Fifty years ago I did not like this story of Abraham going down to Egypt. I simply could not be happy with that experience. When, at that time, I read some messages on Abraham's downward experience, I did not understand it and did not feel good about it. I even questioned God. But now, after many years of experience, I am very happy. How we need to hear this message on Abraham's trial!

It is easy to reach the high point in our experience with God, but it is not easy to remain there. Look at the environment that surrounds you on every side. It was sovereignly arranged before you were born. God is sovereign. Although you may consider yourself a small creature, as far as God is concerned, you are a very important person. Before the foundation of the world, God arranged everything for you. He even arranged that you would be reading this message right now. We are under God's arrangement. Do not try to escape. If you escape to a certain place, you will find that place to be the exact place that God arranged for you. When you reach old age, you will bow down and say, "Lord, I am fully convinced that You arranged everything for me before the foundation of the world."

Abraham's trial was for him to learn a lesson. We all need to learn some lessons. We cannot learn these lessons from our parents or from the experienced brothers and sisters. We all must learn some lessons of God's sovereignty.

FAMINE

As we have seen, the second aspect of Abraham's experience was living by faith. He had to live by trusting in God for his daily needs. In 12:10 we read that there was a grievous famine in the land. This famine was a test to see whether or not Abraham would trust in God in the matter of making a living, in the matter of his daily living.

If you examine 12:10-20, you will see that in this situation Abraham was weak and low. He failed to keep the God-appointed position and went down to Egypt. Behind Canaan was Babel, beside Canaan was Egypt, and close to Canaan was Sodom. Abraham moved gradually southward until he went down to Egypt. As we shall see, in Egypt he sinned by lying. Probably none of us would believe that Abraham could be so weak and low. God had appeared to him at Ur, at Haran, and at Shechem. At Shechem, God said to Abraham, "Unto thy seed will I give this land" (12:7). God told Abraham definitely that He was going to give that place to his descendants. Who was the God that spoke to Abraham? He was the Creator, the Possessor of heaven and earth. This was the very God that appeared to Abraham. When the famine came, Abraham should not have had any doubts but should have said, "I don't care about the famine because I have the living God. I am not concerned about the lack of food because the One who called me, brought me here, and reappeared as a confirmation to my journey is the Almighty God. I have put my trust in Him and now I am living by trusting in Him for my daily need. I don't care whether there is food or not." Abraham should have prayed in this way.

However, what did Abraham do when the famine came? Did he pray? Did he say to his wife, "Dear, let us pray"? No, it seemed that Abraham forgot to pray. When such a period of testing came to him, he did not pray. Do not laugh at Abraham. When everything is going well, you find it easy to pray. But when the famine comes, you forget that you are a Christian and only remember that you are a human being. You forget the living God who appeared to you, only remembering that you have a stomach. Abraham was concerned about his stomach. He looked at the situation: in the land there was famine, and in Egypt there was plenty of food. Abraham and his wife did not talk very much. Immediately they both agreed to go to Egypt. I believe that even before they made this decision, they were already going downward. Both the husband and the wife forgot God. They did not consider where God wanted them to go. It was as if they had no God.

SINNING BY LYING ✦ When Abraham and Sarah came to the border of Egypt, he said to her, "It shall come to pass, when the Egyptians shall see thee, that they shall say, This is his wife: and they will kill me, but they will save thee alive" (12:12). Fearing that the Egyptians would kill him and take his wife, Abraham prayed to Sarah, not to God saying, "Say, I pray thee, thou art my sister: that it may be well with me for thy sake; and my soul shall live because of thee" (12:13). Abraham and Sarah agreed that she should lie about being his wife. Abraham was prepared to sacrifice his wife in order to save his life. It seemed that he had no standard of morality. Among

Christians, Abraham has been uplifted too highly. He was not that high. Many of us would not have done what Abraham did. But Abraham was so low that he was willing to sacrifice his wife, allowing her to be taken to be the wife of another man, in order to save his own life. How shameful that was! Do you believe that God's called one, the father of faith, could do such a thing? We see by this that Abraham was not higher than we are. At the most, he was the same as we are. For the sake of his stomach he was prepared to sell his wife, and Sarah submitted to this. She was certainly the best wife, the standard of all wives. She was submissive, took Abraham's counsel, and did not blame him.

In this matter Abraham was a good prophet, for things happened in Egypt exactly as he had predicted. The Egyptians took his wife away to Pharaoh's palace (12:14-15). In a sense, Abraham did sell his wife. Because of Sarah, Pharaoh gave Abraham many things—sheep, oxen, camels, menservants, and maidservants (12:16). Abraham became rich. I have been unable to understand how Abraham, seeing that his wife had been taken, could have had the peace to receive all of these things from Pharaoh. But he did receive them. He did not fast. He did not say, "Oh, I can't accept this. I want Sarah!" No, he let Sarah go. I believe that Abraham was certain that his wife was lost, that she was gone. According to his figuration, Sarah was gone. More or less, he received as the price of letting her go the cattle, oxen, and servants.

Being kept by God ✦ But God would not let Abraham go. God came in, not to deal with Abraham but to deal with Pharaoh. Verse 17 says, "And the Lord plagued Pharaoh and his house with great plagues because of Sarai, Abram's wife." The Bible says that great plagues came upon Pharaoh and his house. Although it is not confirmed by the word in the Bible, I believe that from the time Pharaoh took Sarah he became seriously ill, becoming sick to such an extent that he was about to die. We are told that great plagues were upon him and his house. What were these plagues? Did a fire burn the palace? I do not believe that. After much consideration, I strongly believe that the plagues were certain diseases that came over Pharaoh and over everyone in the house with the exception of Sarah. The whole palace might have talked about what was happening, wondering why everyone had become sick, why Pharaoh was dying, and why only Sarah had been spared. Perhaps they said, "Who is that woman? Why is she not sick?" They might have asked Sarah the reason. Sarah, seeing the whole situation, began to understand. Then she told Pharaoh that she was Abraham's wife. I believe that this is the way it might have happened. God's hand was on Pharaoh for Sarah. He came in to preserve Abraham and his wife.

When we, the believers, have faith in God, all of the surrounding people receive the benefits, but when we fail to have faith in God, we may bring harm to the people in our surroundings. God was sovereign and Pharaoh suffered. Although I do not say that God took things out of Pharaoh's hand and passed them on to Abraham, the real situation was somewhat like that. Eventually, Abraham did not lose his wife but instead gained great riches.

While he was in Egypt, Abraham experienced God's keeping grace. Without the keeping grace, none of us can remain on the high point of our experience. We all need the keeping grace. Do not trust in your experience—trust in His keeping grace. As far as God's keeping grace was concerned, Abraham was still on the high point even when he was selling his wife in Egypt. Whether he was on the top or on the bottom, he was always in God's keeping grace. In a very good sense Abraham never touched Egypt, for the keeping grace was under him all the time. Although he went down to Egypt, he was still in the keeping grace. Even if you have fallen, you are still in the keeping grace, and the keeping grace will bring you back to the high point. The keeping grace could say to Abraham, "Abraham, don't be naughty anymore. You gave me an opportunity to show you my sovereignty, but it is better for you to trust in me."

HAVING LEARNED THE LESSON THAT GOD TAKES CARE OF HIM IN EVERYTHING AND THAT EVERYTHING IS IN GOD'S HAND   ✦   By this one experience in Egypt Abraham learned that the God who called him also took care of him and that everything was in His hand. As we shall see, the next chapter proves that Abraham had learned this lesson. Through this experience Abraham was disciplined not only to trust in God but to know that God is real and faithful.

As long as you are one of God's called ones, He will take care of you whether or not you believe in Him or trust in Him. If you stay on the high point, He feeds you. If you fall to the bottom, He feeds you the more. Whether we stay on the high point or fall to the bottom is up to us. It does not make any difference to Him, for whether we are on the top or on the bottom, He takes care of us. This is our story as well as the story of Abraham. I can testify to you from my experience that God is real and faithful. Our Father is real and faithful. The One who has called us is real and faithful. Regardless of whether the economy of the world is good or bad, God takes care of us.

We, the called ones, can enjoy God. While we may be selling our wives, our God is taking care of us. While we may be planning to sell our wives to save our lives, God is planning how to preserve our wives, to gain many things for us, and to send us back to His place with all of the riches that we have acquired. When I read this story at first, I did not agree with it. Eventually, I was laughing because our calling God is so good. When Abraham was planning to sell his wife, God was preparing to bless him, preserve his life, and give him many riches. If I had been Abraham at that time, I would have said, "God, what can I say? I have no face to say anything to You." If I had been Abraham and had looked at my wife, cattle, and servants, I would not even have had the face to say, "Father, thank You." I would have said to Sarah, "Dear, let us go back. It doesn't matter whether the servants want to come with us or not. I don't deserve any of these riches that God has given us and I feel ashamed to enjoy them. I am not worthy, but God gives so freely. Sarah, while I was selling you, God gave all of these things to us. You may say that it is good, but I feel ashamed. Sarah, you pray and thank God for me. I just don't have the face to pray for myself." I do believe that this happened to Abraham.

In 13:1 we see that Abraham "went up out of Egypt." He went back to the very place where the high point was, "unto the place where his tent had been at the beginning, between Bethel and Ai; unto the place of the altar, which he had made there at the first: and there Abram called on the name of the Lord" (13:3-4). Abraham returned to the place where he had built an altar and pitched his tent. When Abraham was planning to sell his wife in Egypt, there was no altar, tent, or calling on the name of the Lord. There was no declaration of his anti-testimony to Babel. When he was in Egypt, he lost all of this. But Abraham came back to the beginning, to the place of the altar, and there he recovered his calling on the name of the Lord.

THE STRIVING OF THE BROTHER

After passing through the experience in chapter twelve, it might be easy for Abraham or for us to say, "Praise the Lord, I have learned the lesson!" But some tests are needed to prove whether or not we have truly learned the lesson. One test is the striving of the brother (13:5-13). Abraham had become rich by trying to sell his wife, and these riches caused him some trouble. He became too rich. Lot also acquired riches, and the land was too small to bear them both. In 13:6 we are told that "the land was not able to bear them, that they might dwell together: for their substance was great, so that they could not dwell together." So there was "strife between the herdmen of Abraham's cattle and the herdmen of Lot's cattle" (13:7). This became another trial for Abraham. Many times the second trial comes out of the blessing of the first trial. You may say, "Praise the Lord! When I was walking out of Egypt, I didn't have the face to thank the Lord, but now after three months I can praise Him for His goodness to me. He preserved my wife and has given me all of these riches." If you say this, you may soon find yourself in trouble, for the second trial will come from the blessing of the first trial. This is our experience.

Chapter thirteen indicates that Abraham had learned a lesson. This time he did not fail; he was prevailing because he had learned the lesson in the first trial. If you read carefully, you will see that in this case the fault was not with Abraham but with Lot. Abraham learned the lesson of not striving for himself and of having no choice for himself but of trusting in God's care. He knew that he was in the hand of God and under the care of God. There is no hint in chapter thirteen of any kind of failure on the part of Abraham. He was completely successful. "And Abram said unto Lot, Let there be no strife, I pray thee, between me and thee, and between my herdmen and thy herdmen; for we be brethren. Is not the whole land before thee? separate thyself, I pray thee, from me: if thou will take the left hand, then I will go to the right; or if thou depart to the right hand, then I will go to the left" (13:8-9). Abraham seemed to be telling Lot, "Lot, we are Hebrew brothers, the only Hebrews in the land. All of the others are Gentiles. They are looking at us. There should be no strife between us, for that would be a shame to the God in whom we trust. Lot, look over the land and choose the place where you would like to be. I will not strive or have any choice." Deep within, Abraham must have said,

"My choice is with God. I have learned the lesson by going down to Egypt. Now I know that I am under the care of my God and that under Him everything is mine. I don't need to choose. I will let Lot make his choice." Lot made his choice, departed from Abraham, and "pitched his tent toward Sodom," not caring about the wickedness of Sodom (13:12-13).

It was not a small thing for Abraham to be left without Lot. Abraham did not have a son. His nephew, Lot, a very close relative, was just like a son to him. I believe that Abraham treated Lot as his own son. So when Lot left him, he was alone. But at this point God appeared to Abraham again. In Egypt, God dealt with Pharaoh in the plagues, but He did not appear to Abraham because he was in the wrong position. In Egypt, Abraham was in God's keeping grace, but he did not have God's appearing. Now in chapter thirteen Abraham was not only in God's keeping grace but, having come back to the original place, was also in the right position. Furthermore, he did not strive for himself or choose for himself. As a result of the discipline he underwent in Egypt, he learned that his future and everything were in the hand of God and that he was under God's care. So God appeared to him and said, "Lift up now thine eyes, and look from the place where thou art northward, and southward, and eastward, and westward: for all the land which thou seest, to thee will I give it, and to thy seed forever" (13:14-15). Abraham told Lot to take his choice of the land. Then God came in and seemed to tell Abraham, "I do not allow you to choose. I am giving all the choices to you. Look northward, southward, eastward, and westward—all is yours. You gave the choice to Lot. Now I am giving everything to you." We must learn from this never to strive for ourselves in the church life. Let your brother have all the choices. If you give the choice to your brother, God will come in and give all the choices to you.

This time in His appearing God confirmed the promise concerning the good land in 12:7 and the promise concerning the increase of his seed in 12:2. Our prevailing over any trial always confirms God's promises to us. This happened to Abraham. Moreover, Abraham's prevailing over this trial ushered him to the peak of his experience of God. He removed his tent and came to dwell in Hebron (13:18) where he dwelt for most of the remainder of his time in the fellowship with God (18:1).

7

THE VICTORY
OF THE CALLED

*And Melchizedek king of Salem brought forth bread and wine: and
he was the priest of the most high God. And he blessed him, and said,
Blessed be Abram of the most high God, possessor of heaven and earth:
and blessed be the most high God, which hath delivered
thine enemies into thy hand. And he gave him tithes of all.*

Genesis 14:18-20

*So also Christ did not glorify Himself in becoming a High Priest,
but it was He who said to Him, "You are My Son;
this day have I begotten You"; even as also in another place He says,
"You are a Priest forever according to the order of Melchisedec."*

Hebrews 5:5-6

*For this Melchisedec, king of Salem, priest of the Most High God,
who met Abraham returning from the slaughter of the kings
and blessed him, to whom also Abraham apportioned a tenth part of all;
first being interpreted king of righteousness, and then also king of Salem,
which is king of peace; being without father, without mother,
without genealogy; having neither beginning of days nor end of life,
but likened to the Son of God, abides a priest perpetually.*

Hebrews 7:1-3

In this message we come to the victory in Abraham's experience
(14:11-24). If we read the book of Genesis carefully, we shall see that
apart from chapter fourteen it does not relate much concerning the

international affairs among the Gentiles. But chapter fourteen gives us a record concerning the international fighting among the Gentiles. Why is there such a record? The wording in the Bible is very economical. Not one word is wasted. Nevertheless, chapter fourteen is almost entirely concerned with the international fighting among the Gentile kingdoms. The events in chapter fourteen, however, are not just related to international affairs but are sovereignly related to God's people. Why does this chapter dedicate such a lengthy word to the international fighting among the Gentiles? Although this fighting apparently was international, actually it was sovereignly arranged by the Lord. God is sovereign over the environment and over all the events concerning His people. In the land of Canaan at that time, there were only two families of the Hebrew race—the family of Abraham and the family of Lot. All of the rest were Gentiles. In this chapter we see that God was sovereign, causing something to happen for the good of His people.

Chapter fourteen of Genesis relates the fighting between a group of four kings and a group of five kings. Eventually, the five kings were defeated by the four kings. If you read carefully, you will see this fighting was absolutely for Lot and for Abraham. In other words, both Lot and Abraham, the two Hebrews, were put to the test under God's sovereignty. Was this fighting good or not? Humanly speaking, no fighting is good. However, in this chapter the fighting was good for Lot and especially for Abraham. In this message we need to see the profitable aspects related to God's people in this fighting.

THE CAPTIVITY OF THE BROTHER

The fighting occurred mainly at Sodom. It mainly happened at Sodom because one of God's people, Lot, was living there. Before the time of that fighting, Lot had separated himself from Abraham (13:11). Do you think that it was good for Lot to have separated himself from Abraham? No, it was not good. All of the young people today like to be separated from the older generation. In God's economy, however, it is not good for the young ones to be separated from the older generation. If you do this, you will miss the mark and the protection. At the time of Genesis 13, God's goal and eternal mark were with Abraham. If you had been there and had separated yourself from him, it would have been equal to separating yourself from God's mark. God's goal is with the called ones. If you separate yourself from the called ones, you separate yourself from God's goal. Lot should never have separated himself from Abraham, because God's goal was with Abraham. To leave Abraham was to leave God's mark. Moreover, to leave Abraham was to leave the protection.

Lot was not firstly defeated by the four kings. That defeat was the issue of at least two foregoing defeats. Before Lot was captured by Chedorlaomer, he already had had two defeats. The first defeat occurred when Lot's herdmen were striving against Abraham's herdmen and Abraham offered Lot the choice of the land (13:7-11). When Abraham offered the choice to Lot, Lot should have said, "Uncle, my choice is you. My choice is your choice. I don't like to make any choice of my own. If my herdmen will not listen to me, I will fire them, but I will never go away from you. I have no choice but you and your choice." But, on the contrary, when Abraham gave him his choice, immediately, without much consideration, Lot made his choice and went his way. That was his first defeat.

After separating from Abraham, "Lot dwelled in the cities of the plain, and pitched his tent toward Sodom" (13:12). Lot was going downhill. After taking the first step downward, it was easy for him to take the second and the third. The first step was leaving Abraham, who stood afar off from Sodom. Lot took the way that was toward Sodom. He walked in the direction of Sodom. In the eyes of God, Sodom was a wicked and sinful city (13:13). Lot, as one of the people of God, surely knew this. He should have stayed away from Sodom and not have walked towards it. Nevertheless, because the land around Sodom was rich, Lot journeyed toward Sodom. Eventually, he moved into the city, lived there, and settled there. That was his second defeat.

Do you think that God will allow His people to dwell in such a wicked city? Certainly not. Thus, under God's sovereignty, Chedorlaomer led the attack against Sodom. God allowed that war to take place. Four kings fought against five kings. Humanly speaking, the five kings should have been victorious since their number was greater. But the four kings defeated the five kings, and the city of Sodom was taken. The Bible stresses the taking of Sodom because Lot dwelt there. This fighting was not merely a matter of four kings against five kings; it was a fighting for one of God's people. Lot might have been peaceful as he dwelt in Sodom, but God was not peaceful. God would never allow Lot to stay there in peace. God might have said, "Lot, you may have peace within, but I will stir up some disturbance from without. I will send the four kings to defeat the five kings and capture your city. They will capture you, your family, and all that you have." This is in fact what happened to Lot. Lot suffered defeat after defeat. Eventually, as the last step of his defeat, he fell into the hands of the enemy. He was captured, and the king of Sodom could not help him.

FIGHTING FOR THE BROTHER

In the matter of the capture of Lot, God was sovereign. Genesis 14:13 says, "And there came one that had escaped, and told Abram the Hebrew." The four kings had captured Sodom and all of its food supply, but one person who escaped told Abraham that Lot had been captured. Do you believe that this happened by accident? While so many others were captured, this one escaped. That person was preserved by God's sovereignty. As we shall see, it must have happened because of the intercession behind the scene. The one who escaped did not run away but came purposely to Abraham and told him that Lot had been captured.

Unlike us, Abraham did not count the weak point of his brother and did not take pleasure in Lot's suffering and calamity. Abraham did not say, "Lot should never have separated himself from me. I knew this was going to happen. He got what he deserved. I believe that God is sovereign and that Lot's suffering comes from God. Be at peace and go home. God will preserve Lot." I believe that many of us would have responded in this way. But Abraham was different. When he received this information, he made a strong decision to fight for Lot (14:14). As we shall see, Abraham prayed. In verse 22 he told the king of Sodom that before he went out to war he lifted up his hand to God. How could Abraham have prayed and made such a decision? It must have been due to the fact that someone behind the scene was interceding for him. I believe that the intercessor knew of the fighting that was going on and of the capture of Lot. As a result of this intercession, Abraham made a brief and bold decision.

Abraham decided to take his three hundred eighteen men and fight against the four kings and their armies. The four kings must have had several armies, the number of men in which must have been much greater than the number of Abraham's men. How could Abraham have fought against them with such a small number? Moreover, they were kings and generals who had fought many battles, and Abraham was a layman. How could he fight against those who were experts in war? How could he defeat them with such a small number? Nevertheless, Abraham was bold, having confidence in God.

As far as Abraham was concerned, it was a shame for him to see that his brother had been captured. It is the same in the church today. It is a shame for us to see that any brother or sister has been captured. If a brother in the brothers' house is captured and you see it, that is a shame. You should not tolerate it but should say, "I cannot bear with this. I must rise up and do something about it!" This is what Abraham did.

Abraham's bold decision must have been due to the fact that behind the scene someone was interceding for him. Perhaps you are thinking that there is no record of this in the Bible. Neither is there a record of Melchisedec's parents or genealogy. But do you believe that he had no parents or genealogy? Certainly he did, yet the Bible does not mention them. Many things behind the scene in this chapter are not recorded. I do believe that behind the scene there was some intercession. Someone concerned for God's interest on earth was interceding for Lot, Abraham, and Abraham's fighting.

We have seen that Lot's defeat did not begin at Sodom. In the same principle, Abraham's victory did not start with the slaughter of the kings. Abraham's victory began when Lot departed from him. Abraham had been called by God, and he answered that calling by coming forward to the very land that God intended to give him. At that time, however, Abraham had nearly no experience. All he had was a little experience in answering God's calling and coming forward to the place where God intended him to be. As we saw in the last message, a famine arose as a test to Abraham, and he was not able to withstand that test. Abraham failed God, trying by himself to make a living at the sacrifice of his wife. Under God's sovereign teaching, Abraham learned a great deal by that failure. Abraham learned that God is sovereign over everything and that He knows everything concerning His people. Everything related to God's called ones is in His hand. Abraham saw that, experienced it, and came fully into it.

Afterward, when the problem arose between Abraham and Lot, Abraham was victorious. His victory began at that time because he had learned the basic lesson in his going down to Egypt. We all must learn such a basic lesson. After you have been called and have answered God's calling by coming to the place where He intends you to be, the first basic lesson that God will teach you is that, as a called one of God, everything concerning you is under God's hand. God is sovereign over you. This was the basic lesson that Abraham learned by going down to Egypt. After learning that lesson, he gained the victory with Lot. When the problem arose with Lot, Abraham didn't take his own choice; he knew that his choice was in the hands of God. That was the beginning of Abraham's victory.

Then the time came when Abraham could show the whole universe that he was on God's side. When Melchisedec appeared, two special titles of God are revealed: the Most High God and the Possessor of heaven and earth (v. 19). Both Melchisedec and Abraham spoke of God in this way. Abraham said, "I have lifted up mine hand unto the Lord, the most high God, the possessor of heaven and earth" (14:22). Abraham could say, "By going down to Egypt I have learned the lesson that my God, the One who called me, is the Possessor of both heaven and earth. I don't need to have any choice. My choice is just He. I cannot bear seeing that my brother has been captured. This is a shame to me. I must take him back. I don't care for the number of soldiers and I don't care for the kings and armies. I don't care that I have less than they do. My burden is to get my brother back. If I don't do this, it is a shame to me."

In fighting for his brother, Abraham risked his life. It was not a small thing for him to risk his life in order to rescue his captured brother. But he did it. The fight went smoothly, and Abraham pursued the enemy from the south all the way to Dan in the north. His victory must have been the result of the intercession behind the scene.

Abraham gained the victory by trusting in God. He had confidence in God because he had learned to know Him. Likewise, we all must learn to know God. We must learn that, even today, the earth is God's. God is the landlord. He is not only the landlord but also the heavenlord. Both the heaven and the earth belong to our Father, the One who has called us. We need to have such confidence in Him. If we lack this confidence, we are already defeated and shall become a Lot.

Why was Lot defeated? Because, unlike Abraham, he did not learn the lesson that God is the Possessor of heaven and earth. Even after he had been rescued, there is no record that he thanked Abraham or said a word to the Lord. Lot was absolutely out of function. According to the following chapters, he went back to Sodom. Although his capture was a warning to him not to return to Sodom, he still went back, even after his capture and rescue. We see from this that once you have been defeated it is very difficult to keep yourself away from that defeat.

Although Lot had been defeated, Abraham was victorious. This victory was the peak of his outward experience. Later on, God came in to give him some inward experiences.

THE MINISTRY OF MELCHISEDEC

How was it possible for one who escaped to have come to Abraham, and how could Abraham have made such a brief and bold decision? What happened so that, after a short time, the enemy ran away? Melchisedec came in. Who is Melchisedec? He is a type of Christ. He is very much like Christ. When he came in, it signified that Christ came in. He was a type of Christ as God's High Priest. This is not revealed in Genesis 14, but it is found in Psalm 110. In Psalm 110 we are told that God's anointed One, the very Christ, is the Priest according to the order of Melchisedec, an order which is prior to that of Aaron. Before Aaron came into the priesthood, Melchisedec was God's Priest already.

The Aaronic priesthood dealt with sin, taking care of things on the negative side. The ministry of Melchisedec, on the contrary, is positive. Melchisedec did not come in to take away sin. He did not appear because Abraham had sinned but because Abraham had gained the victory. Melchisedec did not appear with an offering to take away sin but with bread and wine to nourish the victor. Nearly all Christians consider Christ as the High Priest who takes care of sin, but hardly anyone pays attention to Christ as the High Priest according to the order of Melchisedec. As such a High Priest, Christ does not take care of sin but ministers to us the processed God, signified by the bread and wine, as our nourishment.

Do you not believe that before Melchisedec came to minister bread and wine, as the priest of God he was interceding for Lot and Abraham? I believe that he was. I do not believe that Melchisedec was sleeping during all the fighting and that when he heard the news of Abraham's victory he hurriedly appeared to Abraham to minister bread and wine. I believe that Abraham's brief and bold decision to fight for the rescue of Lot was stirred up by the intercession of

Melchisedec. I also believe that the one who came to tell Abraham of Lot's capture escaped because Melchisedec was interceding for Lot. As a priest, Melchisedec must have been taking care of God's people. In answer to his intercession, one escaped from Sodom, told Abraham the news, and Abraham made the bold decision to fight for the rescue of Lot.

While we walk on this earth, many things happen to us. Apparently, these things just happen. Actually, behind the earthly scene, an intercession is going on. Our Melchisedec, our High Priest Christ, is still interceding for us in heaven (Heb. 7:25). His intercession overshadows us and cares for us.

Melchisedec's coming to Abraham was somewhat of an indication of Christ's second coming. What are we, today's Abraham, doing here? We are slaughtering the enemies. Some of God's people, like Lot, have suffered defeat after defeat. By God's mercy, some others need to be today's Abraham who experience victory after victory. We need to learn the basic lesson that our God, the One who called us, is the Possessor of heaven and earth. We are living for Him on the earth and we are His testimony. We do not tolerate any damage to God's interest on earth. When we hear of such damage, we make a quick decision to defeat the enemy and to slaughter the kings.

We need to slaughter some kings daily. We need to slaughter the kings in our mind, emotion, and will. We need to slaughter the kings in our environment, families, and schools. After we have finished our slaughter of the kings, our Melchisedec will come to us, meet with us, and celebrate our victory. The Lord will not come back until we have slaughtered all the kings. Then He will return and drink the fruit of the vine with us, as indicated by His word in Matthew 26:29: "I will by no means drink henceforth of this fruit of the vine until that day when I drink it new with you in the kingdom of My Father." Melchisedec interceded for Lot and Abraham. Today Christ, our High Priest, is interceding for all the overcoming ones. While He is interceding now for us in heaven, we are slaughtering the kings on earth. After the overcoming ones slaughter all the kings, our Intercessor, the High Priest of the Most High God, will appear with the full taste of the processed God.

Melchisedec's coming signified that Christ had come. Our victory always makes Christ manifested. The people in our environment may find it difficult to see where Christ is. However, if we gain a victory, that victory will declare Christ to them. Our victory will bring in Christ in a new aspect. How interesting it is to see that suddenly, in chapter fourteen of Genesis, Melchisedec, whose name means the king of righteousness and who was the king of Salem, which means the king of peace, appeared. What does this signify? It signifies that Christ will be declared to people and brought to them by the overcoming ones. One day the whole earth will be surprised by Christ's appearing. The people in the world do not even believe that there is a Christ, calling such belief nonsense. But after we have slaughtered all of the kings, Christ will suddenly appear. Christ will be made manifest by our slaughter of the kings, and the whole world will be surprised at His coming. To us, the overcomers, Christ's second appearing will not be a surprise, but to the worldly people it will be a great surprise. They may say, "Who is this one? What is his name and where does he come from?" We may answer, "His name is Christ, the real Melchisedec, and He comes from the heavens where He has been interceding for centuries."

We all need to echo the Lord's intercession. If we turn to our spirit and contact Him, there will always be some echoing. If we go according to that echoing, forgetting our environment, enemies, and even ourselves, we shall gain the victory and slaughter the kings. At the end of our slaughter of all the kings, our Melchisedec will appear to us. That will be the second coming of Christ. When Christ comes in, the whole earth will know the Most High God. Then all the earth will realize that God is the Possessor of heaven and earth. The earth is not possessed by any king, president, statesman, or politician, it is possessed by the Most High God, the Possessor of heaven and earth. How can this fact be declared to the earth? Only by our slaughter of the kings.

Abraham's victory in chapter fourteen is not a small thing. In the Bible, God is revealed in a progressive way. In Genesis 1 we do not have the title, "the Most High God." Even up to chapter thirteen we have neither this title nor the special title, "Possessor of heaven and earth." Although you may have been a Christian for years, perhaps you have never realized that God has such titles. God is the Most High God and the Possessor of heaven and earth. He is the heavenlord and the landlord. By our experience of Christ, God's titles are progressively revealed to us. In our experience of Christ, we shall realize that our God is the Most High God and the Possessor of heaven and earth.

This must be our attraction and incentive to go on to slaughter the kings.

Do not be today's Lot, for that is to be timid and cowardly. We all must be brief and bold because we have the Most High God and the Possessor of heaven and earth. Abraham told the king of Sodom that, before he went to war, he lifted up his hand to the Most High God, to the Possessor of heaven and earth. He went to war in such a spirit. Since Abraham had full confidence in the Most High God, the Possessor of heaven and earth, he had to be victorious.

When Melchisedec came to Abraham, he blessed Abraham with the Most High God, the Possessor of heaven and earth (v. 19). This proves that he was greater than Abraham (Heb. 7:6-7). He also blessed God for Abraham's victory (v. 20). Our victory always causes our Melchisedec to grant us blessing and to give blessing to God. Our victory brings in more blessings in Christ, both to us and to God.

At Melchisedec's blessing, Abraham gave him tithes of all, the tithes of his choice spoils (v. 20; Heb. 7:2, 4). This also proves Melchisedec's greatness. Our victory gains the spoils, and the offering of our spoils to Christ always declares the greatness of Christ. Without victory, we have nothing to offer to Christ and His greatness will not be declared.

OVERCOMING THE TEMPTATION OF EARTHLY SUBSTANCE

Abraham's victory regulated and restituted the whole situation and rearranged the entire environment. The four kings had defeated the five kings and had captured everything. The whole situation had been turned upside down. Abraham's victory changed this situation altogether, turning it right side up. He turned the unjust environment into a just one and made the whole situation peaceful. As a result, there was the king of righteousness and the king of peace. Abraham's victory stopped all the fighting and strife and brought in genuine peace.

The king of Sodom could humbly, honestly, and truthfully say to Abraham, "You have gained the victory. Everything that you brought back must be yours. You take it. All I want is my people." If you and I had been Abraham, we probably would have said, "That is right and fair. I rescued your people and recovered everything that you lost. It is good that you have the people and that everything else be mine."

But the environment that was rearranged by Abraham's victory was not at all like this. It was pure. Abraham said to the king of Sodom, "I will not take from a thread even to a shoe latchet," and "I will not take anything that is thine, lest thou shouldest say, I have made Abram rich" (14:23). Abraham seemed to be saying, "If I take a thread from you, you will be able to say that you have made me rich. But I want to give a full testimony to the whole universe that my riches do not come from you. My riches come from the Possessor of heaven and earth, from my Most High God." How pure this was! There in that situation we see righteousness and peace.

Consider the scene in Genesis 14 after Abraham had slaughtered the kings. Abraham had brought back everything, and the kings came out to meet him. Melchisedec, the priest of the Most High God, was there, granting Abraham the blessing and receiving tithes from him. All of the people were watching, wondering to whom the things would go. Even the people who had been captured and brought back by Abraham wondered whose people they would be from then on. Then Abraham said, "I have lifted up mine hand unto the Lord, the most high God, the possessor of heaven and earth." Abraham said that he would not take anything. All the people received a full settlement. In that situation there was righteousness and peace. In a sense, it was like the millennial kingdom, full of righteousness and peace (Isa. 32:1, 16-18; Psa. 72:2-3, 7).

Abraham was fair, saying to the king of Sodom that he would take nothing "save only that which the young men have eaten, and the portion of the men which went with me, Aner, Eschol, and Mamre; let them take their portion" (14:24). Abraham said that his fighters and confederates should have their portion but that he would give his portion to the king of Sodom. What a man he was! He had slaughtered four kings and now he was dealing with another one, the king of Sodom. He was over all of them. We Christians need to be this kind of person today. We must be higher than the earthly kings and presidents. There is only one who is above us—our Melchisedec.

In Genesis 14 we see that Abraham was very high. Can you believe that one who was so high could have been so low as to plan to sacrifice his wife for his living? Can you believe that the one who would sell his wife in Egypt could be so high as to be above all the kings? When Abraham was willing to sell his wife, he was in the lowest hell, but when he dealt with the kings, he was in the highest heaven. We all may be like Abraham in both respects. We may be mean, planning to sell our wives, or, by the Lord's grace, we may be higher than the kings.

Abraham's victory and his being higher than the kings were absolutely due to the intercession behind the scene. Behind the earthly scene, something was going on in heaven that determined the entire situation. We all need to see this.

8

Knowing Grace
for the Fulfillment
of God's Purpose
The Seed and the Land

After these things the word of the Lord
came unto Abram in a vision, saying,
Fear not, Abram:
I am thy shield, and thy exceeding great reward....
And he brought him forth abroad, and said,
Look now toward heaven,
and tell the stars, if thou be able to number them: and
he said unto him, So shall thy seed be.
And he believed in the Lord;
and he counted it to him for righteousness.
And he said unto him, I am the Lord that brought thee
out of Ur of the Chaldees, to give thee this land
to inherit it.

Genesis 15:1, 5-7

In this message we come to a great turn in Abraham's experience of God. Everything that we have seen of Abraham's experience of God thus far has been outward. Abraham was called by God and he answered God's calling by going to the place where God intended him to be. That was absolutely outward. Following that, Abraham's second experience was living by faith and trusting in God for his living.

The first trial that he faced in living by faith was a grievous famine through which he learned to trust God in the matter of eating. Whether in ancient or in modern times, whether in the Orient or in the West, all people, regardless of their attainment, education, or position, are concerned about the matter of making a living. Making a living is completely dependent on eating, on bread and butter. In the Bible and in human history, many times God exercised His control over the human race through this matter of eating. Do not be proud, for once God removes your food supply, you will bow down and say, "O God, help me!"

We have seen in previous messages that after Abraham came to the place where God wanted him to be, the first lesson he had to learn was to trust God in the matter of eating. He failed this test and went down to Egypt. There, in Egypt, he learned the lesson of trusting in God. After learning that lesson, he returned to the place between Bethel and Ai. Immediately after that, there followed another lesson in the same realm, in the realm of eating, when there was strife between the herdsmen of Lot and the herdsmen of Abraham. These herdsmen were fighting for their bread and butter, striving with one another for the sake of a better living. They did not want others to take away their bread and butter. Abraham was victorious in the second trial, having learned in the first trial that God was sovereign in his daily life. Abraham came to know that the God who had called him was the Most High God, the Possessor of heaven and earth. He did not need to take care of his own bread and butter, for he had learned that the One who had called him would take care of this for him.

The fighting between the four kings and the five kings was also related to bread and butter. According to history, all of the warfare among the human race is over this matter. All international warfare is for one purpose—bread and butter. Genesis 14:11 indicates that the fighting between the four kings and the five kings was for this purpose.

Abraham was not afraid of those four kings but went out boldly and fought against them, slaughtering them and recovering the food supply. After Abraham had gained the victory over the four kings,

Melchisedec came to meet him with bread and wine (14:18). This bread was mysterious. There was no need for Abraham to do anything in order to get it and he did not have to fight for it. Abraham just fought the battle and recovered the food supply, and then Melchisedec came to him with bread.

All of Abraham's experiences up to the end of chapter fourteen were outward, being concerned with outward blessing, care, and supply. When Abraham went down to Egypt, God took care of him outwardly, giving him cattle and servants. The victory that he won against the four kings was also outward. Even what Melchisedec brought to Abraham was outward. Everything that Abraham had experienced to that point was outward. Before hearing this, you might have thought that at the end of chapter fourteen Abraham must have been on the peak of his experience of God. Yes, in a sense he was on the peak, but it was the peak of the elementary stage of his experience. All that Abraham had experienced prior to chapter fifteen was elementary. At the beginning of chapter fifteen, God came in to turn him to an advanced stage in experiencing God.

Genesis 15:1 says, "After these things the word of the Lord came unto Abram in a vision, saying, Fear not, Abram: I am thy shield, and thy exceeding great reward." When God came in to speak these words, Abraham was still in an elementary stage. After his slaughter of the kings, a strong enmity had been created between him and the people who belonged to those kings. When Abraham was fighting the battle against the enemy, he was bold and brave. But after gaining the victory and going home he might have said to himself, "What have I done? Those people might come back. What should I do then? I only have three hundred and eighteen men, and they have many more than that." Abraham began to be afraid. Many times we are the same as Abraham. When we are in faith, we are bold, saying, "Hallelujah to the Most High God, the Possessor of heaven and earth. I have lifted up my hand to Him." After gaining the victory and shouting hallelujahs in the meetings, you go home and begin to consider, saying to yourself, "What have I done? What shall I do if the enemy returns?"

When God appeared to Abraham in 15:1, He said, "Fear not." God's saying this to Abraham indicates that Abraham was fearing his enemies. God seemed to be telling him, "Abraham, you don't need to fear. I am your shield. Be at peace. I am also your exceeding great reward." Abraham, still being in an elementary stage at the time, was concerned about two things: that his enemies might return to fight against him and that he still had no child of his own. Abraham might have said, "Look at me—I am old. Look at my wife—she is nearly out of function. We still don't have a child. Lord, don't You know we are getting old in years? When will You give us a child?" When God appeared to him, Abraham was concerned about these two things.

In the presence of God we cannot hide our intention. If we are given the opportunity, we shall sooner or later utter whatever is in our heart. Therefore, in 15:2 Abraham said, "Lord God, what wilt thou give me, seeing I go childless, and the son of possession of my house is this Eliezer of Damascus?" (Heb.). The next word that Abraham spoke to the Lord was not very polite. He said, "Behold, to me thou hast given no seed: and, lo, a son of my house is mine heir" (15:3, Heb.). Abraham seemed to be saying, "Lord, I go childless because You have never given me a child. You must bear the blame for this. Why do I go childless? Because You have never given me a child! Now You come to tell me that You are my great reward. What's the use of Your giving me a reward if I have no child?"

Abraham told the Lord that a son of his house, who was Eliezer of Damascus, would be his heir. In Darby's New Translation the footnote says that "a son of my house" means "one of his domestics." This indicates that Eliezer must have come from Damascus. It might have been that when Abraham was passing through Damascus he obtained him there. None of us has ever answered God's call in a clean-cut way; we all dragged our feet through mud and water. Abraham even suffered two deaths, the death of his elder brother, Haran, and his father, Terah. Eventually, Abraham answered God's calling, being unable to avoid it any longer. He left Haran, where he had been called the second time, taking Lot along with him, and passed through Damascus where he picked up Eliezer. When the Lord appeared to Abraham, saying that He was Abraham's shield and great reward, Abraham seemed to say in reply, "Lord God, I go childless because You have not given me a child. The one whom I intend to have as the heir and possessor of my house must be my domestic servant, Eliezer."

The Lord said to Abraham, "This shall not be thine heir; but he that shall come forth out of thine own bowels shall be thine heir" (15:4). The Lord seemed to be saying to Abraham, "I didn't care for Lot. Neither do I care for this one. There must be a seed born out of yourself, not one of your domestics." Then the Lord said to him, "Look now toward heaven, and tell the stars, if thou be able to number them: and he said unto him, So shall thy seed be" (15:5). It was at this juncture that Abraham believed in the Lord. Verse 6 says that "he believed in the Lord; and he counted it to him for righteousness." Abraham's believing was counted to him by the Lord as righteousness, and at that time Abraham was justified. This is justification by faith.

Abraham's having a seed was absolutely not an outward matter but altogether an inward one. Abraham tried to make this an outward matter, for Eliezer was something outside of him, not something out of him. We need to see the difference here. Today, not many Christians care for the inward experience. Most Christians care for the outward experiences. The things that are taught among Christians today mostly go as far as the end of Genesis 14. Some may argue with this, saying, "Don't they have justification by faith, and is this not in chapter fifteen?" Yes, they do have justification by faith, but even this has been made by them an outward thing.

Abraham was not justified by faith in chapter fourteen when he believed that God was the Most High God, the Possessor of heaven and earth. God did not count that kind of faith to him as righteousness. What kind of faith was it that was reckoned to Abraham as righteousness? It was the faith that believed that God was able to work something into him to bring forth the seed. Believing that God will supply our daily needs, our daily food, is good, but it is not the kind of faith that is precious in the eyes of God. What kind of faith is precious in God's sight? The faith that believes that He is able to work Himself into us to bring forth Christ. Most Christians today only care for the faith that believes that God can do outward things for them. That kind of faith believes that God is able to give them health, healing, a good job, or a promotion. Many Christians only have that kind of faith. Although that kind of faith is good, it is not the faith that is so dear and precious in the eyes of God. He did not count that kind of faith as righteousness to Abraham. The kind of faith that was counted as righteousness to Abraham was the faith that God was able to work something into him to bring forth a seed. In Genesis 15 Abraham did not believe that God would give him bread and butter, cattle, or more servants. He believed that God was able to work something into him and bring forth a seed.

What kind of faith do you have? Most Christians appreciate the faith that believes that God will provide all they need for their daily living. That is the faith that believes in God as the Most High God, as the Possessor of heaven and earth. Perhaps you are thinking that you would be satisfied to have such a faith as that. After reading the last message, you might have tried to believe in the Most High God, believing that our God is the Possessor of heaven and earth. But that faith is not the faith that is so dear and precious in the eyes of God. We need to have the faith that believes that God is working Himself into us, the faith that believes that a heavenly seed will be brought forth by something that has been wrought into us. May this matter be inscribed into our being!

TWO CATEGORIES OF GOD'S DOINGS FOR THE CALLED

FOR HIM TO EXIST ✦ Prior to chapter fifteen, Abraham had experienced God as the One who protected him and provided many material things (12:16). Abraham had given all the choices to Lot and had gained the victory over the four kings. None of these things, however, had anything to do with the fulfillment of God's purpose but were only related to Abraham's existence (12:10; 14:24). He experienced all these outwardly in his environment, not inwardly in his life.

FOR HIM TO FULFILL GOD'S PURPOSE ✦ Do you know what God's purpose is? God's purpose is to have a people to express Him with His image, represent Him with His dominion, and take the earth for His kingdom. Beginning with Genesis 1:26, we see that God's eternal purpose is to have a people expressing Him in His image, representing Him with His dominion, and taking over the earth for His kingdom. When God came in to call Abraham He promised Abraham that he would have the blessing to express God and become a great nation so that through him God might have His kingdom on earth. This is God's eternal purpose today. But everything that had happened to Abraham prior to Genesis 15 had nothing to do with the fulfillment of God's purpose. It is from chapter fifteen through chapter twenty-four that we have a record showing us how God had worked something into Abraham so that he was able to fulfill God's purpose. It was no longer merely outward experiences in environment but inward experiences in life.

Most Christians today only care for their existence, not for God's eternal purpose. Even many among us still have not been deeply impressed with God's eternal purpose. Many are still hoping that the Lord will give them a better job, a good husband or wife, a good education, or an excellent promotion. While all of these things may enable you to exist, they have nothing to do directly with the fulfillment of God's purpose. Everything prior to chapter fifteen was good, helpful, and profitable for Abraham's existence, enabling him to live as a human being, but none of those things had anything to do directly with the fulfillment of God's purpose. Look into Abraham's situation. Could the cattle that Abraham gained in Egypt express God? Could the maidservants represent God? Although God had given Abraham a great deal, nothing that he had was useful for the fulfillment of God's purpose. To exist is one thing, and to fulfill God's purpose is another. The principle is the same with us today. Our education, jobs, and houses are all good for our existence, but none of them are good for the fulfilling of God's purpose.

TWO THINGS NEEDED FOR THE FULFILLMENT OF GOD'S PURPOSE

THE SEED   ✦   Now we need to see the two things that were necessary for the fulfillment of God's purpose in Abraham's day. The first item was the seed (15:1-6; see 13:16; 22:17-18; 12:2). God called Abraham with the intention of fulfilling His purpose. As we have seen, His purpose is to have a people in His image to express Himself and with His dominion to represent Himself. But Abraham did not have a seed. How could Abraham fulfill God's purpose without having a seed? God needs the seed. He needs to have a people through the seed.

Not what Abraham had   ✦   Abraham was the same as we are, and we are the same as he was. When Abraham understood that he needed a seed, he counted on Eliezer (15:2-4). Abraham seemed to say, "Now I realize that I must have a seed for God to have a people. Since I am old and my wife is nearly out of function, the seed must be what I already have." But God will never use for the fulfillment of

His purpose the things that we already have. Whatever we have is altogether no good for this. Do not think that what you have is good for the fulfillment of God's purpose. What you have is just an Eliezer. Nothing that you have is counted. Nothing that we have is useful for the fulfilling of God's purpose. At best, whatever we have is not of God but is something of Damascus.

But what God promised to work out ✦ The seed that was needed for the fulfillment of God's purpose had to be what God promised to work out through Abraham. It had to be something that God worked into him so that he might bring it forth (15:4-5). What then is the seed? If you pray and read Genesis 15 and Galatians 3, you will see that the seed is Christ Himself. Nothing that we have could ever bring forth Christ. Our education, attainments, skills, etc. mean nothing. All of these things are just Eliezers, things which are not what the Lord has wrought into us to bring forth Christ, the seed. None of them are subjective but altogether objective in our environment. Your Eliezer might be your college education. Perhaps even in the church life you might still be trusting in this Eliezer, meaning that you still trust in your college education. All of us have passed through some Damascus, picking up at least one Eliezer. That could never be the seed that God wants. The seed must be something that God works into us, not something that we have picked up. Whatever we picked up from our Damascus can never bring forth Christ. Only that which God works into our being can bring forth Christ as the seed.

In order to fulfill God's purpose we must have Christ wrought into us. This is why Paul told us that Christ was revealed into him (Gal. 1:15-16), that Christ lived in him (Gal. 2:20), that Christ was formed in him (Gal. 4:19), and that for him to live was Christ (Phil. 1:21). Paul lived Christ. When he was Saul of Tarsus, he passed through a Jewish Damascus, gaining many things. All that he acquired during that time was just an Eliezer. The Lord told Paul that he had to forget all of those things—they were dung, garbage, dog food—and to cast them aside. None of the things that Paul had could bring forth Christ. Only that which God worked into his being could bring forth Christ. The Lord seemed to tell Paul, "The things that you had from your religious background can never bring forth Christ. Only what I am working into you will bring forth Christ. What I am working into you is My grace." Eventually, Paul could say, "By the grace of God I am what I am; and His grace unto me was not in vain, but I labored more abundantly than all of them, yet not I, but the grace of God with me" (1 Cor. 15:10).

At this point, I need to say a word about the difference between grace and blessing. What most Christians consider to be grace is actually blessing. What is blessing? Blessing is prosperity, benefit, and bounty. Many Christians, using the adjective form of the word grace, are fond of saying, "Oh, how gracious God is to us." But this is far short of the meaning of the real grace. The Hebrew word for gracious in Numbers 6:25 means to bend or to stoop oneself in order to be kind to an inferior person. For example, in kindness, a king may stoop to give something to a beggar. That is what it means to be gracious. However, in the Bible, grace is nothing less than God Himself. In the Bible grace is simply God Himself coming into us to be our enjoyment. John 1:17 says, "For the law was given through Moses; grace and reality came through Jesus Christ." John 1:14 says that "the Word became flesh...full of grace and reality," and John 1:16 tells us that "of His fullness we all received, and grace upon grace."

Blessings are for our existence, but grace is for the fulfillment of God's purpose. We do need God's blessing for our existence. If God did not bless us, we would lose our jobs, health, and perhaps even our physical lives. I have no doubt that, for my existence, I am fully under God's blessing.

Merely to exist, however, is vanity of vanities. What are we doing here in this country? Are we just here to make a living for our existence? If this is the case, it is vanity of vanities. All the cars, houses, degrees, and jobs are vanities. Some people may say, "Praise the Lord, we have three sons and two daughters. The sons are medical doctors and the daughters are professors. What a blessing this is!" This is a blessing for you and your family to exist in the vanity of vanities, if your existence is not for the fulfillment of God's purpose. Others may say, "Five years ago I was only making $5,000 a year, but this last year I made $25,000. What a blessing this is!" This also is a blessing for people to exist in the vanity of vanities, if they are not for God's eternal purpose.

Recently, the Lord awoke me early one morning and pointed out to me that not one of the New Testament books ends with the words, "Blessing be with you" or "Blessing be with your spirit." However, nearly all the Epistles end with the words, "Grace be with you" (Gal.

6:18; Eph. 6:24; Phil. 4:23; Col. 4:18). To say, "Blessing be with you," means that you will be prospered with material things. But our Bible never says anything like that. The Gospel of John does not say that the Word became flesh full of blessing, or that blessing came with Christ. No book ends by saying, "Blessing be with you."

In the Old Testament we mainly have blessings, but in the New Testament the physical blessings immediately are replaced by spiritual blessings. Ephesians 1:3 says that God has blessed us with all spiritual blessings in Christ, and the last verse of the same book says, "Grace be with all those who love our Lord Jesus Christ." The last verse of the whole Bible also speaks of grace. Revelation 22:21 does not say, "The blessing of the Most High God, the Possessor of heaven and earth, be with you all." No, it says, "The grace of the Lord Jesus be with all the saints." Do you remember the blessing that the priests used to give the children of Israel in Numbers 6:24-26? It went like this: "The Lord bless thee, and keep thee: the Lord make his face shine upon thee, and be gracious unto thee: the Lord lift up his countenance upon thee, and give thee peace." Paul's blessing in 2 Corinthians 13:14, on the contrary, is in another category: "The grace of the Lord Jesus Christ, and the love of God, and the fellowship of the Holy Spirit be with you all." I repeat, blessings are for our existence, and grace is for the fulfillment of God's purpose.

God's promise and Abraham's faith counted for righteousness ✦
After rejecting Abraham's proposal, God promised him that He would do something for him so that he might have seed born of himself, even as many as the stars in heaven (15:5). Abraham believed in the Lord according to His word, and the Lord counted his believing to him for righteousness (15:6). It is the kind of faith that believes that God will work in us to bring forth Christ, the seed, that is precious to God and is our righteousness in the eyes of God. This is the faith for receiving God's grace, not for receiving His blessing.

Today, most Christians care for blessing, not much for grace. Although this is the New Testament age, many Christians still live in the Old Testament dispensation, caring only for blessings, not for grace. In the Lord's recovery we do need the blessings. It is a great blessing to meet together all of the time. But, more than this, we need grace. We need God to come in and say, "What you have does not count. What you can do and will do does not count either. I will work something into you, and this will bring forth the seed. Do you believe in this?" If we believe this, this kind of faith is precious to God. This is not the faith that believes that God will give us all that we need for our existence; it is the faith that believes that God is working Himself into us in order to bring forth Christ as the unique seed, the seed that is needed for the fulfillment of God's purpose.

THE LAND   ✦   The second thing needed for the fulfillment of God's purpose was the land (15:17-21; see 12:7; 13:14-15, 17; 17:8).

The definition of the land   ✦   What is the land? Many Christians think that the land is heaven, considering physical death as the Jordan River. This concept is altogether not according to the proper understanding of the Holy Word. During Abraham's time, the land was a place in which he could live. Abraham needed a place to live in and to live on. Hence, the land is a place for God's people to live in and to live on. Furthermore, during Abraham's time, the land was a place in which Abraham could defeat all of his enemies in order that God might have a kingdom on earth. Moreover, the land was the place where God could have a habitation as the expression of Himself. Thus, we see five points concerning the land: that it was a place for God's people to live in, a place for them to live on, a place where God's enemies could be defeated, a place where God could have His kingdom, and a place where God could have a habitation for His expression. Eventually, in the land, the kingdom of God was established, the temple was built for God's habitation, and the glory of God was manifested. All of that was a miniature of the fulfillment of God's purpose. This was altogether a different matter from Abraham's existence. It was one thing for Abraham to exist; it was another thing for him to have the seed and the land for the fulfillment of God's purpose.

What is the land for us today? Undoubtedly, the land is Christ who is living in us and in whom we are living. Today, we must live in Christ and on Christ. But many Christians do not practice this. They care neither for Christ's being wrought into them as the seed nor for their living in Christ as their land for the fulfillment of God's purpose. To them, Christ is not the land for them to live in and to live on; neither is He the land for them to slaughter all their enemies. Where can we slaughter our enemies? In Christ our land. Christ is the very place in which we slaughter our Chedorlaomer and all of the other kings. Christ is also the land for the kingdom of God where God's habitation can be built.

If we see this, then we know how greatly most Christians have missed the mark in seeking only for God's blessings. We do not need to pay that much attention to our existence or to be so concerned about God's blessings, because our Father knows what we need. We should let Him take care of us. He will never leave us nor forsake us (Heb. 13:5).

In this matter of God's purpose we should not count on what we have or on what we can do. What we have is Eliezer and what we can do is Ishmael. Eliezer was what Abraham had and Ishmael was what Abraham could do, and neither of them counted for the fulfillment of God's purpose. What we have and what we can do does not count. It has to be God Himself. After a certain time, when we truly have become nothing, God will work Himself into us, and that which He has worked into us will bring forth Christ as the seed and will also bring us into Christ as our land. Christ should be the seed within us. Christ should also be the land in which we live. Do we not have Christ in us? Yes, but He must be the seed. Are we not in Christ today? Yes, but we must live in Him as our land.

Today the land is also the church, for the church is the enlargement of Christ. The Body of Christ, the church, is the expansion of Christ. In the church we live in Christ and on Christ; in the church we slaughter the enemies; and in the church we have the kingdom of God with the habitation of God. For this reason, when we came into the church, we immediately had the sensation that we had come home. Now we are no longer wandering but have a place in which and on which to live, a place in which to slaughter all our enemies, a place in which we may have the kingdom of God with the habitation of God. Before we came into the church, we did not have the proper Christian living, but after coming into the church, what a positive change has happened to our living!

Before coming into the church, it was difficult for us to defeat any of our enemies, but after coming into the church, it was so easy. Chedorlaomer is afraid of the church. Where can we slaughter all of our enemies? In Canaan. What is today's Canaan? It is the church, the enlarged Christ. Where is the kingdom of God with God's habitation today? Also in the church. The church, the enlarged Christ, is our good land today.

Both the seed and the land are Christ. The seed is Christ in us and the land is the Christ in whom we live. Christ lives in us as the seed, and we live in Him as the land. He is both the seed and the land for the fulfillment of God's eternal purpose.

God's promise and Abraham's lacking of faith ✦ In this chapter God not only repeated His promise to Abraham concerning the seed but also the promise to him concerning the land. The promise concerning the seed is fully covered in the first six verses. Abraham believed in the Lord for that promise concerning the seed. The promise concerning the land is affirmatively made by God in verse 7, but Abraham lacked faith to believe in God for this promise concerning the land. By this we can see that believing in God for the seed is easier than believing in God for the land. It is easier for us to let Christ live in us as the seed than it is to live in Christ as the land. To take Christ as the seed living in us is easier than to take Christ as the land for us to have the church life for God's kingdom with God's habitation. Because Abraham was like us, lacking faith in God in this respect, God was forced to make a covenant with him to confirm His promise concerning the land. In the next message we shall see the details concerning the covenant that God made with Abraham. ✖

9

KNOWING GRACE FOR THE FULFILLMENT OF GOD'S PURPOSE GOD'S COVENANT WITH ABRAHAM

And he said unto him, I am the Lord that brought thee
out of Ur of the Chaldees, to give thee this land to inherit it.
And he said, Lord God, whereby shall I know
that I shall inherit it? And he said unto him,
Take me a heifer of three years old, and a she goat
of three years old, and a ram of three years old, and
a turtledove, and a young pigeon. And he took unto him
all these, and divided them in the midst....
And it came to pass, that, when the sun went down, and it was dark,
behold a smoking furnace, and a burning lamp
that passed between those pieces.
In that same day the Lord made a covenant with Abram,
saying, Unto thy seed have I given this land...

Genesis 15:7-10, 17-18

In the last message we saw that whatever Abraham experienced prior to Genesis 15 was a matter of God's blessing for his existence.

But God's calling of Abraham was not merely that Abraham should exist; it was that God's eternal purpose might be fulfilled through him. Beginning with chapter fifteen, God came in to show Abraham that he needed grace for the fulfillment of God's eternal purpose. Abraham not only needed outward blessings in his environment but also grace in his life. If we read Genesis 15 through 22 carefully, we shall see that in these chapters God was dealing with Abraham in order to bring him to the realization that he needed His grace in order to fulfill His eternal purpose. So God came in not simply to bless Abraham outwardly but to work Himself into him as grace in order that Abraham might have something substantial for the carrying out of God's eternal purpose.

As we saw in the previous message, two things were needed for Abraham to fulfill God's purpose—the seed and the land. If you read Genesis 15 again, you will see that these two things, the seed and the land, are mentioned repeatedly. We have seen that both the seed and the land are Christ. Firstly, the seed is the individual, personal Christ, and eventually it is the corporate Christ. Galatians 3:16 reveals that Christ is the seed of Abraham. Initially the seed was the individual Christ, but ultimately it has become the corporate Christ—the Christ who is the Head with all of us as His Body. This is the seed that is needed for the fulfillment of God's purpose.

Christ is also the land. The concept that Christ is the land may seem rather new or strange because in the past many of us were told that the good land of Canaan was a type, a symbol, of heaven. This concept is held by many Christians, but if we return to the pure Word, we can see that the land actually symbolizes Christ. In type, the land is the place where God's people have rest and where God can defeat all of His enemies and establish His kingdom with His habitation for His expression and representation. Please remember the following points regarding the land: that it is the place where God's people may have rest; that it is the place where all of God's enemies can be slaughtered; and that it is the place where God establishes His kingdom and builds up His habitation that He may be expressed and represented on this rebellious earth. What is qualified to be such a land? Nothing other than Christ. In Christ, we have rest and we slaughter the enemies. In Christ, God establishes His kingdom and builds His habitation, the church, for His expression and representation. Have you seen that both the seed and the land are Christ? The seed that God promised

Abraham is today the corporate Christ, and the land that God promised him is the wonderful resurrected and elevated Christ in whom we rest and slaughter our enemies and in whom God establishes His kingdom and builds up His habitation that He might be expressed and represented.

When God promised Abraham that he would have a seed, Abraham believed God for this immediately (15:6). When Abraham believed in God for the promise concerning the seed, his faith, which was so precious to God, was counted as righteousness to him by God. At that time, Abraham was justified by faith, by the faith that believed that God would give him the seed to accomplish God's eternal purpose. When Abraham believed in God for that, God was happy with him. After this, however, when God also promised Abraham that He would give him the land, Abraham fell short, saying to the Lord, "Lord God, whereby shall I know that I shall inherit it?" (v. 8). Although he was able to believe in God for the promise concerning the seed, he could not believe in Him for the promise concerning the land.

The principle is the same today. To believe that Christ is the seed is easy, but to believe that Christ is the land is difficult. It is easier to believe that Christ is our life than it is to believe that Christ can be our church life. Many Christians believe in God for Christ's being their life, but when they come to the matter of the church life, the good land where we can rest, slaughter the enemies, and afford God the ground to establish His kingdom and build up His habitation, they say that it is impossible for us to have this today. Many Christians seem to be saying, "It is possible for us to live by Christ, but it is impossible to have the church life." It is easier for them to believe that Christ can be their life than that the church can be their living. They cannot believe that it is possible to have the church life today. Once again we see that we are the same as Abraham, finding it easy to believe in God for the seed but finding it difficult to believe in Him for the land. Do you have Christ as the seed? Do you also have Him as the land? It is not such a simple matter to have Christ as the land for us to live in so that we may have the church life and that God may have His kingdom with His habitation for His expression and representation.

Years ago, before we came into the church life, we ministered on the matter of living by Christ, but we ourselves were not in the rest. We wandered restlessly until one day, by His grace, we came into the church. When we came into the church, we began to have the sensation that we were in the rest. Before we came into the church life, it was very difficult for us to slaughter the enemies, but after coming into the church life, we found that it was easy to slaughter them all. In the church life God's kingdom is set up, His habitation is built up, and God is expressed and represented. This is the fulfillment of God's eternal purpose today.

GOD CONFIRMING HIS PROMISE BY MAKING A COVENANT WITH ABRAHAM THROUGH CHRIST

Because Abraham found it difficult to believe in God regarding the promise of the land, God was forced to make a covenant with him. In 15:9-21 we see that God confirmed His promise by making a covenant with Abraham through Christ. The way in which God made this covenant with Abraham was very peculiar. This portion of the Word is difficult for people to understand. We need to see that God was forced to make this covenant with Abraham. As far as God was concerned, there was no need for Him to do this. If Abraham had immediately believed in God for the promise of the land, Genesis 15 would have been much shorter than it is now. There would have been no need for many things that are mentioned there: the dividing of the heifer, the she-goat, and the ram; the offering of the turtledove and the young pigeon; the deep sleep that fell upon Abraham; the horror of great darkness that came upon him; God's passing through the pieces as a smoking furnace and as a torch of fire; and the mention of the four hundred years. It seems that nothing was pleasant. It was not the time of sunrise but of sunset, and God did not come in a lovely way but as a smoking furnace and a flaming torch. If we had witnessed such a scene, we probably would have been frightened to death, being unable to withstand it and finding it altogether a terrifying thing. This scene, however, has a very sweet flavor because in it God made a covenant with His dear called one; He had no intention of terrifying him.

I have spent much time in trying to understand this portion of the Word. In the early days I could not understand it because I lacked experience. I looked into some books, but none of them said anything helpful about this matter. But eventually by experiences through the years the Lord has shown me the real significance of this portion of the Word. This incident in Genesis 15 is the consummation of a covenant, the record of God's enacting of a covenant. The first covenant that God made was with Noah (9:8-17), a covenant that had a rainbow as its sign. Here, in Genesis 15, is the second covenant made by God with man. We need to keep this fact firmly in mind.

THREE CATTLE SIGNIFYING THE CRUCIFIED CHRIST ✦ In making His covenant with Abraham, God told him to take a heifer, a she-goat, a ram, a turtledove, and a young pigeon (v. 9). The three cattle, all of which were three years of age, were divided in half, but the two birds were not; they were kept alive. It was through these that God made His covenant with Abraham, implying that it was in this way that Abraham could fulfill God's eternal purpose.

We need to see the significance of the three cattle and the two birds. In typology, all things offered to God by man are a type of Christ. Based upon this principle, each of these five things undoubtedly is a type of Christ. Christ is firstly the crucified Christ, the cut Christ, and secondly He is the resurrected, living Christ. If we see this, then we can immediately understand that the three cattle, which were cut and killed, are types of the crucified Christ. The crucified Christ was the One who became flesh, living on earth in His humanity. John chapter one says that the Word who was God became flesh (v. 14). Then it speaks of this One as the Lamb of God (v. 29). The Lamb of God was the One who was the Word of God becoming flesh. Thus, the three cattle in Genesis 15 should signify Christ in His humanity being crucified for us.

If we read Genesis 15 along with the book of Leviticus, we can see that the female heifer was for a peace offering (Lev. 3:1). Why does the peace offering come first? Because when God was making a covenant with His called one, there was the need of peace. In making a covenant or any agreement between two parties there is the need of peace. In order for God to make a covenant with His called one, there was firstly the need of a peace offering. And Christ was that peace offering. The she-goat was a type of Christ as our sin offering (Lev. 4:28; 5:6). Regardless of how good we may be as God's called ones, we are still sinful. Thus, following the peace offering we need the sin offering. Hallelujah, the problem of sin has been settled! It has been taken away by Christ as our she-goat, as our sin offering. Following this there was the need of the burnt offering, the offering which signifies that everything must be for God (Lev. 1:10). After the peace offering, there was the sin offering, and after the sin offering, there was the burnt offering. Christ was all of the offerings that God passed through in making a covenant with His called one.

Why were the three cattle all three years old? Because Christ was not killed in death but in resurrection. He was not offered in death but in resurrection. Referring to His crucifixion, the Lord told the Jews, "Destroy this temple, and in three days I will raise it up" (John 2:19). The Lord was killed when He was "three years old," meaning that He was killed in resurrection. Even before He was killed He was already in resurrection because He was always in resurrection (John 11:25). Therefore, when He was killed, He was killed in resurrection, and this was why He could be resurrected. Christ offered Himself to God in resurrection. He was nailed to the cross in resurrection. Regardless of how strong you may be, if you were to be killed, you would be killed in death, not in resurrection. But the Lord Jesus was killed in resurrection.

TWO BIRDS SIGNIFYING THE RESURRECTED CHRIST   ✦   The two birds, neither of which was killed, signify the resurrected, living Christ (Lev. 14:6-7). This resurrected Christ is mainly in His divinity because, according to the Bible, a dove in typology signifies the Holy Spirit (John 1:32). Therefore, while the cattle typify Christ in His humanity, the birds typify Him in His divinity. So the birds in Genesis 15 signify the heavenly Christ, the Christ who came from and who still is in heaven (John 3:13), the Christ who was and who still is living. Christ has been crucified, yet He lives. He was killed in His humanity, but He lives in His divinity. He was killed as a man who walked on this earth, but now He is living as the heavenly One soaring in the heavens. While His humanity was good for Him to be all the sacrifices, His divinity is good for Him to be the living One. He was sacrificed for us in His humanity, and He is living for us in His divinity.

In typology, the turtledove signifies a suffering life and the young pigeon signifies a believing life, a life of faith. While He was living on earth, the Lord Jesus was always suffering and believing. In His suffering life He was the turtledove and in His believing life He was the young pigeon.

There were two birds, and the number two means testimony,

bearing witness (Acts 5:32). The two living birds bear testimony of Christ as the resurrected One living in us and for us (John 14:19-20; Gal. 2:20). The living Jesus is the testimony, the One who constantly bears witness. In Revelation 1 the Lord Jesus said, "I am...the living One, and I became dead, and behold, I am living forever and ever" (v. 18). His living forever is His testimony, for the testimony of Jesus is always related to the matter of being living. If a local church is not living, it does not have the testimony of Jesus. The more living we are, the more we are the testimony of the living Jesus.

There were three cattle and two birds, making a total of five items. The number five is the number of responsibility, indicating here that Christ as the crucified and living One is now bearing all the responsibility for the fulfillment of God's eternal purpose.

As FOWL FROM THE AIR, SATAN AND HIS ANGELS COMING TO MAKE CHRIST OF NONE EFFECT   ✦   When the sacrifices were made ready, the fowl from the air came down trying to eat them (v. 11). This signifies that Satan and his angels come to make Christ of none effect for the church life (Gal. 5:2, 4). Today Satan and his angels (2 Cor. 11:13-15) are doing their best to rob Christians of the enjoyment of Christ for the church life (Col. 2:8). As Abraham drove the fowl away, so we must drive Satan and his angels away from what Christ is to us for the church life.

THE COVENANTING GOD PASSING BETWEEN THE PIECES OF THE SACRIFICES   ✦   It was through the sacrifices as types of Christ that God passed to make a covenant with Abraham (vv. 17-18; cf. Jer. 34:18-19). After Abraham divided the cattle and arranged all the sacrifices, "when the sun was going down, a deep sleep fell upon Abram; and, lo, an horror of great darkness fell upon him" (vv. 11-12). When Abraham was in this kind of situation, God came in. Verse 17 says, "And it came to pass, that, when the sun went down, and it was dark, behold a smoking furnace, and a torch of fire that passed between those pieces" (v. 18, Heb.). God did not come in a very lovely way but as a smoking furnace and as a flaming torch. A furnace is for refining, and a torch is for enlightening. In the midst of a dark situation God came in to refine and to enlighten. This happens quite often in the church life. Suddenly the sunrise becomes the sunset, a dark night descends upon us, many saints are sleepy and out of function, and there is suffering on every side. During such a time of affliction, we may begin to doubt, saying, "What is this? Is something wrong with us?" At such a time God will always come in as a furnace to refine us, to burn us out, and also as a torch to enlighten us. People often say of those in the church life, "How can you people have so much light? What light there is among you! How the torch is flaming!" The light mainly comes from the sufferings. Look at Abraham's situation: the sun went down, night came, Abraham was sleeping, and God came in, not as a comforter but as a furnace to burn and as a torch to enlighten. On the one hand God is burning us and we are suffering; on the other hand He is enlightening us and we are under the light. At such a time, even if we are in a dark night, we shall be so clear.

It was in this kind of a situation that God passed between the pieces of the sacrifices, and that was the enacting of God's covenant. God made a covenant with Abraham in the way of passing through all of the sacrifices as a smoking furnace and a torch of fire. It was in this way that God confirmed His promise to Abraham by making a covenant with him for the fulfillment of His eternal purpose.

THE CALLED ONE IDENTIFIED WITH CHRIST BY OFFERING HIM TO GOD ✦ Whenever people offered something to God in the Old Testament, they laid their hand upon the sacrifice, signifying their union or identification with it. God's asking Abraham to offer the cattle and birds to Him implied that Abraham had to be one with all of the things that he offered to God. God seemed to be saying to him, "Abraham, you must be in union with all of the things that you offer to Me. You must be identified with the cattle and the birds." This indicates that we also have to be cut in Christ's being cut and crucified in His crucifixion. Our natural man, our flesh, and our self must be cut and crucified. As we are identified with Him in His crucifixion, we are also identified with Him in His resurrection. We are dead in His death (Rom. 6:5a, 8a) and we are living in His resurrection (Rom. 6:5b, 8b) to fulfill God's purpose. We were terminated in His crucifixion and we were germinated in His resurrection. It is in this way that we are enabled to fulfill God's eternal purpose.

It is impossible for the natural man to have the church life. Among us we have many different kinds of brothers and sisters. Humanly speaking, it is impossible for us to be one. Nevertheless, in the church we are truly one by the crucified and resurrected Christ. We are so one in Him that even the Devil has to admit that we are one. Our old man was terminated in Christ's crucifixion. Whenever my terminated old man comes out of the grave, I immediately rebuke him, saying, "What are you doing here? You have been terminated already. It is wrong for you to come here." We all have been terminated in Christ's crucifixion and germinated in His resurrection. In His resurrection we all are living, not living by ourselves but by the resurrected Christ who lives within us and who enables us to have the church life.

Now we see how God can have such a wonderful seed and land as the people and the sphere in and with which He can establish His kingdom and build up His habitation for His expression and representation. How can God do this? Only by Christ's being crucified as our peace offering, sin offering, and burnt offering and being resurrected to be our life. Now we, the called ones, those who offer Christ to God and are identified with Him, are one with Christ. When Christ was crucified and resurrected, we also were crucified and resurrected with Him. We were crucified in His crucifixion and resurrected in His resurrection. Now we can all declare, "It is no longer I who live, but Christ lives in me" (Gal. 2:20). It is by this fact that we can be living today in order to have the church life. In the church life we have Christ within as the seed and Christ without as the land. How can we get into such a land, into such a church life? Only through the crucified and resurrected Christ, through the heifer, she-goat, ram, turtledove, and pigeon. On the one hand, we all have been crucified; on the other hand, we all are living. So here God can have the seed and the land for the fulfillment of His eternal purpose. Hallelujah for such a Christ as the seed for us to live by and as the land for us to live in!

THE AFFLICTION OF THE PROMISED SEED

SIGNIFIED BY THE GREAT DARKNESS   ✦   Verses 12 through 16 speak of the affliction of the promised seed. This affliction was signified by the great darkness that fell upon Abraham. As the sun was going down, Abraham fell into a deep sleep, and a horror of a great darkness came upon him. In that darkness God prophesied concerning Abraham's seed, saying, "Know of a surety that thy seed shall be a stranger in a land that is not theirs, and shall serve them; and they shall afflict them four hundred years...but in the fourth generation they shall come hither again" (vv. 13, 16). God seemed to be telling Abraham, "Abraham, you should not doubt that I will give you the land. Your seed will inherit the land. But your descendants are going to suffer affliction for four hundred years." The Lord's prophecy here is very meaningful. In the church life today, at a certain point the sun will go down, the dark night will come, and most of the people will be sleeping, that is, they will be out of function and no longer useful. Such a time is a time of affliction. Here with Abraham we see three things: that the sun was going down, that a deep sleep fell upon Abraham, and that a horror of a great darkness fell upon him. It is during such a time that God's called people are under suffering. God told Abraham that his seed would be suffering like that for four hundred years. Those four hundred years were to be one long night, a dark age when all the children of Israel would be sleeping, out of function, and suffering affliction. Abraham's sleep signified that the four hundred years were to the children of Israel a dark night through which they passed.

FROM ISHMAEL'S PERSECUTION OF ISAAC TO THE EXODUS OUT OF EGYPT　　◆　　History proves that Abraham's seed did suffer affliction for a period of four hundred years beginning with Ishmael's persecution of Isaac (21:9; Gal. 4:29) about 1891 B.C. until the exodus out of Egypt about 1491 B.C. (Exo. 3:7-8; Acts 7:6). Ishmael's mocking of Isaac was the start of the affliction of Abraham's seed that was to continue for four hundred years. What is the significance of the number four hundred? This number is composed of ten times forty. In the Bible, the number forty is the number of trials, sufferings, and tests. Thus, four hundred indicates ten times of trials. Before the children of Israel were tested in the wilderness for forty years, they had been tested for ten times forty years already. From Ishmael's persecution of Isaac, the promised seed, until the exodus out of Egypt was four hundred years. Why then does Exodus 12:40-41 (cf. Gal. 3:17) speak of four hundred thirty years? This four hundred thirty years began with Genesis 12:1-6, from about the year 1921 B.C. From the day that Abraham was called in Genesis 12 to the persecution of Isaac by Ishmael was exactly thirty years, the period in which God's called ones lived in a strange land. While Abraham was in Canaan, it was a strange land to him, and it remained a strange land to God's called ones until the day they entered into it as the good land. The persecution of the seed began thirty years after Abraham was called in Genesis 12 and continued for four hundred years.

This is not merely a doctrinal matter, for the principle is the same in the church life today. While we are enjoying Christ as the seed within and as the land without, a dark night may fall upon us and some trials and testings may come. What is the purpose of this? For the purpose that, in the midst of the dark night, the lack of function of the called ones, and the affliction, God might come in as a smoking furnace to refine us and as a flaming torch to enlighten us that we may fulfill His purpose by the seed and by the land.

AS A SIGN FOR THE FULFILLMENT OF GOD'S COVENANT   ✦   In making the covenant with Abraham, God sovereignly made an environment of darkness in which He told Abraham that his descendants would suffer affliction for four hundred years. This prophecy, which was fulfilled accordingly, was a sign for the fulfillment of God's covenant made here. The affliction of the promised seed was a sign that God would fulfill His covenant. By suffering the affliction as God prophesied, God's people should be assured that God would fulfill His covenant. It is the same with us today. The suffering of the church in dark times is a strong sign that God will fulfill His covenant for the church life with Christ as the seed and the land.

In verse 18 the Lord made a covenant with Abraham and said, "Unto thy seed have I given this land, from the river of Egypt unto the great river, the river Euphrates." Abraham's seed was given a spacious land, from the river of Egypt to the great river of Euphrates. The nation of Israel today has only a narrow strip of land, but the promised land is more spacious than this. In typology, this means that after all of the experiences of affliction, the church life will be expanded and become spacious. Then we shall have a richer seed and a wider, broader church life. The seed within us will be richer, and the land without us will be broader. It is here that we fulfill God's eternal purpose.

I believe that now, by the Lord's mercy, Genesis 15, a chapter which has been so difficult to understand, has been made clear to us. In this chapter we have the seed and the land. Here we have Christ as the crucified One and as the resurrected and living One. Here we also have our identification with Him. In this chapter there are the four hundred years of affliction and God's coming in as a furnace and a torch. It is here that God enacted His covenant that we might fulfill His eternal purpose. How did God enact His covenant? In the way of Christ's being crucified as the peace offering, sin offering, and burnt offering and being resurrected as the living One; in the way of our offering Christ and being fully identified with Him in His crucifixion and resurrection; and in the way of our realizing that we shall have the dark night, the affliction, and God's coming in as the furnace and the torch to refine and enlighten us. It is here in Genesis 15 that we are in the covenant made through Christ that enables us to fulfill God's eternal purpose. It is here that in the church life we enjoy Christ as the seed and as the good land. It is here that we enjoy Him as the all-sufficient grace for the fulfillment of God's purpose.   �֎

10

KNOWING GRACE
FOR THE FULFILLMENT
OF GOD'S PURPOSE
THE ALLEGORY
OF THE TWO WOMEN

God said unto Abraham,...Sarah shall her name be.
And I will bless her, and give thee a son also of her:
yea, I will bless her...
And Abraham said unto God, O that Ishmael might live before thee!

Genesis 17:15-16, 18

For it is written that Abraham had two sons,
one of the maidservant and one of the free woman.
However the one of the maidservant was born according to the flesh,
but the one of the free woman was born through promise.
These things are spoken allegorically,
for these women are two covenants...

Galatians 4:22-24

Genesis is a book of the riches of God's divine revelation. The more I stay with this book, the more I enjoy its sweet riches. When we read the book of Genesis, we need the divine enlightenment, for by our human mentality we cannot get anything out of this book except historical records and some interesting stories. When I was young, I was happy to hear the stories in this book, but if we only understand Genesis as a story book, we shall miss a great deal.

Sarah and Hagar, the wife and the concubine of Abraham, God's called one, are an allegory of two covenants (Gal. 4:24). If the Apostle Paul had not written the book of Galatians in which he tells us that these two women are an allegory of two covenants, none of us would ever have dreamed of such a thing. Although some Christians criticize the allegorization of the Bible, Paul took the lead to allegorize the Old Testament. If we are going to appreciate the treasures in the book of Genesis, we must realize that Genesis is a book of allegories. Abraham's biography is an allegory. His wife and his concubine especially are a very meaningful allegory. In this message we shall do our best to probe into the meaning of this allegory.

Before we come to this allegory, however, we need to see something about the book of Genesis. Why is Genesis so sweet and precious? Because it is a book containing many seeds of the divine revelation that were sown by God Himself. This book contains all of the main aspects of God's divine revelation. In the very first chapter we see that God has an intention to express Himself through man and that for this purpose He created man in His own image (1:26). Man was made according to God's image with the intention that he might become God's exact expression and that through this expression God might have a dominion, a kingdom, in which He could exercise His authority. This is God's ultimate intention, His eternal purpose. If you read the Bible with this heavenly light, you will see that the whole Bible covers this divine intention. In order for God to fulfill His intention of having Himself expressed and of obtaining a dominion on earth, He needs to have the seed and the land, both of which are related to Christ. This Christ must be wrought into God's people. God wanted to do this with Adam, but Adam failed. Eventually, God had a new start with a new race, the race of the called ones, the first one of which was Abraham. If you read Abraham's biography, you will see that again and again God came to him with a promise concerning two things—the seed and the land (12:7; 13:15-16; 15:5, 7, 18). Abraham was not young when he was first called by God; he was seventy-five years of age when he answered God's calling in a full way.

Although Abraham was seventy-five years of age, he still did not
have a child. As far as God was concerned, that was very good. If
when God calls you you have nothing, that is very good, for if you
have too much, that will frustrate God's calling. When Abraham was
called by God, he did not have a child and he lived in a condemned,
demonic land, a land out of which God called him. After he was
called, Abraham had no child and no land. Suppose a man and his
wife today would have no child and no land. Would they not think of
themselves as the most pitiful people on earth? Perhaps Abraham said
to his wife, "What are we here for? I am seventy-five and you are
sixty-five, and we don't have even one child. We have also been
called out of our land. Where are we? What are we doing here?
Where are we going?" It seems that they were in a pitiful situation.
But the more pitiful we are in this way, the better it is for God's purpose. I hope that none of us has a child within nor a land without. If
both within and without we have nothing, that would be wonderful.
Why? Because God does not want us to have anything for the fulfillment of His purpose. What God wants is to work Christ into us as the
seed and then to work Christ out of us as the land. Firstly, the seed
must be wrought into us; secondly, it must be worked out of us to
become the land. Both the seed and the land are Christ.

We have seen that Abraham answered God's calling in the way of
dragging his feet through mud and water. Since God did not give
Abraham a child, Abraham took Lot, his nephew, along with
him. Abraham could not say that he had nothing, because he had
taken Lot with him. Furthermore, it might have been that as he was
traveling through Damascus, he found Eliezer and took him along
with him. Following that, it might have been that after Abraham fell
into Egypt, drifting downstream like a piece of driftwood, he acquired
Hagar. Although he planned to sacrifice his wife in Egypt, under
God's sovereignty his wife was preserved, and, according to God's
good plan, Abraham acquired many riches, including an Egyptian
maid named Hagar. In Haran Abraham picked up Lot, in Damascus he
found Eliezer, and in Egypt he secured Hagar. But in the good land he
did not gain anything. All he obtained in the good land was God's
promise in plain words regarding the seed and the land.

Although Abraham was not free to argue with God, within himself
he probably said to God, "God, You don't need to promise me over
and over again that You will give me a boy. You already told me that

my descendants will become a great nation. You have told me three times that I would have a seed, but why don't You do anything? God, don't You realize that one action is better than a thousand words? You've not only made a promise to me but also a covenant. You tell me that the rain is going to come, but I have not yet seen even one drop of water. Also, You told me that You would give me this land. Why don't You give it to me right now? You always say, 'I will give it to you,' but don't You know that I need it now?" This was a real testing to Abraham. Firstly, Abraham relied upon Lot. Eventually Lot became a problem to him and separated from him. After that, Abraham put his trust in Eliezer, telling God that Eliezer would be his heir. When God said that Eliezer would not be the heir, Abraham might have said, "God, what are You doing? You have just robbed me. You say no to this and no to that. You don't give me even one yes." In order to strengthen Abraham's faith, God made a covenant with him in a very extraordinary way, using three cattle and two living birds. That covenant made by God was much stronger than just His promise.

After this, Abraham and Sarah might have had a lot of sad fellowship. Abraham might have said to his wife, "Sarah, many years ago God promised that we would have a seed. Where is it? God also promised to give us the land. In order to strengthen our faith, He made a covenant with us. We cannot say that the covenant is not believable or trustworthy, because I offered the cattle and the birds as the Lord told me to. But we still don't have anything." In times like this, the wives are often like Sarah. Often the wives are finer and look at things in more detail. It might have been that while Abraham was talking in such a sad way that Sarah presented him with a good proposal saying, "Abraham, we cannot say that God's word is not trustworthy, but look at how old we are. Didn't God tell you that someone born out of you would be your seed? Now I have a good proposal. It must have been sovereign that we acquired Hagar in Egypt. Why don't you go to her and have a child by her? Then we shall have the seed to fulfill God's purpose." If we had been Abraham we probably would have said, "This is a wonderful idea. I never thought of it, but thank God that you had the wisdom to propose such a plan." Abraham took Sarah's counsel and Ishmael was produced. Perhaps after Ishmael was born Abraham said, "Who can deny this one? He was certainly born of me. Don't you believe that God was sovereign in giving us Hagar in Egypt and in the fact that she gave birth to a boy, not to a girl? God has been sovereign in three respects—in giving us Hagar, in causing her to conceive, and in giving us a boy through her. Praise the Lord! This is surely the sovereignty of God." But after the birth of Ishmael, God stayed away from Abraham for thirteen years (16:16; 17:1).

On the one hand, during that period of time Abraham might have been happy because he had a child, but on the other hand, he was suffering because he did not have God's appearing. He might have said to his wife, "Why don't we have God's appearing? What has happened? We didn't go down to Egypt again or do anything wrong. We acted on your proposal to have a seed to fulfill God's purpose. What is wrong with us? We have a child, but we don't have God's presence." As we shall see in the next message, after thirteen years, God finally came in, saying to Abraham, "I am the all-sufficient God; walk before me, and be thou perfect" (17:1, Heb.). God seemed to be telling Abraham, "Abraham, you must be perfect. Although you have done no wrong, it is certain that you are not perfect." Then God told him that a seed would be born not only out of him but also out of his wife, saying that He would give Abraham a son by her (17:16). Ishmael had been born out of Abraham but not out of Sarah. Abraham, being very reluctant to give up Ishmael, said to God, "O that Ishmael might live before thee!" (17:18). God answered Abraham, saying, "Sarah thy wife shall bear thee a son indeed; and thou shalt call his name Isaac" (17:19). God seemed to be telling Abraham, "Abraham, you have misunderstood Me. The seed must not only be out of you but also out of Sarah. And his name shall be Isaac, not Ishmael." God had rejected Ishmael.

In Galatians Paul tells us that Sarah and Hagar, the two women, are an allegory symbolizing two covenants. Paul could only have seen this through God's revelation. Without Paul's telling us about this, would you ever have dreamed that Sarah was a symbol of the covenant of grace and that Hagar was a symbol of the covenant of law? We should not be content with just knowing the stories in Genesis but should press on to understand the meaning of the allegory.

In Galatians 3:17 Paul said, "And I say this a covenant ratified beforehand by God, the law having come four hundred and thirty years after does not annul, so as to make the promise of none effect." This four hundred thirty years covers the span of time from

Genesis 12:1 to the giving of the law in Exodus 20. Before the law was given, there was an allegory. In other words, before the law was given, God took a photograph of what would happen with the law four hundred thirty years later. We all must see this.

THE FREEWOMAN, SARAH,
SIGNIFYING THE COVENANT OF PROMISE (GRACE)

Sarah, the freewoman, signifies the covenant of promise (Gal. 4:23). God's covenant of promise with Abraham was a covenant of grace. In that covenant God promised that He would give Abraham the seed, without having any intention that Abraham needed to do anything in order to have it. God would work something into him that he might bring forth a seed to fulfill His purpose. It would be God's doing, not Abraham's. This is grace. Sarah, as the freewoman, the proper wife of Abraham, was a symbol of this covenant of grace. She brought forth Isaac not by man's strength but by God's grace.

THE BONDWOMAN, HAGAR,
SIGNIFYING THE COVENANT OF LAW

Hagar, the bondwoman, signifies the covenant of law (Gal. 4:25). It was when the children of Israel ignored God's work of grace upon them and attempted to please God by themselves that the law was brought in. When man is ignorant of God's grace, he will always endeavor to do something to please God, and this brings in the law, of which Hagar, the bondwoman, the improper wife of Abraham, was the symbol. Since she was the improper wife, she should not have come in. What she brought forth could not remain in God's economy. This signifies that the law should not have come in and that the produce of the law has no position in fulfilling God's purpose. Hagar brought forth Ishmael, who was rejected by God, by man's effort, not by God's grace. The produce of man's effort through the law has no share in the fulfillment of God's purpose.

According to God's economy, a man should only have one wife. Thus, Sarah's proposal that Abraham have a seed by Hagar was absolutely against God's economy. Hagar was not a proper wife but a concubine. Hagar, Abraham's concubine, was a symbol of the law. By this we can see that the position of the law is the position of the concubine. While grace is the proper wife, the mother of the proper heirs

(Gal. 4:26, 28, 31), the law is the concubine, the mother of those who are rejected as heirs. According to the ancient custom, men mainly took concubines because their wives could not bear children. This is quite meaningful. When grace has not yet worked and you are in a hurry, you will join yourself to a concubine, to the law. Sarah was a symbol of grace, of the covenant of promise, and Hagar was a symbol of the law. Grace is the proper wife and the law is the concubine.

THE COVENANT OF PROMISE (GRACE) BEING MADE FIRST

The promise was given in 12:2, 7; 13:15-17; 15:4-5, and the covenant was made in 15:7-21. According to God's intention, the covenant of promise came first. God had no intention of bringing in the law and of having man endeavor to keep it for the fulfillment of His purpose. What He originally intended to do was to work Himself into man to fulfill His purpose through man.

THE COVENANT OF LAW BEING BROUGHT IN LATER

The covenant of law was brought in later by the effort of the flesh in Genesis 16. What we have in Genesis 16 is the effort of the flesh that brought in Hagar, the symbol of law. The promise was given when Abraham was called in Genesis 12, about 1921 B.C., and the law was given in Exodus 20, four hundred thirty years later, after the exodus out of Egypt about 1491 B.C. (Gal. 3:17). Grace always comes first, but the law follows to frustrate. Not very many Christians see that the position of the law is that of a concubine, that it is against God's economy, and that its produce is under God's rejection. Nevertheless they appreciate the law and try their best to keep it, making themselves Ishmaels, the children of the bondwoman.

THE PRODUCE (ISHMAEL)
BY THE EFFORT OF THE FLESH WITH THE LAW

Without exception, every Christian is like Abraham. After we were saved, we came to realize that God wants us to live a Christlike life, a heavenly life, a victorious life, a life that constantly pleases God and glorifies Him. Yes, God does want us to live such a life, but He will work Christ into us to live for us a heavenly life to please Him and glorify Him. However, all of us focus on the intention and neglect the grace. The intention is that we live a heavenly life for the glory of God, and the grace is that God will work Christ into us for the fulfillment of His purpose. So firstly we rely upon our Lot, that which we brought with us from our natural background, trying to use him to fulfill God's purpose in living a heavenly life for the glory of God. When God does not allow us to rely upon Lot, then we turn to Eliezer, expecting that he will enable us to live a heavenly life for God's glory. Eventually God tells us, "I don't want that. I don't want anything objective but something subjective from within your own being." Once we realize that God wants this, then we begin to exercise our own energy, our natural strength, to fulfill God's purpose. We all have a Hagar, a maid who is always willing to cooperate with us. We may not have the law given by Moses, but we do have many self-made laws. We all are lawgivers and make laws for ourselves.

Let us consider some examples of these self-made laws. Perhaps you say that never again will you lose your temper with your husband or have a negative attitude towards him. This is your first commandment. The second commandment is that, as a Christian lady and a Christian wife, you need to be nice, sweet, and humble. Your third commandment is never to criticize others, and the fourth is to always love people and never to hate them. These self-made laws are our Hagars. Whether we succeed or not in keeping our laws makes no difference in the eyes of God because in His eyes even our successes do not count. In the past years some sisters nearly succeeded in fulfilling their self-made laws. They had a strong character, a strong will, and a strong intention, and all day long they tried their best to control their temper and to be nice, sweet, and humble. Although such sisters might have been successful at this, what they produced was just an Ishmael. These sisters were happy with their Ishmael and, in a sense, they were proud of him. The principle is exactly the same with the brothers.

Although we may gain an Ishmael who is good in our eyes, we have the deep sensation that we are missing something. We have lost God's presence. Moreover, this Ishmael will always mock the spiritual things (21:9). On the one hand, we do not like this mocking element, but, on the other hand, we still feel that since Ishmael was produced by us, he is not that bad. But, having lost God's presence, we find ourselves in trouble. Just as the descendants of Ishmael are a problem to Israel today, so the Ishmael that we have produced remains a problem to us. Once we are clear about this, we would pray, "Lord, keep me in Your grace. Keep me in the promise. Whether Your promise will be fulfilled today or many years from now does not matter. I only want to care for Your promise." Although it is easy to say this, it is not easy to live it.

What is true in our Christian life is also true in our Christian work. The New Testament tells us that after we are saved we need to preach the gospel and bear fruit. But how much natural effort and strength are exercised in the matter of so-called soul winning! Many kinds of Hagars, all of whom were acquired in Egypt, are used to win souls. Every worldly means of soul-winning is a Hagar. Yes, you may use Hagar to win souls, but what kind of souls will you win? They will not be Isaac but Ishmael. According to the New Testament, the proper fruit-bearing and gospel preaching are by the overflow of the inner life, by God working Christ into, through, and out of us. This means that the proper gospel preaching is by Christ as grace to us.

There are a great many Hagars in the Christian world today. Do you want to live a Christian life by yourself? It is better for you to stop. Do you want to preach the gospel with worldly means? It is better that you stop this as well. Stop living the Christian life by yourself and stop working for the Lord with worldly means. Then you may say, "If I stop, I'll be finished." That is right. That is exactly what God expects. Although Abraham fully answered God's call when he was seventy-five, God did not do anything with him until he was ninety-nine because until then he still had his natural strength. He had Lot and Eliezer to rely upon and Hagar to match his natural strength. Eventually God was forced to stay away from him. Likewise, as long as we have a Lot and an Eliezer to rely upon, or a Hagar to endeavor with, God cannot do anything. As long as we still have the strength to produce an Ishmael, God cannot do anything. After the producing of that Ishmael, He will stay away for a period of time. When Abraham was ninety-nine years of age, according to his figuration, he was a dead person. Romans 4:19 says that "he considered his own body already become dead, being about a hundred years old." Romans 4 also indicates that Sarah was out of function. Both Abraham and Sarah were fully convinced that they were finished and could do nothing themselves. At that point God came in.

All of the revival preachers stir up people, telling them to live for Christ and to work for Him. But in our ministry we are saying that you have to stop living a Christian life by yourselves and doing a Christian work with worldly means. Do not be bothered at our saying this, for regardless how much we tell people to stop, hardly anyone will stop. If anyone will stop trying to live a Christian life by himself or to work for the Lord by worldly means, blessed is he. It is not easy to stop your self-effort in the Christian life and your natural zeal in Christian work. Although it is easy to be called by God, it is most difficult to stop your natural zeal. If the Lord would come in to stop you, you might say, "No, Lord. Look at today's situation. Hardly anyone works for You in what I am burdened to do. I'm nearly the only one. How could I stop my work for You?" But blessed is the one who will stop, for when you stop, God comes in. The end of humanity is the beginning of divinity. When our human life ends, the divine life begins.

When Abraham was eighty-six years of age, he still had too much of his own strength, causing God to wait for another thirteen years. Perhaps God, sitting in the heavens and looking at Abraham, said, "Abraham, you are now eighty-six, but I still have to wait for another thirteen years." While you are praying that God will do something, God is praying that you will stop. While you are saying, "O Lord, help me to do something," God is saying, "It would really be good for you to stop." While Abraham was so busy on earth, God might have looked at him and said, "Poor Abraham, you don't need to be that busy. Won't you stop and let Me come in? Please stop and let Me do it. Since you won't stop, I have to wait until you are ninety-nine years old." God waited until Abraham was a dying person out of function. Then He came in and could say, "Now is My start. Now is My time to begin something."

The produce of the effort of the flesh was Ishmael, but Ishmael was rejected by God (17:18-19; 21:10-12a; Gal. 4:30). Not only was Ishmael rejected by God, but he also frustrated God's appearing. Our experience today tells us the same thing, for our Ishmael breaks our fellowship with God and keeps us from God's appearing. We see by this that it is not a matter of what we do or of what we are; it is altogether a matter of whether or not we have God's presence. Do you have God's appearance all the time? We must forget our doing and our working and take care of God's appearing. When God's appearing is with us, we are in the grace, in the covenant of grace. But most Christians today only care for their doing and work, not for God's appearing and presence. Although they may produce many Ishmaels, they do not have God's presence. What we need is God's presence. What we need is not the outward fruit of our outward work but the inward appearing of our God. Do you have the presence of God within you? This is a most crucial test.

THE PRODUCE (ISAAC) BY THE PROMISE OF GRACE

The produce of the promise of grace, which is Isaac, is the seed for the fulfillment of God's purpose (17:19; 21:12b). The seed for the fulfillment of God's purpose is nothing less than Christ Himself wrought by God into, through, and out of us. What God has wrought into us brings in Christ as the seed (Gal. 3:16). This seed will eventually become our land. Now we have the seed as our life and the land as our living. Within we have Christ as the seed by whom we live, and without we have Christ as the land in whom we live. This is the church life with Christ as our life. This is the only way for us to fulfill God's purpose.

No longer should we consider this story in Genesis merely as a kind of prediction but as an allegory of today's situation. Grace, law, and our natural strength are all here, and we are always being tempted to exercise our natural strength to coordinate Hagar to produce an Ishmael to fulfill God's purpose. But we have a safeguard—to check whether or not we have God's presence in our daily life and in our Christian work. The safeguard is not how much fruit we have; it is God's presence. Do you have the assurance, the confidence, that day after day Christ is being wrought into your being to be the inner life by whom you live? Do you have the assurance that this Christ is even becoming the realm in which you live? This realm is the church life. We need to have the seed and the land, the proper Christian life plus the church life. We need to live by Christ within and we need to live in Christ without. This is the proper way for us to fulfill God's purpose. We need to see this not for others but for ourselves. Abraham's biography is our autobiography, and the allegory of the two women is a portrait of our life. As we live today, we need Christ as the seed and as the land.

11

KNOWING GRACE FOR THE FULFILLMENT OF GOD'S PURPOSE GOD'S COVENANT CONFIRMED WITH CIRCUMCISION

The Lord appeared to Abram, and said unto him, I am
the Almighty God; walk before me, and be thou perfect....
Neither shall thy name any more be called Abram, but thy name
shall be Abraham; for a father of many nations have I made thee....
This is my covenant, which ye shall keep, between me and you and
thy seed after thee; Every man child among you shall be circumcised.

Genesis 17:1, 5, 10

And he received the sign of circumcision, a seal of the righteousness
of the faith which he had while in uncircumcision, that
he might be the father of all those in uncircumcision who believe,
that righteousness might be accounted to them also.

Romans 4:11

In this message we come to Genesis 17, a record of God's crucial dealing with Abraham in confirming His covenant. We have seen that

Abraham was called and that he received God's call, promise, and covenant. After God called Abraham, He gave him the promise and then He confirmed the promise by making a covenant with him. After Abraham received the covenant, he accepted his wife's proposal to exercise his flesh along with the expediency of Hagar to produce a seed. The result was Ishmael. Here we see three things: Sarah's proposal, Hagar's expediency, and Abraham's exercise of the flesh to produce Ishmael.

GOD'S DISAPPEARING FOR THIRTEEN YEARS BECAUSE OF ABRAHAM'S EXERCISE OF THE FLESH

Abraham might have thought that it was not serious for him to exercise his flesh to produce Ishmael, but according to God's economy for His eternal purpose, it was very serious. If we compare the first verse of chapter seventeen with the last verse of chapter sixteen, we can see that between these two chapters there was a period of thirteen years and that there was no record of Abraham's life during those thirteen years. When Abraham brought forth Ishmael, he was eighty-six years of age, and thirteen years later, when he was ninety-nine, God appeared to him again. During that long period of thirteen years, Abraham, a man called by God, a man who was living by faith and who was learning to know grace for the fulfillment of God's purpose, missed God's presence. How serious it is not to have God's presence!

After Abraham had answered God's calling and had begun to live a life by faith in God for his existence, he had a failure. Being short of faith, he went down to Egypt where he was even planning to sacrifice his wife. According to the human concept, that was much worse than using Hagar to produce Ishmael. But if we read these chapters attentively, we shall see that God was not as displeased with Abraham's going down to Egypt as He was with his using Hagar to produce Ishmael. Of course, it was not good for Abraham to go down to Egypt, but that did not offend God as much as his exercise of the flesh to bring forth Ishmael. Going down to Egypt was a failure without, but taking Hagar to produce Ishmael was failure within. It was deeper, for it was not merely related to circumstances but to life. Taking Hagar to produce Ishmael was not simply a matter of right or wrong or of committing a sin; it was a matter of life. Nothing that we do by ourselves is life. Whatever we work by ourselves is not life. Life is God Himself. It is God being something to us in our very being. We should not do anything by ourselves but by God's being wrought into us. Whatever we do by ourselves is not life but death, for it is the issue of our natural self.

In the eyes of God, our natural self is more dirty and more defiling than sin. Although sin is unclean in the presence of God, it is not as offensive to God as our natural self is. While we all recognize the seriousness of sin, not many people realize the seriousness of our natural self. If we commit a sin, we would immediately confess it to God, but if we do certain good things by our natural self, we do not have the sense that we are offending God. If I hate a particular brother, it is easy for me to recognize that this hatred is a sin and confess it as such to God. But if I love this brother by my natural self, it would be difficult to realize that this is against God. Sin only offends God's righteousness, but our natural self offends God Himself. God wants to come into us to be our life and our everything that we may live, work, and do everything by Him. But when we do things by our self, our natural self, we put Him aside. By this we can see that the natural self is against God Himself. It is not only against God's righteousness or holiness but against God Himself.

God's intention with Abraham was that He would work Himself into Abraham so that Abraham might bring forth a child to fulfill God's purpose. God did not intend that Abraham do this by his natural strength. Nevertheless, Abraham used his natural strength to bring forth a child to fulfill God's purpose. Nothing offends God more than this kind of natural doing. Working by our natural self is the most offensive thing to God. To Abraham, it was not so serious for him to take Hagar. His wife, Sarah, even proposed this, thinking that it would help Abraham to produce the seed since Abraham was old and she was out of function. But God had promised that they would have a son. Since they did not know how this could come about, they took the expediency of using Hagar, the Egyptian maid, to produce a child, not realizing how offensive that was to God. It was an insult to Him. Therefore, God disappeared from His dear called one for thirteen years. It was as if God had turned His face away from Abraham and had refused to speak to him for that length of time. There is no record in the Bible of what happened during that period of time. We only know from the last verse of chapter sixteen and the first verse of chapter seventeen that God reappeared to Abraham thirteen years later. According to the Bible record, thirteen years of Abraham's life were wasted. In the heavenly record those years were lost because Abraham exercised his natural self to do something for the fulfilling of God's purpose.

PERFECTION REQUIRED BY GOD'S ALL-SUFFICIENCY

Genesis 17:1 says, "And when Abram was ninety years old and nine, the Lord appeared to Abram, and said unto him, I am the all-sufficient God; walk before me, and be thou perfect" (Heb.). Here we see that God charged Abraham with two things—that Abraham had to walk before the all-sufficient God and that he had to be perfect. In chapter sixteen, Abraham did not walk before God; he walked before Sarah, Hagar, and Ishmael. Since he had not walked before God, God came and told him to walk before Him and to be perfect. God's telling Abraham to be perfect indicates that before that time he was not perfect. In chapter sixteen, Abraham was imperfect; he lacked something.

Before we consider further what it means to walk before God and to be perfect, we need to learn the meaning of the title of God in 17:1, the all-sufficient God. In Hebrew this title is El-Shaddai. El means the Strong One, the Mighty One, and Shaddai, implying the meaning of breast, udder, means all-sufficient. El-Shaddai is the Mighty One with an udder, the Mighty One who has the all-sufficient supply. An udder produces milk, and milk is the all-sufficient supply, having water, minerals, and many vitamins in it and containing all that we need for our daily living. So El-Shaddai means the all-sufficient Mighty One.

When Abraham did things by his natural self, he forgot the source of his supply. In other words, he forgot God as his all-sufficient source of supply. Therefore, God came to Abraham and seemed to say, "I am the Mighty One with an udder. Are you lacking something? Why don't you come to this udder? Are you hungry or thirsty? Come to this udder. The source of your supply is not your natural self, but I, the Mighty One with an udder. I am the all-sufficient One who can supply everything you need for your living and everything you need for the fulfillment of My eternal purpose. I am the source. You are not the source. You should not live on your own or by yourself. You have to live by Me as the source of your supply."

In chapter seventeen it is not a matter of the Most High God or of the Possessor of heaven and earth as in chapter fourteen; it is absolutely a matter of the Mighty One with an udder. When Abraham was afraid of his enemies, God came in and said, "Fear not, Abram: I am thy shield, and thy exceeding great reward" (15:1). At that time God seemed to say to Abraham, "You don't need to be afraid of your enemies. I am your shield and protection." But after Abraham had done something of his own natural self to fulfill God's purpose, doing something that was against God Himself, God came in and seemed to say, "I am El-Shaddai, the Mighty One with an udder. You should not do anything on your own or by yourself. You must realize that I am your supply." An udder does not give us weapons with which to kill people but milk that comes into us as our supply. God's supply must come into us as milk. God does not want you to energize your strength to produce a seed for the fulfillment of His purpose; He wants you to drink of His milk, to take something of Himself into you so that you might produce a seed. If we did not have the New Testament, we could never understand adequately this title of God, but now we can understand this title adequately. Today we may constantly live by taking the supply of the Mighty One with an udder. Are you receiving the supply from the divine udder day by day? This is not the protection of the shield against the enemy; it is the supply of the udder for producing the seed. This is not a matter of receiving a good job in place of a poor one but of rendering us the supply which, when taken into us, will become the very constituent to produce a child for the fulfilling of God's eternal purpose. What supply are you receiving day after day? We are receiving the supply from the Mighty One with His divine udder. Day by day we are under His udder and have the all-sufficient supply. God is such an all-sufficient Mighty One to us.

In 17:1 God told Abraham to walk before Him. What does this mean? It means to enjoy the Lord. Walking before the Lord means that we constantly enjoy Him and the supply of His udder. Will you walk before Him, enjoying the all-sufficient supply of His divine udder? To walk before God does not mean that we walk before Him fearfully as before the Holy One. No, the Mighty One with the all-sufficient udder supplies all of our daily need. As we are enjoying His supply, we are walking in His presence.

God also told Abraham to be perfect. What does it mean to be perfect? For Abraham to be imperfect did not mean that he was not good; it meant that he was short of God. None of us can be perfected without God. Without God, there is no perfection. Without Him we are always lacking something. Regardless of how perfect we may be in ourselves, we are still short of God and need to be perfected by and with God. If your home life is without God, your home life is not perfect. If God is not in your married life, your married life is imperfect. There is no perfection without God. Suppose your hand had only four fingers. Although it might be a good hand, since it did not have the thumb, it would not be perfect. Your hand would need to be perfected by the addition of the thumb. If one day the thumb would come to be added to your hand, your hand would be perfect. Hence, to be perfect means that we need God to be added to us. To walk before God means to enjoy Him, and to be perfected means to have God added to us. Have you ever realized that your perfection is God Himself? Have you ever realized that regardless of how good you are or how perfect you are in human eyes, without God you are short of something? We do not have the perfecting factor in ourselves, for the perfecting factor is God Himself. God must be added into our lives. If He is not added into our lives, our lives will remain imperfect.

Why did God require Abraham to be perfect? Because God was and still is the all-sufficient Mighty One. Since He is the all-sufficient Mighty One, there is no reason or excuse for us to be imperfect. Whatever we lack, God is. Do you lack strength? God is strength. Do you need energy? God is energy. God is whatever we need. Thus, God's all-sufficiency requires us to be perfect. There is no reason for us to be poor; we have a large deposit in the heavenly bank.

Practically speaking, to be perfect means that we do not rely upon the strength of the flesh but trust in the all-sufficient Mighty One for our life and work. We should not rely upon the exercise of our natural self or upon the energy of our flesh. We must always trust in God's all-sufficiency for everything. Many of us, for example, are troubled by our temper. Why do we lose our temper at certain times? Because at those times we do not trust in God. The losing of our temper should force us to learn one lesson—never to stay away from God but to trust in Him every moment. Do not try to overcome your temper. If you forget your temper and trust in God every moment, your temper will be overcome. Every imperfection is due to one thing: that we keep ourselves away from the all-sufficient Mighty One. When we keep ourselves away from Him, we are like an electrical appliance that will not work because it is cut off from the supply of electricity. We all must learn to keep ourselves constantly in God. This is the way to be perfect.

When as a young Christian I read 17:1, I realized that I was not perfect. I lacked kindness, humility, patience, love, and many other virtues and attributes. Therefore, in my prayer I made the decision that with the help of the Lord I would have love, patience, humility, kindness, and the other virtues that I lacked. But I must tell you that I never succeeded. Whenever I read 17:1 I could not understand what it meant to be perfect. Eventually I saw that the perfecting factor in our life is God Himself and that I needed to have God added into me. The most that we have is four fingers; we do not have the thumb. Regardless of how much we might train our four fingers to do things, they will still be imperfect because they are without the thumb. We need the thumb to be added to our hand to make it perfect.

THE CHANGING OF NAME

Now we come to the changing of name. In 17:5 God said to Abraham, "Neither shall thy name anymore be called Abram, but thy name shall be Abraham; for a father of many nations have I made thee." Abram means an exalted father, and Abraham means the father of a great multitude. Although Abraham was a high father, he was not the father of a multitude, the father of many nations. But in 17:5 his name was changed from exalted father to the father of a multitude. In Hebrew the name Abram is composed of just four letters represented by the English letters A-b-r-m. The name Abraham is composed with one additional letter—h. This indicates four plus one. Four is the number of the creature, and one is the number of the Creator. Hence, as four fingers plus one thumb makes a complete hand, so man plus God equals perfection. Four plus one equals five, the number of responsibility. Regardless of how good we may be as the number four, we are still short of the number one. In order to be the number five, bearing the responsibility to fulfill God's eternal purpose, God must be added to us. What was the significance of the changing of Abraham's name? It was that God was added into him. Before Genesis 17, Abraham was just Abram, a man who did not have God added to him. But in Genesis 17 the man, and not only his name, was changed by having God added into him. One unique letter was added to the four letters, and God was added into man. God is the perfecting factor. Without Him we are imperfect. We all need God to be added into us. This is perfection.

As the person is the reality of one's name, so the changing of Abraham's name signifies the changing of his person. His original name indicated that he was an exalted father. Now God changed his name to indicate that he would be the father of a great multitude. What is needed to fulfill God's eternal purpose is not an exalted father but a father of a great multitude, not an exalted individual but a multiplied person, a person with a great multitude as his multiplication. God needed a great multitude of people to fulfill His purpose, and for this He needed a producing father. Most Christians desire to be a person with exalted spirituality. The more they seek this kind of spirituality, the more they become barren and individualistic, producing no seed. But God needs us to be multiplied in producing seed, not exalted in seeking spirituality. For this we need the changing of name, the changing of our person. The exalted father has to be changed to the father of a great multitude. The exalted-spirituality-seeking person has to be changed to the multitude-producing person. This requires the termination of the spirituality-seeking self. Even this kind of self has to be terminated so that we may be a multiplied person, not an exalted one, for the fulfilling of God's purpose.

In 17:15 we see that Sarah's name was also changed. "And God said unto Abraham, As for Sarai thy wife, thou shalt not call her name Sarai, but Sarah shall her name be." Sarai means my princess and Sarah means princess. The word "my" before princess indicates narrowness, but princess by itself indicates broadness. Sarai's name was changed to Sarah because in a broad way, not in a narrow way, she was to be a mother of many nations. In 17:16 God said, "And I will bless her, and give thee a son also of her: yea, I will bless her, and she shall be a mother of nations; kings of people shall be of her." When God is added into us, we become wider and broader. Without God's being added into us, we are not only imperfect but also narrow. Although you may be a brother or sister, if you do not have God added into you, you are a narrow brother or sister. If you are a husband who does not have God added into you, you are a narrow husband. If you are a wife who does not have God added into you, you are a narrow wife. What can widen us? Only God Himself. If you are going to be a broadened person with a broadened view and with a broadened mind, heart, and spirit, you need God to enlarge you. Regardless of who we are, as long as we do not have God added into us, we always say things such as, "my interest," "my profit," "my future," "my growth in life," "my seeking of the Lord," "my function in the church meetings." Unless God enlarges us, we shall not care for others. Our name, which is "my princess," must be changed to "princess." We say, "This is my day, my house, my time, my this, and my that," because we are short of God, but once we have God added to us, we immediately become broadened. When we have God added into us, we shall not only become a father of a great multitude but also a princess of many nations for the fulfilling of God's eternal purpose. We all need such a change, a change which comes from God being added into us to broaden our narrow person.

We all need to be changed from "my princess" to "princess," transformed from our narrow concept of spirituality to a broadened and general spirituality that we may be no longer "my" princess but a "mother of nations," caring for others and having the seed for the fulfillment of God's purpose. This also requires the termination of our old and natural man so that we may be transformed into a new person, producing the seed, caring for many others, and enabling God's purpose to be fulfilled with a great multitude. For God's eternal purpose we need to be the "father of a great multitude" and the "mother of nations." We need to be transformed into a multiplied and multiplying person and into a broadened and general person.

THE COVENANT CONFIRMED WITH CIRCUMCISION

In order for us to have God added into us and to be broadened we need to be circumcised. The covenant that God made with Abraham in Genesis 15 was confirmed in Genesis 17 with circumcision. There was no need for God to confirm it again, for He had confirmed it once already, but it had to be confirmed from Abraham's side. While God was faithful to His covenant, Abraham was not because he had used his natural strength to produce Ishmael. Since Abraham's use of his natural energy with Hagar to produce Ishmael was the cause of the trouble, God confirmed His covenant by having Abraham circumcised (17:9-11, 13).

In the New Testament we can find out the significance of circumcision. The spiritual meaning of circumcision is to put off the flesh, to put off the self and the old man. Colossians 2:11-12 says, "In whom also you were circumcised with a circumcision not made with hands, in the putting off of the body of the flesh, in the circumcision of Christ, buried together with Him in baptism, in whom also you were raised together through the faith of the operation of God, who raised Him from among the dead." Circumcision is a matter of putting off the flesh, the old man; it is not a matter of dealing with sin. In a strict sense, circumcision has nothing to do with the dealing with sin; it is a matter of being crucified and buried with Christ. Circumcision means to terminate your self, to terminate your flesh. Abraham exercised his flesh in Genesis 16, but here, in Genesis 17, God wanted his flesh to be cut off. In Genesis 16 he had energized his natural strength, but in Genesis 17 his strength had to be terminated. This is circumcision.

The problem is the same today. As long as our natural strength remains, it is difficult for God to come in to be our everything for the fulfillment of His purpose. God wants to come into us to be everything to us, but our flesh, our natural being and strength, our old man and our old self, are a frustration to God's being everything to us. This self, this old man, must be terminated. It must be circumcised, that is, crucified. I want to tell you the good news that our old man has been crucified already (Rom. 6:6). With Abraham, it was to be crucified, but with us, it has been crucified already. We all must see this, reckon on it, and take it by faith. By faith we can declare that our flesh, our natural man with its strength, has been crucified. "I have been crucified with Christ, and it is no longer I who live, but Christ lives in me" (Gal. 2:20). We all need to live with the realization that the old man, the self, has been crucified. If we declare this and live according to it, then the God of resurrection immediately has the way to come into us and to be everything to us for the carrying out of His economy.

Circumcision is a sign, a seal, of justification by faith (Rom. 4:11). However, many Christians neglect this sign. Although they may realize and declare that they have been justified by faith, after having been justified by faith they do not have the sign of the termination of the self. How can you show people that you have been justified by God? You must live a life of the termination of the self. You must show that you are no longer living by yourself but that you are living by Christ. Then your living becomes a sign of your having been justified. To live a crucified life in the resurrection of Christ is a sign of our being justified. Suppose I, a saved person who has been justified by God, still live, act, and work by myself, doing everything by myself. If such is the case, it will be difficult for anyone to recognize that I am a justified person. People may even doubt that I am saved. But if I live a crucified life, putting myself aside and taking Christ as my life, no one could doubt that I have been justified by faith. Everyone would have to say, "Praise the Lord! There is no doubt that here is a brother who has been justified by God." The life of the termination of the self is a sign and a seal of our justification.

The confirmation of the covenant by circumcision concerned the seed and the land for the fulfillment of God's purpose (17:2-8). In order to fulfill God's eternal purpose that man express and represent Him, we need to have Christ as our seed and as our land. In order to have Christ as the seed and the land for the fulfillment of God's purpose, we need to be circumcised and to live a crucified life. Circumcision is for the fulfillment of God's purpose. When the flesh, the self, and the old man have been terminated, the door is open for God to come in and bring forth Isaac.

Among the Jews, circumcision was always practiced on the eighth day (17:12). The eighth day was the first day of a new week and denoted a new start, a new beginning in resurrection. Whenever we live a crucified life, we have a new beginning in resurrection. When we reject and deny our self and live a crucified life, we immediately have a new beginning in resurrection. Although you might have been married for many years, if today you begin to live a crucified life, you will have a new beginning in resurrection in your marriage, and your marriage will be renewed. Whenever there is circumcision there is the eighth day. In other words, whenever we live a crucified life, we are in resurrection.

All of the uncircumcised people were cut off from this covenant. In 17:14 God said to Abraham, "And the uncircumcised man-child whose flesh of his foreskin is not circumcised, that soul shall be cut off from his people; he hath broken my covenant." This is true today. If we do not live a crucified life, we are cut off from Christ, from the church life, and from the supply of the divine udder. Whenever we are unwilling to be circumcised, we are finished with the fulfilling of God's eternal purpose. Today our enjoying God, our living by Christ, and our practicing the church life all depend upon one thing—upon circumcision, upon living a crucified life.

THE BIRTH OF ISAAC PROMISED

In 17:15-21 we see the birth of Isaac promised more definitely than ever before. We know that it is more definite because the name Isaac was mentioned and his mother was designated. In the foregoing chapters, God said that He would give Abraham a seed and that Abraham would bring forth the seed, but God did not mention that the seed would be out of Sarah. Neither did He say that the seed would be named Isaac. But in these verses we see that God promised in a definite way that the seed would be Isaac and that Isaac would be born of Sarah.

AFTER ABRAHAM HAD BECOME AS OLD AS DEAD AND SARAH HAD BECOME OUT OF FUNCTION ✦   The promise of the birth of the seed was confirmed definitely at the time when Abraham was as old as dead and Sarah was out of function. Perhaps Abraham said to Sarah, "Sarah, I am a hundred years old and you are ninety. I am dying and you are out of function. We both have become nothing and we can do nothing." It is wonderful to become nothing, for then the Mighty One with an udder can come in to do everything for us. I would like to be a hundred years of age and become nothing. Becoming nothing would afford the Almighty One, the all-sufficient One, the best opportunity to feed me and to supply me with whatever He likes. Even today there are times when God would like to give me a new portion of milk, and I say, "No, I still have some way, some energy, some strength." We all need to become a hundred years of age. But do not try to act as if you are already a hundred years of age. After reading this message telling you that you need to be a hundred years of age and become nothing, you may pretend to be a hundred years of age. But you cannot become nothing overnight. The Lord knows how much we still are. Nevertheless, the principle is that we all need to become nothing so that the all-sufficient Mighty One may come in to be our everything with His all-sufficient udder to render us the supply that we need.

NOT BY ABRAHAM'S NATURAL STRENGTH BUT BY GOD'S VISITATION ✦   After Abraham and Sarah had become nothing, God promised that Isaac would be born of Sarah (17:16, 19, 21). This means that the birth of Isaac was not the result of Abraham and Sarah's energy but that it was absolutely the result of God's gracious visitation. In 18:10, 14 we see clearly that the birth of Isaac was due to God's return to Abraham at the time of life. His gracious visitation to Abraham included His feeding and supplying him with all that He was. God had to be the udder supplying the milk that Abraham needed to bring forth Isaac. Isaac was not produced by any element in Abraham's natural being; he was brought forth by God's all-sufficient supply out of the divine udder.

ISHMAEL, THE SEED PRODUCED BY THE FLESH, BEING REJECTED BY GOD ✦ Ishmael, the seed produced by the flesh, was rejected by God (17:18; 21:10). Whatever we do by our ability or by our natural self will always be rejected by God. Although you may do good by keeping the law, that will be rejected by God. Whatever we live, do, and work by the natural self and the old man will be altogether rejected. Not many Christians realize that even their natural goodness is rejected by God. Whatever we do by our natural self, natural strength, natural ability, or natural man, regardless of whether it is good or bad, will be rejected by God.

ISAAC, THE SEED BROUGHT FORTH BY GOD'S GRACE, ESTABLISHED FOR THE FULFILLMENT OF GOD'S PURPOSE ✦ Only Isaac, the seed brought forth by God's grace, by the supply out of the divine udder, was established for the fulfillment of God's eternal purpose (17:19, 21; 21:12; Rom. 9:7-9). God will only honor what is out of Him because only the seed that is produced out of Him by the supply of His grace can fulfill His purpose. This means God will only honor Christ, not anything out of our self, our natural man. Only the Christ whom we experience of the divine udder as our supply of grace can accomplish God's purpose. Only this Christ will be established as the real seed for the fulfillment of God's purpose. Our Ishmael was rejected, but our Isaac, Christ, has been and will be established in God's economy.

Now we can see what grace is. Grace means that God transmits some element out of His being into us to be our supply and that this supply becomes the very element by which we bring forth Isaac for the fulfillment of God's eternal purpose. After Abraham was called, he learned to live by faith in God for his existence. Then, beginning with Genesis 15, God began to train him in the matter of knowing grace for the fulfillment of God's purpose. We have seen this clearly in chapters fifteen, sixteen, and seventeen. Our self, flesh, natural strength, natural man, and old man must be terminated so that we might take God as our supply and that some of God's divine being might be wrought into us to be the element to produce Isaac for the fulfillment of God's promise. This is grace.

12

KNOWING GRACE FOR THE FULFILLMENT OF GOD'S PURPOSE

THE UNVEILING OF THE DIVINE TITLE AND THE CHANGING OF HUMAN NAMES FOR THE FULFILLING OF GOD'S PURPOSE

The Lord appeared to Abram,
and said unto him,
I am the Almighty God....
Neither shall thy name any more be called Abram,
but thy name shall be Abraham.

Genesis 17:1, 5

If we are to understand Genesis 17, we must know what God's purpose is. God's purpose, which He made in eternity past, is to express Himself through a body of people on earth. In order to have a collective people as His expression, God created the universe and within the universe, as its center, He created man in His image with the intention that man would express Him and represent Him so that He may have a dominion on earth as His kingdom. This was God's purpose with Adam and with the children of Israel in the past, it is His purpose with the church today, and it shall be His purpose in the millennium and throughout eternity. Throughout all the ages, God's purpose has remained the same: to have Himself expressed and represented by man on earth.

For the fulfillment of His purpose, God needs a people. If God can gain a people, He will be able to accomplish His purpose, but if He cannot gain a people, He will be defeated. But our God cannot be defeated! God created Adam, and Adam became a failure. Then God called Abraham to be the head of a new race. Although God called only one person, Abraham, this person had to become a race so that God could be expressed and represented on earth. God called Abraham for this purpose. It is impossible for an individual to fulfill God's purpose, for what God needs is not just an individual but a people. One Abraham must be multiplied into a great many Abrahams. But this cannot be accomplished according to man's natural understanding or by his natural ability, strength, or being.

GOD'S DESIRE TO WORK HIMSELF INTO MAN

The Bible reveals that God's way to express Himself is to work Himself into man. God's way is extraordinary. Although God wants us to do things for Him, His desire is not that we do anything but that He come into us to do everything through us for Himself. His desire is to work Himself into us, making Him one with us and us one with Him. But no one is willing for God to do this. Everyone seems to say, "O Lord, if You ask me to do something, I'll do it for You, but I cannot bear to have You come into me to annul me and dethrone me. When I do something for You, I like to do it by myself." Nevertheless, God would say, "Before you do anything for Me, I must work Myself into you. By coming into you, I will have you crucified and then I will make you alive by, with, and for Me. Are you willing for this?" Abraham did not wait for God to do this, but, as Genesis 16 reveals, he acted on his own to bring forth a seed.

THE UNVEILING OF THE DIVINE TITLE

In 17:1 God came in to unveil His divine title, unveiling what He, the very God, is. To unveil a name is to unveil a person, for a name always represents a person. Since God's divine title denotes His divine Person, the unveiling of the divine title is actually the revelation of the divine Person. In 1:1 God was unveiled as Elohim, which primarily means the Mighty One, the Strong One, and which is mainly related to God's creation. In Genesis 2 God was revealed as Jehovah, the great I Am. The name Jehovah means "I Am that I Am," implying that God is the self-existent and ever-existing One. This title of Jehovah refers to God's relationship with man. Furthermore, God revealed to Abraham that He was the Most High God, the Possessor of heaven and earth (14:22). This is mainly related to God's care for His people's existence. But now in chapter seventeen, God comes in to unveil Himself further, revealing Himself to Abraham as El-Shaddai, the all-sufficient Mighty One with an udder.

God's all-sufficiency is in His divine udder. Perhaps some readers are unhappy with the use of the word udder and prefer that we use the word breast. However, if we were to use the word breast, most people would associate it with the matter of love. But the divine title in 17:1 denotes that God is the rich source of supply as grace to His people for them to fulfill His purpose. Although He wants us to fulfill His purpose, He does not need anything from us. He wants to be our supply. Our God has an all-sufficient source of supply, and this source is likened to an udder. This is the meaning implied in the title El-Shaddai. Everything that is supplied to us from the udder of a cow comes into us and even becomes our constituent. All of the elements and ingredients of the riches of the milk we drink become our constituent, our organic tissue. It seemed that God was saying to Abraham, "You have known Me as the Most High God. Although that is wonderful, it is no longer adequate. I am not only the Most High God to you objectively, but I want to be the divine milk to you subjectively. I must be the One that you drink into your being."

Our mind may be bothered at the thought of such a divine drinking. The first time that I gave a message on the eating of Jesus was in 1958. After that message, a very highly educated brother said to me, "Brother Lee, that message was very good, but the term 'eating Jesus' is too wild." I replied, "Brother, I am not the first one to use this term. In John 6:35 and 57 the Lord Jesus said, 'I am the bread of life' and 'He who eats Me shall also live because of Me.'" Are you troubled by the likening of God's rich breast to the udder of a cow? Although I would prefer to liken God to a nice, tender, gentle mother with a loving breast, it is more meaningful to liken God to a cow with a rich udder, as the Scripture implies. We all have been positioned under this divine udder.

Many verses in the Bible give us the ground to speak of God in this way. Exodus 3:8 says, "I am come down to deliver them out of the hand of the Egyptians, and to bring them up out of that land unto a good land and a large, unto a land flowing with milk and honey." The good land is a type of the all-inclusive Christ. With this Christ there is the flowing of milk. Before the children of Israel came into the good land to drink of the milk, they drank of the water that flowed from the riven rock which also was Christ (Exo. 17:6; 1 Cor. 10:4). In Revelation 22 we see that in the New Jerusalem there will be a river flowing from the throne of God and of the Lamb. If we put all of these verses together, we can see that our God today is One out of whom something is flowing to quench, supply, and satisfy us. Regardless of whether we call it milk or living water, it flows out of God's being to supply us. Hence, 1 Corinthians 12:13 says that we have all been made to drink of one Spirit, who is God Himself (John 4:24). When we are drinking of the Spirit, we are drinking of God. Our God is so rich that one type or symbol cannot give us a complete understanding of Him, so the Bible uses different types and symbols to reveal the various aspects of His riches. The milk and the living water both reveal how rich God is to us. The principle in each case is the same: that the riches of His divine being are flowing out to be our supply as grace to us for us to fulfill His purpose. We all must drink of the rich supply that flows out from our God that we may be able to fulfill the divine purpose.

None of us is qualified to fulfill God's purpose. Although religion tells us that we must do certain things for God, what God wants us to do is to take Him in as our supply so that He may become our constituent and that we may become one with Him. The Bible reveals that God's intention is to get into us and that we must eat and drink of Him, taking something of Himself into our being. As we take into our being some element of His divine being, partaking of His divine nature, this divine element will work in and through us to fulfill His purpose.

At the time of Genesis 17, God needed to reveal this divine title of His to Abraham. In Genesis 16 Abraham did something not for his own purpose but for the fulfillment of God's purpose. However, what Abraham did for the fulfilling of God's purpose was accomplished by his natural being and natural strength. Since he did something for God by his natural strength, God was displeased and disappeared from him for thirteen years. After that long absence, God came in and seemed to say, "Abraham, you must know that I am the all-sufficient One with an udder. You must drink of the supply of this udder and not do anything for Me by your natural strength or natural ability. Doing something for Me by your natural strength is an insult to Me. I don't want anything from you. I want you and I need you, but I do not want you to use your natural strength and natural ability to bring forth the promised seed. You must bring forth a seed by My supply. Stop using your strength, deny your natural being, and put aside your natural ability. Since I am the all-sufficient Mighty One, you should not do anything by yourself or apart from Me. Apart from Me, it is impossible for you to fulfill My purpose because apart from Me you can do nothing for My economy. Abraham, in order to fulfill My purpose, you must drink of the supply out of My udder and take Me in. I am not here now as the Most High God or as the Possessor of heaven and earth. You have learned that already. I am now here before you as El-Shaddai, the all-sufficient Mighty One with an udder out of which is flowing a rich supply for you. Abraham, you must walk before Me. This means that you must drink of My udder and live by Me." The Divine Word is deep, and we cannot understand it superficially. We must dive into it before we can see what is revealed there. How good it is that God revealed Himself to Abraham as the Mighty One with an udder full of the all-sufficient supply for His people to fulfill His purpose.

THE CHANGING OF HUMAN NAMES

Immediately after the divine title was revealed to Abraham, God told him that his name was to be changed (17:5). This is very meaningful. Not only must God's title be unveiled to us, but our names need to be changed, meaning that we need to be changed. The name Abram has to be changed to Abraham. As we pointed out in the previous message, Abram means exalted father and Abraham means the father of a great multitude, that is, a multiplied father, "a father of many nations." If you had a choice between being highly exalted and being multiplied, which would you choose? Instead of being highly exalted to the heavens, would you choose to be flattened out and multiplied? According to our natural concept, we would all desire to be exalted rather than multiplied. It is troublesome to be multiplied, for the more children we have, the more problems we have. Everyone likes to be exalted; however, God does not want to exalt us but to multiply us, making us a father of a great multitude. Are you willing to be multiplied?

It is impossible for an exalted father, who is only good for exhibition, to fulfill God's purpose. For the fulfillment of God's purpose, there must be a multitude. So we need to be multiplied, not exalted. Today most Christians want to be spiritual giants, and religion encourages them in this way. When I was young, I was taught and encouraged to be a spiritual giant, but I was never told that I needed to be multiplied. While our natural tendency is to be exalted, God wants to change our name from the father of exaltation to the father of multiplication. How our concept needs to be changed! What is the multitude that God wants? It is the church, a corporate people. God needs the church, the multitude. If you remain by yourself, God has no way of fulfilling His purpose through you. For the sake of the fulfillment of His purpose, we need to forget our old name and be changed from being exalted to being multiplied. To be multiplied is for the fulfilling of God's purpose, not for anything else. It is not merely for the increase or for the expansion of our work; it is for God to be expressed and represented on the earth.

To change the name is to change the person. It is not that originally I am a frog and that now you change my name to fish. Although you may call me a fish, I am still a frog. The title has been changed, but the person has not. The proper changing of the name is the changing of the person. When our person has been changed, the change of title follows.

In the church life today we do not need any exalted fathers; we need many multiplied fathers. This is why the Lord has led us to have the communal life in so many homes. It is not easy for a family to live together with several young people because we all like to have our privacy and stay by ourselves. If the husbands are honest, sometimes even living with their wives is too much for them, and they would prefer to be left alone. But if we all stayed in private, how could we take care of the young ones? The changing of names helps the communal life. Why does the increase take place so slowly in the proper church life? Simply because we lack the fatherhood and because there are not enough homes to take care of the new ones. We need the multiplied fathers' homes to take care of the multitude.

One of the qualifications of an elder is hospitality (1 Tim. 3:2). If you are not hospitable, meaning that you are unwilling to take care of others but only care to be individually holy, you are not qualified to be an elder. If we are going to be hospitable, our name must be changed from the father of exaltation to the father of multiplication. Only a multiplied father is hospitable. The more we take care of others, the better it is for the church life. This is the real changing of names and the real changing of our person.

Not only Abraham's name was to be changed but also Sarah's. The name Sarai, which means my princess, has to be changed to Sarah, which means princess. "My princess" has to be changed to "princess," to "a mother of nations." Your particular character has to be changed into a general one so that you can be a mother of nations and take care of many people.

While every brother likes to be an exalted father, every sister wants to be a "my princess." When our name is Sarai we say, "My husband, my home, my day, my children, my position, my function in the meetings, my everything." Although the sisters may say "my princess," God wants them simply to become "princess" without any "my," to be general, not particular. We should not be exalted but multiplied, not particular but general. Particularity always goes with exaltation; they make a good couple. In the church life, none of us should be for exaltation or in particularity. We all have to be multiplied and general, to be a "father of nations" or a "mother of nations" (17:5, 16).

The church life depends a great deal upon the changing of names. If the brothers still insist on being exalted and if the sisters still prefer to be particular, how could we have the church life? We could only have a religion with a Sunday morning service and come together once a week, greet one another, and then go our separate ways until the next Sunday. In order to have the church life, there must be a great multitude of people that has been built up and compacted together, a people who truly know and practice the communal life. When the brothers no longer want to be exalted but multiplied and the sisters no longer want to be particular but general, then we shall be able to live together and have the proper church life and the multitude for the fulfilling of God's purpose. Then we shall live together day by day and be a churching people all the time. Nearly every time will be a meeting time. We shall be meeting together constantly because no one will want to be exalted but multiplied and because no one will want to be particular but general. This is not merely a doctrine. The changing of names is not only a change of term but a change of our being, of our person. Thus, we may change the title of this message to "the unveiling of the divine Being and the changing of the human person for the fulfilling of God's purpose." Although God's divine being has been unveiled, if we remain the same, His being unveiled will not profit us. His unveiling depends upon our changing. We need to be changed not only in name but also in person. Then we can enjoy the unveiled God and drink at His rich udder.

The changing of names in the sense of changing the person is also seen in the case of Jacob and Peter. For the fulfilling of God's purpose, Jacob's name was changed to Israel (Gen. 32:27-28); a heel-holder, a supplanter (Jacob), was changed into a prince of God (Israel). If Jacob had remained a supplanter, he could never have been used by God in the fulfillment of the divine purpose. Jacob had to be changed into a prince of God. For the building of the church, Peter's name, Simon, was changed to Cephas, which means a stone (John 1:42). Peter's natural being was muddy, and he had to be transformed into a stone, even a precious stone, for God's building (1 Pet. 2:5) to fulfill the divine purpose.

THE SUFFICIENT GRACE FOR FULFILLING GOD'S PURPOSE

By the Lord's mercy, we have no confidence in ourselves or in anyone else. We do not have confidence in people because we have learned that no one is qualified to fulfill God's purpose. Whatever we can produce is just an Ishmael. The proper church life is not concerned with anything human or natural. The proper church life is that which carries out God's eternal purpose through being supplied with the riches of God Himself. Whatever we are able to do means nothing in the fulfilling of God's eternal purpose. All that is needed for the fulfillment of God's purpose is the supply of the divine udder. So we must drop ourselves, depreciate our natural strength and ability, and walk before God, drinking of the riches of His udder. If we do this, spontaneously some element of His divine being will be wrought into us to produce the seed for the fulfillment of His purpose. This is the proper church life.

We have seen that both the seed and the land are Christ. Now we need to see that the seed and the land are not only Christ but also we. After drinking of God's rich supply, we all shall become the seed and the land. Eventually, the seed becomes the land. For the fulfilling of His purpose, God needs a people to possess the land. In that land, God will have a kingdom to be built up with His habitation for His name. This is God's purpose. Since we are the seed, the people to fulfill God's purpose, we, the seed, shall also become the land. Among and within us God has His dominion, and in this dominion God has a kingdom in which He may build up His habitation.

We become the seed and the land by enjoying the riches of God and by having God wrought into us. God and we, we and God, are one in producing the seed and possessing the land. This is something heavenly on earth. It is Bethel, the gate of heaven, with the heavenly ladder joining earth to heaven and bringing heaven down to earth. Here we have God and man, man and God, joined together to be a mutual habitation. How is this fulfilled? By the unveiling of the divine Being and the changing of the human person. Once we have been changed, then we are qualified to enjoy the unveiled God as our grace. God has been unveiled, but this unveiled God needs the changed person. Regardless of who or what we are, we all need to be changed from having natural character to having spiritual character, changed from our source to the divine udder for the supply we need to fulfill the divine purpose. We need to forget ourselves, cease from our natural source of supply, walk before God, and drink of His udder all day long. Then the riches of the unveiled divine Being will be wrought into our human being as the all-sufficient grace for us to fulfill the divine purpose. The Apostle Paul labored more abundantly than all the apostles; yet it was not he but the grace of God that was with him. By the grace of God he was what he was (1 Cor. 15:10). He fulfilled God's purpose in his ministry by enjoying the Lord's sufficient grace (2 Cor. 12:9). Paul surely was drinking of the divine udder to receive the sufficient supply of grace. He did not exercise his natural strength to produce Ishmaels but enjoyed the rich supply of the sufficient grace to bring forth many Isaacs. He lived and worked in the way of "no longer I who live, but Christ" (Gal. 2:20). The real changing of a name is the change from I to Christ—El-Shaddai, the all-sufficient grace Supplier. Only Christ, not I, can fulfill God's purpose.   ✳

13

KNOWING GRACE FOR THE FULFILLMENT OF GOD'S PURPOSE CIRCUMCISION FOR THE FULFILLMENT OF GOD'S PURPOSE

And God said unto Abraham, Thou shalt keep my covenant therefore, thou, and thy seed after thee in their generations. This is my covenant, which ye shall keep, between me and you and thy seed after thee; Every man child among you shall be circumcised.

Genesis 17:9-10

In Him also you were circumcised with a circumcision not made with hands, in the putting off of the body of the flesh, in the circumcision of Christ.

Colossians 2:11

In the book of Genesis, nearly all the divine truths are sown as seeds. In this message we come to a great and basic truth in the holy Word that is sown as a seed in Genesis 17—circumcision.

In order to understand circumcision, we need to see two main points of the divine revelation unfolded in the Bible. The first is that God's eternal purpose is to have Himself expressed and represented by man on earth. This matter is revealed throughout the whole Bible, from the first chapter of Genesis through the last chapter of Revelation. The second point concerns God's way of accomplishing His purpose. God's way to fulfill His purpose is to work Himself into man as man's life and everything so that man may become His expression and representation. The accomplishment of God's purpose does not depend upon what we can do but upon God's working Himself into us. If we see these two points, then we can understand the basic truths in the Bible.

For the fulfillment of His divine purpose, God called Abraham out of Chaldea, a land of demons and idolatry. As we have seen, Abraham did not give a clear-cut answer to God's call but dragged his feet through mud and water. His father brought him to Haran, the halfway place. By God's mercy, Abraham answered God's call nearly in a full way at Haran, crossed the great river, and came to the very place where God wanted him to be. That place was close to the sinful city of Sodom. It was not easy for Abraham to remain in the place where God wanted him to be and not long afterward he drifted down to Egypt. But by God's sovereignty, Abraham, who had left demonic Chaldea, had forsaken halfway Haran, and had overcome sinful Sodom, was delivered out of worldly Egypt and was brought back to the place of God's choosing.

We need to recall the names of three very important persons related to Abraham—Lot, Eliezer, and Hagar. Abraham took Lot with him when he left Haran, and he probably acquired Eliezer at Damascus and Hagar in Egypt. None of these three was a help to Abraham; each one was a problem. God rejected all three of these persons. Abraham used his natural strength to coordinate with Hagar to produce his masterpiece—Ishmael. But Ishmael was absolutely rejected by God.

With this as the background, we come now to the matter of circumcision (17:9-14). At the time of Genesis 17, Abraham had been robbed of all the places where he had been and of all the important persons he had acquired. Chaldea and Haran were past, and he had nothing to do with Egypt. Although he was in the land that God had promised to give him, it had not yet been given to him. Thus, Abraham did not have Chaldea, Haran, Egypt, Sodom, or a portion of the promised land. Furthermore, Lot had separated from him, and both Eliezer and Ishmael had been rejected by God. Abraham was left alone with Sarah. They were two old people who had gained nothing and who were able to do nothing. Perhaps Abraham looked at Sarah and said, "What shall we do? We don't have anything and we can't do anything." At that juncture God came in, revealing Himself to Abraham as El-Shaddai, the all-sufficient Mighty One. It was then that God told Abraham that his name had to be changed from Abram to Abraham and that his wife's name had to be changed from Sarai to Sarah. After that, God told Abraham that he had to be circumcised. Abraham had been robbed of every place and every person. The only thing that still remained with him was himself. God came in to deal with Abraham's self, with his flesh, natural strength, and natural ability. This self, the flesh and natural strength, had to be cut off, circumcised. If we had been Abraham, we probably would have said, "God, don't You know that You have robbed me of so much? There is no one like me on the whole earth. Everyone else has a place of his own, but I have nothing. What will You do now—get rid of me?" God might have answered, "Abraham, you are right. I have robbed you of Chaldea, Haran, Egypt, Lot, Eliezer, Hagar, and Ishmael. I will not rob you anymore, but I will cut you. What you have acquired has been taken from you, and what you are must now be cut." This is circumcision.

Why is there the need of circumcision? On the one hand, God needs man for the fulfillment of His purpose. On the other hand, God does not want anything of man. However, none of the called ones would say, "God, I want to be for You, but I don't want anything of me to be for You. I am willing for You to take all that I have and terminate all that I am." On the contrary, everyone says, "Praise the Lord that He has called me. From now on, whatever I have and whatever I am will be for Him." Consider the example of Peter. For three and a half years the Lord told His disciples that they had to love Him and follow Him. But none of the disciples understood that the Lord did not want anything of them. When the Lord told the disciples that they all would be offended because of Him, Peter said, "If all shall be stumbled in You, I will never be stumbled," and "Even if I must die with You, I will by no means deny You" (Matt. 26:33, 35). But the Lord told Peter, "Truly I say to you, that this night, before a cock crows, you will deny Me three times" (Matt. 26:34). The Lord seemed to be saying to Peter, "Peter, don't boast. You have nothing to boast in. Tonight you will deny Me three times." Peter did deny the Lord three times, and those denials were his actual and practical circumcision. The proud, self-confident Peter was cut into pieces by the circumcising knife of his denial of the Lord.

We all must see that although God does need us for His recovery, He does not want anything of us. It is difficult for us to realize this. We either stay away from the Lord or we come to Him with everything that we have. A Japanese brother may say, "We Japanese are the most patient people on earth. I shall serve the Lord with my Japanese patience." But the Lord does not need this kind of patience. Some sisters may say, "The Lord certainly needs us sisters, and we are willing to be for Him. As sisters, we are not rough like the brothers; we are quite fine. In the church life, our fineness will be for the Lord." Sisters, it is absolutely right for you to be for the Lord, but it is absolutely wrong that anything of yourselves be for Him. Since God does not want anything of us, we all need to be circumcised.

The seed of circumcision was not sown in Genesis 12 or 15 but in Genesis 17, after Abraham had been robbed of so much. Then God appeared to Abraham again, unveiled Himself as the all-sufficient Mighty One with an udder, and told Abraham to change his name. Abraham had to have a radical change. God seemed to say, "Abraham, you must now be circumcised. If you are not circumcised, there is no way for Me to fulfill My purpose through you. In order to have a people for My purpose, there must be the seed. Out of that seed will come the people who will possess the land wherein I shall have dominion, build My temple for My expression, and find rest. This is My purpose. But for the fulfillment of My purpose, I don't need anything of you. I will do everything for you and be everything to you. This is why I have taken every place and everyone away from you. Now I am asking you to agree with Me and cooperate with Me to get rid of yourself. I want your flesh to be cut off, but I don't want to do it directly. I want you to do it for Me. I want you to cut off your flesh. Are you willing to cooperate with Me?" We must not take this as a doctrinal teaching or as an exposition of the stories in the Bible. We all must realize that our need today is to have ourselves circumcised.

How grateful I am to the Lord that so many among us have left Chaldea and Haran and do not care for Sodom or Egypt, but remain in the very place where the Lord's recovery is. But how can the Lord have the seed? How can He take possession of the land so that He may have the proper church life for His dwelling place, dominion, satisfaction, and rest? It is not by our doing anything for Him. It is only by the way of His robbing us of so many things. Our intelligence, wisdom, natural ability, natural strength, and all that we are in our natural being must be taken away by the Lord. Do you agree with this? If you do, then you must pick up the circumcising knife and cut your flesh, your natural being. This is not a matter of overcoming sin or the world; it is a matter of terminating yourself so that the all-sufficient One may have a way to come in to be your life, your everything, and even your very self. This is circumcision. May the Spirit speak this word into us all.

The greatest frustration to the Lord's move in His recovery of the church life is our natural ability. What frustrates the Lord's move is not what we cannot do; it is what we can do. Abraham's exercise of his natural strength kept God away from him for thirteen years. What a frustration that was! Although Abraham had been robbed of so much, he still had his flesh, natural ability, and natural strength. It was by and with his flesh that he produced Ishmael with Hagar. By the time of Genesis 17 the time was ripe for God to touch the frustrating element of Abraham's flesh. God seemed to say, "Abraham, I have taken so much away from you. Only one thing is left to frustrate My gracious work in you—your flesh. I want to take this away from you, but since it is such a subjective matter in your being, I will not force you. I want you to cooperate with Me to cut yourself, to circumcise yourself for Me. Abraham, nothing that you can do by yourself will ever please Me. It can only offend and insult Me. As long as your natural strength remains, I have no way to come into you and bring forth Isaac. Abraham, your natural strength, your flesh, must be cut off." This matter of circumcision in Genesis 17 is most crucial.

What is the meaning of circumcision? It is to get rid of yourself. God has a purpose and He has the called ones, but there is a frustration to His coming in to bring forth the seed—our flesh. Many among us have come to the crucial point of dealing with the flesh. Throughout the years, we have been robbed of so many things, but our flesh, our natural strength, our natural ability may still remain. If we keep using our flesh, Isaac cannot be brought forth from us or even be conceived in us. Our need, then, is to be circumcised and to terminate the self, the flesh. This is what the Bible calls circumcision.

THE SIGNIFICANCE OF CIRCUMCISION

TO PUT OFF OUR FLESH   ✦   What is the significance of circumcision? Firstly, it is to put off our flesh (Col. 2:11, 13a; Deut. 10:16; Jer. 4:4a; Acts 7:51). Many Christians today talk about the overcoming of sin, but that is not the basic dealing. The basic dealing is to put off the flesh. The flesh does include the sinful flesh. However, in the Bible, the flesh includes much more than this, for it also includes our natural strength, ability, power, and talents. Moreover, the flesh includes our natural man, the ego, the "I." Hence, to put off the flesh means to put off the very "I"; it means to terminate the self.

Many years ago I was seeking for the overcoming of sin, but I was only partially successful until I saw that my need was not to overcome sin but to terminate myself. I began to see that once I was terminated everything would be all right. This is why Paul said that he who has died is free from sin (Rom. 6:7). The more we try to overcome sin, the more we are involved with and troubled by it. The best way to overcome sin is to be dead and buried. Then sin will have nothing to do with us. Thus, the basic dealing in the Bible is not to overcome sin but to terminate ourselves.

Although the book of Genesis contains nearly all the seeds of the biblical truths, it does not contain the seed of the overcoming of sin. The real dealing with sin is not to overcome it but to get rid of ourselves, to circumcise ourselves. Once we have been circumcised and have ourselves terminated, we shall have no problem with sin. If you are still trying to overcome sin, it means that you are still living. If you terminate yourself, you will be through with sin. Therefore, it is not a matter of dealing with sin or of trying to overcome it; it is a matter of terminating ourselves. This is the negative significance of circumcision.

TO BRING US INTO RESURRECTION   ✦   The positive significance of circumcision is to bring us into resurrection (Col. 2:12). Circumcision was always performed on the eighth day (17:12). In figure, the number eight signifies resurrection. This means that we cannot have circumcision without resurrection. Circumcision must be in resurrection, and it will always usher us into resurrection, just as death ushers people into resurrection. On the one hand, we have been crucified with Christ and have been buried with Him. On the other hand, this crucifixion and burial will usher us into His resurrection. When we have been terminated and ushered into resurrection, we become a new person. We are still we, but we are now another person because we have another life, nature, and constitution. We are people in resurrection. Only by being in resurrection are we able to fulfill God's eternal purpose. In our natural strength, we can do nothing to please God or to fulfill His purpose. Our self and our natural strength must be cut off in circumcision. Then in resurrection we shall become another person.

EQUAL TO BAPTISM   ✦   Circumcision in the Old Testament is the equivalent of baptism in the New Testament (Col. 2:11-12). Both baptism and circumcision have the same purpose—to terminate our natural being and bring us into resurrection. Why are we baptized after believing in the Lord Jesus? Because we realize that our old man has been crucified with Him and that we must be buried so that we may be one with Him in His resurrection. Hence, Abraham's circumcision has the same significance as our baptism. In both circumcision and baptism the principle is the same. Although Abraham was justified in Genesis 15, he was circumcised in Genesis 17. As circumcision was the sign of Abraham's being justified, so baptism is the mark of our being saved. How can we prove that we have been saved? By living a life of baptism, a life of one who has been crucified, buried, and resurrected. If we live such a life, everyone will be able to see upon us the mark of our salvation.

CORRESPONDING TO THE CHANGING OF HUMAN NAMES   ✦   Circumcision corresponds to the changing of human names (17:5-6, 15-16). As we have seen, to change the name is to change the person. When Abraham's name was changed, his person was changed also. This was especially true of Jacob. When Jacob's name was changed to Israel, his person was changed (32:27-28). This change of name can only be accomplished through circumcision, through having ourselves terminated and ushered into resurrection. Then we are no longer a natural person but a resurrected person. Being terminated and ushered into resurrection is the real changing of a person. Hence, circumcision corresponds to the changing of names. Now we can understand why the changing of names and circumcision are both revealed in the same chapter. These two things are actually one. The changing of names and circumcision both mean to terminate our old being and to bring us into resurrection so that we may be another person.

NOT OUTWARDLY IN THE FLESH, IN THE LETTER, BUT INWARDLY OF THE HEART, IN THE SPIRIT

Romans 2:28-29 says that circumcision is not "outward in the flesh," but "of the heart, in the spirit, not in the letter." Circumcision is not an outward matter; it is an inward one (Phil. 3:3). The same is true of baptism. Baptism should not just be a form; it must be an inward reality. Let me tell you a story that I heard more than forty years ago. In Central America, the Catholic Church accepted and baptized as members many people who were not saved. One day, a certain priest sprinkled a few drops of water on a boy's head and changed his name to John. At that time, the Catholic Church insisted that on Fridays its people eat only fish, not meat. One Friday, this John had only meat to eat. Since the priest had sprinkled water on his head and had changed his name to John, he thought that he could do the same to the meat. Therefore, he sprinkled water on it and called the meat fish. He then proceeded to cook the meat by boiling it. As he was boiling the meat, the priest came by. Smelling the aroma of boiling meat, he was angry with John and asked him what he was doing. John replied, "I am doing nothing wrong. This is not meat; it is fish. Don't you remember sprinkling water on me and changing my name to John? I followed your way and sprinkled water on the meat and called it fish." This is not real baptism nor the genuine changing of names. Baptism must be an inward reality in the spirit, not an outward form of sprinkling a few drops of water on a person's head.

THE CIRCUMCISION OF CHRIST

Colossians 2:11 speaks of "the circumcision of Christ." Real circumcision is in Christ. The circumcision of Christ, like baptism, means to terminate our old being and to make us a new creation, a new person. Galatians 6:15 says, "For neither is circumcision anything nor uncircumcision, but a new creation." The book of Colossians reveals that Christ is our eternal portion (1:12), our life (3:4), and our hope of glory (1:27), and that we must live by Him as the seed and walk in Him as the land (2:6). If we a*re to walk in Christ, we must not be distracted by other things. The way to live by Christ and walk in Christ is to be buried with Him. We who have been buried with Christ have been brought into His resurrection, not by our effort but by the operation of God, which is carried out by the Spirit of God. When we realize that we have been terminated with Christ, buried with Him, and ushered into His resurrection, the indwelling Spirit will honor our realization with an operation, minister the riches of Christ into us, and make us a person in resurrection. This is not a matter of mere teaching; it is the operation of God, the exercise of the living Spirit within us. This is the circumcision of Christ.

Colossians 3:9-10 tells us that we have put off the old man and have put on the new man. This is the real changing of names, the true significance of circumcision, and the genuine experience of baptism. To circumcise the flesh is to put off the old man and to put on the new man. Then as the new man, we shall have the seed for the fulfillment of God's purpose. Moreover, when we are in the new man, we are in the land, the church. This is altogether a matter of the experience of Christ. When we see that we have already been terminated with Christ and ushered into His resurrection, the indwelling Spirit will honor this by operating within us so that we can put off the old man and put on the new man. In this way, God has the seed and the land for the fulfillment of His eternal purpose.

NOT I, BUT CHRIST

Galatians 2:20 says, "I have been crucified with Christ, and it is no longer I who live, but Christ lives in me." The real changing of names is the change from I to Christ. This is the significance of circumcision and the meaning of baptism. The circumcision of Christ works out one thing—the change from I to Christ. Then it is no longer I, but Christ who lives in me.

NOT I, BUT THE GRACE OF GOD

Eventually, the "not I, but Christ" becomes "not I, but the grace of God" (1 Cor. 15:10). The Apostle Paul said that he labored more than the other apostles; yet it was not he, but the grace of God. What is grace? As we have seen, grace is God coming to us to be everything for us.

In Genesis 18:10 and 14 we find a very strange saying: "At the time appointed I will return unto thee, according to the time of life, and Sarah shall have a son." What does this mean? There was no need for God to come in order for Sarah to have a son. If we had been Abraham, we probably would have said, "Lord, You don't need to do that much. You can simply stay in heaven and say a word, and Sarah will have a son." But the Lord said that the birth of Isaac would be His coming, His arrival. It seems that the coming of God was very nearly the birth of Isaac. God seemed to be saying, "The delivery of Isaac will be My arrival. Isaac will not be out of you, but out of My coming. When I return to you, Sarah will have a son. My coming will be the birth of Isaac." I am not saying that Isaac is God or that God is Isaac, but I do say that it appears that the return of God nearly was the birth of Isaac. Isaac was an unusual person. Although he was a human being, his birth was the result of a divine visitation. What was that divine visitation? It was grace. Hence, both Abraham and Sarah could say, "It is not I, but the grace of God."

God called the time of Isaac's birth the appointed time. The appointment was made in 17:21, when God said, "My covenant will I establish with Isaac, which Sarah shall bear unto thee at this set time in the next year." God called that appointed time the time of life, saying that according to the time of life He would return and Sarah would have a son. This is very meaningful. Everything we do must be according to the time of life and by God's visitation. The seed that we bring forth must be the coming of the Lord in His visitation of grace. This visitation of grace is the birth of Isaac. This proves that only the very Christ whom God has wrought into our being can be the seed to possess the land for the fulfillment of God's purpose. This is absolutely a matter of grace. It is not I, but Christ. It is not I, but the grace of God. Praise the Lord that we do have Christ and the grace of God worked into us so that we can have the seed and possess the land. We have Christ as our seed and the church life as our land. This is altogether the result of circumcision.   ❉

14

LIVING IN FELLOWSHIP WITH GOD
COMMUNION WITH GOD ON THE HUMAN LEVEL

And the Lord appeared unto him in the plains of Mamre:
and he sat in the tent door in the heat of the day; and he lifted up
his eyes and looked, and, lo, three men stood by him: and when
he saw them, he ran to meet them from the tent door,
and bowed himself toward the ground, and said,
My Lord, if now I have found favor in thy sight,
pass not away, I pray thee, from thy servant.

Genesis 18:1-3

And the Scripture was fulfilled which says, "And Abraham
believed God, and it was accounted to him as righteousness";
and he was called the friend of God.

James 2:23

In this message we come to Genesis 18, which contains an intimate record of Abraham's experience with God. If we take an overall view of Abraham's experience with God as found in chapter eleven through chapter twenty-four, we shall see that his experience is in four major sections. Firstly, while he was living in the demonic land of Chaldea, he was called by God. Suddenly, much to his surprise, the God of glory appeared to him (Acts 7:2). That was the beginning of his experience with God.

Secondly, in chapters twelve through fourteen, Abraham experienced living by faith in God for his existence. He had been called by God for the fulfillment of God's divine purpose, but, as a human being, he still had to have food, protection, and all that was necessary to maintain his existence. He was a stranger in a new land, having no property of his own. Thus, God trained him to exercise the very faith which God had infused into him to trust in God for his existence.

Following that, in chapters fifteen through seventeen, the third section, God trained him to know grace for the fulfillment of His purpose. Here Abraham learned not to do anything by himself or on his own but to do everything by and with God. Although God needed him, God did not need anything of him. All that Abraham had, was, and could do was absolutely repudiated by God. God spent at least fifteen years to train Abraham in this matter. For thirteen years, God disappeared from him because he did not behave himself properly. Abraham was trained, disciplined, and very much in God's favor, but he did not walk in the presence of God. Rather, he walked in the presence of his wife, the one who proposed that he exercise his flesh to produce a seed for the fulfillment of God's purpose. Abraham expected that Ishmael, his seed, could fulfill God's purpose. Nevertheless, God seemed to say, "No, I don't approve of Ishmael. He is the issue of your effort, the produce of your doing. I reject him and you must not keep him. Abram, you must learn that nothing that you can do means anything to Me. I only need you, not your ability and strength. I don't need your Lot, Eliezer, Hagar, or anything of you. You must walk before Me, not doing anything by yourself or on your own. You must be nourished and supplied by the sufficiency of My divine udder. Then you will be able to produce something not only for Me but also of Me. I only accept and approve what is out of Myself. I shall not produce an Isaac without you. I shall produce an Isaac through you, but not out of you. You are My channel, not the source. Whenever you consider yourself to be the source, you insult Me. I am the unique, all-sufficient source. You have known Me as the Most High God, the Possessor of heaven and earth. Now you must know Me as El-Shaddai, as the all-sufficient Mighty One with an udder. Stay under My udder and be supplied and nourished constantly by My all-sufficiency. This is the way to walk before Me." As Abraham learned to know grace for the fulfillment of God's purpose, God changed him in both name and in nature. God changed Abraham's constitution by having him circumcised. Abram was terminated and Abraham came into being. This is the third major section of Abraham's experience of God.

Immediately after this, he was ushered into a glorious section—living in fellowship with God (18:1—24:67). Abraham had been called, had learned to live by faith in God for his existence, and had come to know grace for the fulfillment of God's purpose. Now he has been brought into constant fellowship with God. The fourth section of his experience is found in chapters eighteen through twenty-four. Everything revealed in these seven chapters is an aspect of Abraham's intimate fellowship with God.

In the first section of his experience, God appeared to Abraham as the God of glory. In the second section He revealed Himself as the Most High God, the Possessor of heaven and earth. In the third section He came to Abraham as El-Shaddai, as the all-sufficient Mighty One with an udder. In the fourth section God came in a very different way—as a mortal man. As Abraham sat in the door of his tent during the heat of the day, he saw three mortal men approaching (vv. 1-2). In Hebrew, the word translated "men" in verse 2 means mortal men, human beings. God appeared to Abraham in such a form. At first, Abraham did not realize that one of these men was the Lord, Jehovah, and that the other two were angels.

Of these forms of God's appearing—as the God of glory, as the Most High God, as El-Shaddai, and as a mortal man—which do you prefer? Do you prefer that God appear to you as the God of glory? If He did, you would be terrified. Would you like Him to come as the Most High God? If the president of the United States were to come to me and say, "I am the most high president of the United States coming to visit a little man," I would feel uneasy. But if he were to come as a man the same as me, I would say, "Sir, how are you? Please come in and rest and be refreshed." If he were to come in this way, revealing later that he was the president of the United States, I could have a very good time with him. Of these four ways of God's appearing, I prefer that He come to me in the form of a mortal man, not in His divine glory, in His most high position, nor in His all-sufficiency.

We all need to experience our God to such an extent. At the beginning of our experience, we sense Him as the God of glory. But the more we experience Him, the more we realize that He comes in a human form, the same as we are. If God had not come to Abraham in such a human form, how could Abraham have been called His friend? Genesis 18 reveals that Abraham and God spoke with one another like friends. Abraham said to Him, "My Lord, if now I have found favor in thy sight, pass not away, I pray thee, from thy servant: let a little water, I pray you, be fetched, and wash your feet, and rest yourselves under the tree" (vv. 3-4). Abraham prepared water for God to wash His feet, and God rested under a tree in front of Abraham's tent.

Very few Christians think that God would ever come in the form of a mortal man, rest under the shade of a tree, and wash His feet with the water that was prepared by a man. Which do you think is more pleasant—for God to sit on His throne demanding that we bow down to Him and worship Him, or for God to sit under a tree and wash His feet? Before the feet of the Lord Jesus were washed with the woman's tears in the house of Simon (Luke 7:38, 44), God's feet were washed in front of Abraham's tent. While Jesus was in the house of Simon having His feet washed and anointed, the priests of Judaism were worshipping God in the temple. Where was God at that time—in the temple in Jerusalem or in the house of Simon? Surely He was in the house of Simon. Likewise, where was God in Genesis 18— sitting on His throne waiting for Abraham to worship Him, or washing His feet beneath the tree in front of Abraham's tent? How marvelous it was that He was in the form of a mortal man washing His feet in front of Abraham's tent! Where is your God in your experience? Is He sitting on a throne in heaven or washing His feet at your tent? Do you prefer to have your God sitting on the throne, waiting for you to say, "Holy, Holy, Holy" to Him, or do you prefer to have Him sitting at your tent door? God came to Abraham on his level and in a human form. Since He came in this way, He and Abraham could be friends. In this chapter there is no religious worship or fear, just sweet intimacy. How wonderful! Who is your God today? Is He only the God of glory, the Most High God, and the El-Shaddai, or One in the form of a mortal man, the same as you are?

I do not say that God was a mortal man in Genesis 18; for He was just in the form of a mortal man. One of the three men who appeared to Abraham in Genesis 18 was Jehovah God. Verse 13 mentions "the Lord." In Hebrew, the Lord here is Jehovah. It was Jehovah who came to Abraham in the form of a man!

When I read Genesis 18 years ago, I was troubled by it. In this chapter Abraham certainly saw the Lord, but the New Testament says that no man has ever seen God (John 1:18). Abraham did not see God in His divine form, but God in a human form. God appeared to him as a man. It was the same when the Lord Jesus was on earth. People did not see God in His divine form; they saw God in the man Jesus. Firstly, God appeared to Abraham in His divine glory. Then He came in His most high position and as the El-Shaddai, the all-sufficient Mighty One with an udder. Lastly, He came in the form of a man. Abraham did not see the form of God but the form of man. He saw three mortal men, not realizing at first that one of them was Jehovah.

God likes to appear to us in this way. He does not come in the form of God but in the form of man, without making any declaration that He is Jehovah God. God talked with Abraham as one man talks with another. Suddenly He asked Abraham, "Where is Sarah thy wife?" This might have shocked Abraham, and he might have thought, "This man knows my wife! How could He know her? Isn't he a stranger?" Then the Lord said, "I will certainly return unto thee according to the time of life" (v. 10). Abraham might have said, "Who are you? You must be the very El-Shaddai who gave me the promise of Isaac's birth" (17:19, 21). Probably Abraham was still uncertain about this until God said, "Sarah thy wife shall have a son." Sarah laughed when she heard this. No human being could have known at that time that Sarah was laughing within, but the Lord said, "Wherefore did Sarah laugh, saying, Shall I of a surety bear a child, which am old?" (v. 13). At this juncture, the Lord clearly unveiled to Abraham that He was Jehovah God by saying, "Is anything too marvelous for the Lord [Jehovah]?" When Sarah denied laughing He said, "Nay; but thou didst laugh" (v. 15), indicating that He was the omniscient God, the One who knows everything, even what is in man's heart. At this time Abraham was clear that this man was the Almighty Jehovah, the very El-Shaddai. In like manner, the disciples of Jesus gradually came to know that the man Jesus was God.

We all need to experience God in this way. We should not practice a religious form of meeting with God, saying, "Now is the time to worship God. I must dress up, comb my hair, and reverently walk into the cathedral where I shall be with God." If we take this way, God may not appear to us. Many times God comes to us while we are sitting at our tent door. Although we may be unprepared to worship God, we may see someone approaching and ask him to stay with us for a while. Eventually we learn that this One is God. Have you not had this kind of experience? According to religion, God visits people in a cathedral or chapel. But God often visits us in a very normal way, in a way which is extraordinary as far as religion is concerned. I like the God who appeared to Abraham in the form of a mortal man at his tent door. Many sisters have the experience that while they are cooking in their kitchens or doing the laundry, the Lord comes to them in a very intimate, human way, and they have a pleasant time of sweet fellowship with the Lord, conversing with Him as with a friend. Many brothers have the same kind of experience. While they are working on their jobs or resting at home, the Lord comes to them as a dear friend, and they have an intimate conversation with the Lord. This is the experience of the Lord coming to visit us on our human level so that we can commune with Him as with an intimate friend.

In which of the four sections of Abraham's experience are you? Are you experiencing God as the God of glory, as the Most High God, as the El-Shaddai, or as the One in the form of a mortal man? Are you living in intimate fellowship with God on a human level? How sweet it is when God comes to us not with His divine glory or in His high position but in the form of a mortal man!

AFTER ABRAHAM'S CIRCUMCISION

Abraham's fellowship with God began after he was circumcised and had been terminated (17:24-27). He had not only been called and learned to live by faith in God for his existence, but he had learned to reject and deny his natural strength and to trust in God for everything for the fulfillment of His purpose. After becoming such a person, he began to live in fellowship with God. In his circumcised state, God came to visit him, and as a circumcised person Abraham had an intimate communion with the visiting God. He did not need to go to God; God came to visit him. Religion always charges people to go to God, but Genesis 18 reveals that God came to visit His circumcised one. The circumcised one did not need to go to a temple or cathedral; his tent became God's tabernacle, the place where God enjoyed His circumcised one's ministry of water and food. It is after our flesh has been circumcised and our natural man has been terminated that God comes to visit us and we minister water and food to Him for His refreshment and satisfaction in our intimate fellowship with Him.

AS A FRIEND OF GOD

As Abraham lived in fellowship with God, God considered him to be his friend (James 2:23; Isa. 41:8; 2 Chron. 20:7). The conversation between Abraham and God in this chapter resembles that between two friends. This happened by the oaks of Mamre in Hebron, where Abraham lived according to God's pleasure (13:18). The name Hebron in Hebrew means fellowship, communion, and friendship. It was at this place of fellowship and friendship that God came to visit Abraham as a friend, and Abraham welcomed God as a friend, preparing water for God to wash His feet for His refreshment and feeding God with a rich meal for His satisfaction. Abraham did all this in the intimate fellowship with his Friend at his tent door under the shadow of the oak trees, not in the religious worship of "God" in a cathedral or sanctuary under the service of a "priest" or "minister."

When Abraham was sitting in the tent door to cool himself in the heat of the day, God appeared to him with the two angels. When he saw them approaching, he ran to welcome them and asked them to stay with him. He prepared water for them to wash their feet and served them a rich meal of three cakes of fine wheat flour baked on embers, a tender and good calf, and butter and milk (vv. 4-8). In ancient times, three measures, or three seahs, were the equivalent of an ephah. According to 1 Samuel 1:24 and Judges 6:19, the normal portion for a meal was an ephah of fine flour. Why then does 18:6, like Matthew 13:33, mention three measures, not one ephah? Because in both Genesis 18 and Matthew 13 three measures of fine flour signify the resurrected Christ in His humanity. Such a Christ is the fine flour baked into cakes to be food for both God and man. Abraham also prepared a tender calf. This calf, like the fatted calf used to feed the prodigal son in Luke 15:23, was also a figure of Christ.

Abraham also served God and the angels butter and milk. God drank the milk of the good land much earlier than the children of Israel did. The cakes, the calf, and the butter and milk all signify the riches of the all-inclusive Christ for the satisfaction of both God and man.

Although the Bible does not say that Abraham presented this meal to God as an offering, in actuality he did so. Years later, when the children of Israel went to their yearly feasts, they offered God the produce of the good land, offering Him the produce of either the vegetable or animal life. In principle, Abraham did the same thing in Genesis 18. Whenever we enjoy a good time with God, having intimate fellowship with Him, at that time Christ not only is supplied to us, but we offer Christ to God, offering Him the riches of Christ for His enjoyment. In other words, we offer Christ to God as three measures of fine flour, as a tender and good calf, and as butter and milk. Thank the Lord that we have had at least some experience of this. While we were enjoying intimate fellowship with God, we not only received Christ from God but also offered Christ to God as God's food. We offered Christ in His resurrected humanity as three measures of fine flour, we offered Christ as the tender and good calf, and we presented all the riches of Christ to God for His enjoyment. A good number of times at the Lord's table I have not enjoyed the Lord as much as when I have offered Christ to God for God's enjoyment. When guests come to visit you in your house, you do not expect them to feed you. Rather, you enjoy feeding them. The sisters especially enjoy serving a meal and watching the guests eat it. The more the guests eat, the happier the sisters are. We all need to be in such an intimate fellowship with God that we not only enjoy Christ but also offer Christ to God for His enjoyment. The highest fellowship is not when we enjoy Christ so much before God but when God enjoys Him in us more than we do. The highest and richest meeting in the church is the meeting in which we offer Christ to God for His satisfaction.

RECEIVING REVELATION FROM GOD

As Abraham was enjoying such sweet fellowship with God, he received revelation from Him regarding the birth of Isaac and the destruction of Sodom. These are the two basic things concerning which God will always deal with us. The birth of Isaac is related to

Christ, and the destruction of Sodom is related to God's judgment upon sin. Isaac must come and Sodom must go. This means that Christ must come in and sin must go out. Today God is not only accomplishing His plan to fulfill His purpose, but as the Lord over all men He is also judging sin. The principle is the same in every aspect of our lives: in our married life, home life, personal life, Christian life, and church life. God's concern is to bring Christ forth through us and to eliminate all the sinful things. He intends to produce Christ and to destroy the "Sodom" in our home life, work life, and even in our Christian and church life. All the revelation that we have received and shall receive from God mostly concerns these two items. If you consider your own experience, you will find that this is so. Whenever you have received revelation from God during the course of your fellowship with Him, it has always concerned Christ on the positive side and sin on the negative side. Positively we see more of Christ and say, "I have seen something new of Christ. How I hate that I have not lived more by Him." This is the revelation regarding the birth of Isaac, the revelation that Christ will be brought forth in your life. But negatively we see our sins and say, "O Lord, forgive me. There is still so much selfishness, hatred, and jealousy in me. I have so many failures, shortcomings, and even sinful things. Lord, I judge these things and want them destroyed." This, in principle, is God's judgment upon and destruction of sin. In our Christian life, Christ must be brought in and "Sodom" must be destroyed. Likewise, in the church life, Christ must increase and sin must be abolished.

CONCERNING THE BIRTH OF ISAAC THROUGH SARAH   ✦   *The promise confirmed*   ✦   How can Christ be brought forth? Firstly, there is the promise. The promise made to Abraham regarding the birth of Isaac in 17:19 and 21 was confirmed in 18:10. Not only did God promise Abraham that he would give birth to Isaac through Sarah, but in the whole Bible, especially in the New Testament, there is the rich promise concerning Christ. We have the promise that Christ will be our life, our supply, and our everything. How much the New Testament promises concerning Christ! All these promises can be fulfilled by the gracious visitation of God.

At the time of life, the appointed time   ✦   The birth of Isaac was at the time of life, at the appointed time (17:21; 18:10, 14). Christ always has been and always will be increased in us and brought forth through us at the time of life. We need to have many such times of life. I would like to have one every day. The time of life is always the appointed time, the time appointed by God. God made the appointment, not Abraham. It is the same with us today, for it is God who makes the appointments, not you and I. Our past experiences will help us to understand this. Whenever God comes to visit us to bring forth Christ, that time is the appointed time, the time of life.

Abraham becoming old as dead and Sarah becoming out of function   ✦   The time of life for Abraham and Sarah was the time when they had become nothing. Isaac was born when Abraham had become as old as dead and Sarah had become out of function (vv. 11-13). Likewise, whenever we become nothing, that is a good time, a divinely appointed time, for us to participate in more life.

A wonderful and marvelous doing of the Lord   ✦   In verse 14 the Lord said, "Is anything too marvelous [or wonderful] for the Lord?" (Heb.). Every experience of Christ is marvelous in our eyes; it is a wonderful doing of the Lord. How could Sarah have brought forth Isaac? It was humanly impossible. If that had happened to us, it would have been a wonderful and marvelous thing in our eyes. Christian experiences are always like this because the Christian life is a life of impossibilities. How marvelous it is that all the impossibilities become possibilities with Christ! We can do what other people cannot do and we can be what others cannot be because Christ is marvelous and wonderful in our experience of Him.

CONCERNING THE DESTRUCTION OF SODOM   ✦   *Abraham walking with God to bring Him on the way*   ✦   The second revelation that Abraham received concerned the destruction of Sodom (vv. 16-21). After enjoying such intimate fellowship with Abraham, God and the two angels were satisfied, strengthened, and refreshed. Verse 16 says that then "the men rose up from thence, and looked toward Sodom: and Abraham went with them to bring them on the way." Abraham walked with them for a certain distance to conduct them, to send them away. Often when guests come to visit us, we walk them out to their car after their visit, seeing them on their way. Abraham's walking with his visitors was like one sending his friend away.

God not hiding His intention from Abraham   ✦   As Abraham was bringing God on His way, "The Lord said, Shall I hide from Abraham that thing which I do?" (v. 17). God could not hide His intention from Abraham, but told him of His intention to judge Sodom saying, "Because the cry of Sodom and Gomorrah is great, and because their sin is very grievous; I will go down now, and see whether they have done altogether according to the cry of it, which is come unto me; and if not, I will know" (vv. 20-21). God's heart was concerned about Lot, but He could do nothing for him without an intercessor. As we shall see in the next message, God here was seeking for an intercessor. Although God did not mention Lot's name, He knew within His heart that Abraham understood what He was doing. God and Abraham spoke to one another in a mysterious way, neither of them mentioning Lot's name. The outsiders did not understand what they meant, but they each understood.

REMAINING IN THE PRESENCE OF GOD

Verse 22 says, "And the men turned their faces from thence and went towards Sodom: but Abraham remained still standing before the Lord" (Heb.). When the two angels left, Abraham did not tell the Lord good-bye. No, he remained standing before the Lord. As we shall see, the purpose of his standing before the Lord was for intercession.

In Genesis 18 we see that Abraham, a circumcised man, had peace with God. Although Abraham did not expect such a visitation, God appeared to him in the form of a mortal man, conversing with him as with a friend. There was nothing religious about such intimate fellowship. In that fellowship Abraham received revelation from God positively concerning the birth of Isaac and negatively concerning the destruction of Sodom. Then, after the angels had left for Sodom, Abraham remained in the presence of God. God had found a man to whom He could commit what was on His heart, a man to respond to His heart's intention and echo His heart's desire. In this chapter we see that the sweetest and most intimate experience of God is like what we have with our most intimate friend.   ❈

15

LIVING IN FELLOWSHIP WITH GOD A GLORIOUS INTERCESSION

And the Lord said,
Shall I hide
from Abraham that thing which I do?
Abraham stood yet before the Lord.
And Abraham drew near, and said,
Wilt thou also destroy the righteous
with the wicked?
That be far from thee to do after this manner,
to slay the righteous with the wicked;
and that the righteous should be as the wicked,
that be far from thee:
Shall not the Judge of all the earth do right?

Genesis 18:17, 22b-23, 25

In this message we come to another seed of the divine revelation sown in the book of Genesis—the seed of intercession. In the first seventeen chapters of Genesis, there is no record of any intercession. Although we may suppose that Melchisedec was interceding behind the scene for Abraham, there is no record of this. The first clear mention of intercession in the Bible is in Genesis 18, where we see that Abraham was the first intercessor. This record of intercession is not simply a seed, for it contains a certain amount of development. In Genesis 18 we not only have a story of intercession but a clear revelation of the basic principles of intercession. Intercession is a great thing in the Bible. Without it God's economy cannot be accomplished. The excellent ministry of Christ today as our kingly and divine High Priest is a ministry of intercession. Romans 8:34 and Hebrews 7:25 both tell us that Christ is interceding for us. Since this matter of intercession is so important, we must devote an entire message to it, mainly considering the basic principles of intercession.

ACCORDING TO GOD'S REVELATION

The first basic principle of intercession is that it must be according to God's revelation (18:17, 20-21). The only intercession that counts in the eyes of God is that which is according to His revelation. This means that proper intercession is not initiated by us but by God in His revelation. This is clearly portrayed in Genesis 18. Abraham did not wake up one morning concerned for Lot and then kneel down to pray to the One on the throne in heaven regarding him. No, while Abraham was sitting at his tent door to cool himself in the heat of the day, God came to him in the form of a mortal man. Since God did not come to Abraham in His glory with His majesty, Abraham did not recognize at first that it was Jehovah God who was visiting him. Eventually, Abraham realized that this One was the very God. Nevertheless, Abraham was not terrified; he was very restful, conversing with God as with an intimate friend. This conversation must have lasted for several hours, for it took time to prepare the meal and to eat it. When God and the two angels were about to leave, Abraham did not bid them good-bye but conducted them on their way, probably walking with them for a good distance. Here we see that our God is not only a loving God but also a testing God. Although He loves us and knows everything, He often tests us. He knows our heart, the innermost part of our being, but He often says nothing. By testing He draws out what is within us.

What was God's purpose in coming to Abraham in Genesis 18? He surely did not come for a meal; neither did He come to confirm

His promise regarding Sarah's giving birth to a son. God came to Abraham because He was seeking an intercessor. On His throne in heaven, God had decided to execute His judgment on the wicked city of Sodom. But God would never forget that one of His people, Lot, was in that city. Lot did not even realize that he had to be rescued from Sodom. What could God do? He had to find someone to intercede for Lot. God knew that there was no one on earth who was as concerned for Lot and who was so much with God as Abraham was. Hence, God came to Abraham for the purpose of finding an intercessor. Without an intercessor to intercede for His people, God cannot do anything. God has His divine principles. One of them is that without intercession He cannot save anyone. The salvation of every Christian has been accomplished through intercession. God did not stay on His throne in heaven waiting for such intercession to occur. Rather, He came down to visit Abraham in the form of a mortal man so that Abraham might easily talk with Him and intercede for Lot. In Genesis 18 Abraham did not pray to God or call on the name of God; he talked to God as with an intimate friend. Thus, the purpose of God's visit to Abraham in this chapter was that Abraham might take up the burden to intercede for Lot according to God's desire.

Although God remained at Abraham's tent door for several hours, talking a great deal to him, God did not say a word about His purpose in coming to secure an intercessor. We often act in the same way. Perhaps you want a brother to do a certain thing for you. If you are wise, you will not come to him and immediately ask him to do what you desire. You will first determine his mood by having a talk with him about various matters. At the very end of your visit, as the brother is seeing you to the door or conducting you on your way, you may open yourself to him and tell him of your desire. However, if he does not linger with you but says, "See you in the meeting tonight," you will realize that his heart is too cold and that he would not be interested in doing what you want him to do. But if he says, "I would like to stay with you for a while longer," then you will know that you can open yourself to him.

When God came to Abraham, Abraham welcomed Him, providing Him water and serving Him a good meal. Although God spoke to Abraham during the preparation and eating of the meal, He did not disclose the purpose for which He came. Only when God rose up and

walked away from the tent and Abraham accompanied and conducted Him and the two angels on their way, did God tell Abraham
of His intention. While Abraham walked with them, the Lord said,
"Shall I hide from Abraham that thing which I do?" (18:17). God
could not hide His intention from Abraham, His dear friend and
called one.

As Abraham lingered in God's presence, even after the two angels
had left for Sodom, remaining standing before Him (18:22), God
opened up to him. God did not open to Abraham directly but in the
way of implication. God did not say, "Abraham, I shall soon destroy
Sodom. Lot is there, and I am very concerned about him. I have come
to ask you to intercede for him." God was not that simple. Instead,
He said, "Because the cry of Sodom and Gomorrah is great, and
because their sin is very grievous; I will go down now, and see
whether they have done altogether according to the cry of it, which is
come unto me; and if not, I will know" (18:20-21). Although God
did not say a word about Lot, His intention in speaking about Sodom
was for Lot. These two friends talked about Lot, but neither of them
mentioned his name. They spoke about him in a mysterious way, in a
way of implication. Abraham knew that God's concern was for Lot,
and he interceded for Lot without mentioning him by name. Nevertheless, God knew Abraham's intention as Abraham knew God's
intention.

Do not think that God's revelation regarding intercession comes in
a sudden, miraculous, "Pentecostal" way. In order to receive such a
revelation from the heart of God, we must pass through a long
process. We must come all the way from Ur of Chaldea through many
places to the tent door at the oaks of Mamre in Hebron. Firstly God
called Abraham by appearing to him as the God of glory. At that time
Abraham was neither prepared nor qualified to receive a revelation
from God's heart. He was not in intimate fellowship with God. Even
after he had slaughtered Chedorlaomer and the other kings, Abraham
was not ready to converse with God in an intimate way. In chapters
fifteen and sixteen we see that although Abraham was a man who
sought God and loved Him, he was still so much in his flesh. In chapter seventeen he was circumcised and terminated, his name was
changed from Abram to Abraham, and he became another person.
Then, in chapter eighteen God came to him at the oaks of Mamre
in Hebron not as the God of glory nor as the Most High God, the

Possessor of heaven and earth, nor as the El-Shaddai, but as a mortal man to enjoy a meal with His intimate friend. At that time God had found a man who was after His heart. The glorious intercession which Abraham made before God in Genesis 18 was not a prayer from man on earth to God in heaven; it was a human conversation between two friends. God came down from heaven, lowering Himself, putting on the form of a mortal man, and conversing with Abraham. Eventually, He indicated to Abraham that He was the Almighty God; yet they continued to talk as two friends. When Abraham was in this condition, he was prepared and qualified to receive a revelation from God's heart concerning His desire. Intercession is an intimate talk with God according to the unveiling of His heart's desire. This is the first principle of intercession.

In order for God to reveal His heart's desire to a man, that man must be prepared. Although millions of people belong to the name of God, very few have been prepared, disciplined, trained, circumcised, and terminated. Although we are not very much like Abraham, occasionally we have had similar experiences. We were willing to abandon ourselves and reject our flesh. Then, much to our surprise, God came to us as a human friend. We did not pray to Him or call on His name; we talked to Him as to an intimate friend.

In order to fulfill the first basic principle of intercession—that it should be according to an intimate revelation of God's heart's desire—we need to pass through a long process. We need to be dealt with, circumcised, and terminated. Then we shall be ready for intimate fellowship with God. God will come to us on a human level, not on a divine level, just as He came to Abraham. Suppose God would come to you in this way today and you would serve Him a meal and talk with Him, speaking with Him face to face. How good it is to talk with God in this way! When we have fellowship with God like this, we do not have the sense that we are talking to the almighty, majestic God, but to another human being. This is the meaning of intercession being according to the revelation of God. This intercession is always intimate, mysterious, and in the way of implication.

APPARENTLY FOR SODOM, ACTUALLY FOR LOT

When God revealed to Abraham what was on His heart, Abraham immediately understood what God meant. Apparently Abraham interceded for Sodom; actually he interceded for Lot. "Abraham drew near, and said, Wilt thou also destroy the righteous with the wicked?" (18:23). Lot is implied here. Abraham seemed to be saying, "Lord, don't You know that in Sodom, the wicked city which You are about to destroy, there is a righteous person? There might also be other righteous ones with him. Do You intend to destroy the righteous with the wicked?" God did not mention the name of Lot to Abraham, but Abraham understood. Likewise, Abraham did not mention Lot to God, but God knew. They spoke to one another in a mysterious way. None of the outsiders knew what they were talking about, but they understood each other because they were intimate friends. How can we prove that Abraham was actually interceding for Lot? The proof is in 19:29: "And it came to pass, when God destroyed the cities of the plain, that God remembered Abraham, and sent Lot out of the midst of the overthrow, when he overthrew the cities in the which Lot dwelt." We are not told that God remembered Lot but that He remembered Abraham. This verse tells us clearly that God answered Abraham's intercession by rescuing Lot from Sodom. Thus, Abraham's intercession in chapter eighteen actually was not for the city of Sodom but for Lot.

In principle, Abraham's intercession for Lot was like the intercession in the church in the New Testament. In Abraham's time, God's people on earth were composed of two families, the families of Abraham and Lot. A part of God's people, Lot's family, had drifted into the wicked city of Sodom. In like manner, some of the church people have drifted into the world. Just as Abraham interceded for that part of God's people who had drifted into Sodom, so we must intercede for the brothers and sisters who have drifted into the world. Abraham's intercession was the first that resembles the intercession in the church life.

ACCORDING TO GOD'S HEART

Since all proper intercession is according to the revelation which is out of God's heart, it must also be according to God's heart. Intercession is not according to God's word. As I have already pointed out, although God did not mention Lot by name, Abraham realized what was on God's heart. Abraham did not intercede according to the outward word of God but according to the inward intention of God's heart. Proper intercession must always touch the heart of God. While Abraham was interceding, God was happy and could say within Himself, "How good it is that I have found a man on earth who knows My heart!"

I say once again that proper intercession must always be initiated by God's visitation on the human level. Whenever we have the deep sense that God has come to us on a human level, we shall realize that this is the time when God will initiate an intercession for us to carry out. For this we must learn to linger in the presence of God. If He would begin to walk away, we must stay in His presence and tell Him, "Lord, I don't want to lose Your presence. I want to linger here with You." Your lingering in His presence will open up His heart and draw out His desire. We have seen that Abraham did not abruptly say good-bye to the Lord but walked with Him for a certain distance. This reveals that, in a certain sense, God is very human. If we would linger in His presence, He would be so human as not to leave us. He would remain with us because of our lingering with Him. I have experienced this many times. I did not leave God's presence and He did not leave mine. As a result of that lingering, God opened His heart to me and the proper intercession came forth.

Intercession is not merely prayer; it is an intimate conversation. In this chapter Abraham was not praying; he was talking to his intimate Friend on a human level, saying, "Wilt thou also destroy the righteous with the wicked?" Abraham seemed to be saying to God, "Is this Your way? Let me remind You that You should not do it this way. There might be fifty righteous people in the city. Will You not spare it for the fifty righteous people who might be there?" This was a conversation. Then Abraham continued, "That be far from thee to do after this manner, to slay the righteous with the wicked; and that the righteous should be as the wicked, that be far from thee: Shall not the Judge of all the earth do right?" (18:25). This was a strong challenge to the Lord. Have you ever had such a challenging talk with God? Very few have ever done this. But when you have come into intimate fellowship with God on the human level and know His heart's desire, you can challenge Him, saying, "Lord, is this Your way?" This is neither praying nor begging; it is challenging God in a very friendly conversation. The Lord answered Abraham, saying, "If I find in Sodom fifty righteous within the city, then I will spare all the place for their sakes" (18:26). A basic principle of intercession is that intercession is a challenging talk, not a praying or a begging. God wants us to challenge Him. When Abraham challenged God, God might have said, "I have found a man on earth who knows My heart so well that he does not pray, ask, or beg; He challenges Me. I must do what he says because I have been challenged by My dear friend. Now I am not as concerned for Lot as I am for Myself." Have you ever experienced this kind of intercession, talking with God in a challenging way, saying, "Lord, is this Your way of doing things? Will not the Judge of all the earth do right? Is it Your way to slay the righteous with the wicked? Surely it isn't!" This is real intercession.

In verses 27 through 32 we see that Abraham continued to talk to God about the number of righteous people it would take to spare the city. After the Lord had said, "If I find in Sodom fifty righteous within the city, then I will spare the city for their sakes," Abraham asked if He would destroy the city if the number was five less than that. To this the Lord replied, "If I find there forty and five, I will not destroy it." The number forty-five was spoken by the Lord, not by Abraham. The Lord seemed to be saying, "The number forty-five is all right, but I can't find that many there." Then Abraham asked about forty, and the Lord said, "I will not do it for forty's sake." When Abraham proposed that thirty be the number, the Lord said that He would spare Sodom if thirty were found there. Then, on Abraham's side, the number was reduced to twenty. Once again, the Lord said that He would not destroy the city for the sake of twenty. Finally, reaching the bottom number, Abraham made his sixth proposal, asking the Lord to spare the city if ten righteous people were found there. God said that even for the ten He would not destroy the city. Abraham made six proposals to the Lord, reducing the number from fifty to ten. After that, he did not have the burden to make a seventh proposal. He might have been led by God's presence not to do so. When God told Abraham that He would not destroy the city for the sake of ten righteous persons (18:32), Abraham was disappointed. Lot had his wife, two unmarried daughters, and some married daughters with their husbands. According to Abraham's figuration, there must have been at least ten people in Lot's family, if all his sons-in-law were included. Abraham was surprised and disappointed to learn that there were not even ten righteous people in Sodom.

ACCORDING TO GOD'S RIGHTEOUS WAY

Abraham's challenge to God was according to God's righteous way (18:23-25). Abraham said to the Lord, "You are the Judge of all the earth. Shall You do this? This is not Your righteous way." Proper intercession is neither according to God's love nor according to His grace, but according to His righteousness. The strongest challenge to God is not to say to Him, "God, are You not a loving God?" If we say this, God might say, "Yes, I am a loving God, but to love is up to Me. When I feel happy, I love. But if I don't feel happy, I don't love. What's wrong with My doing this?" We have nothing to say to this. We should say to God, "God, are You not the righteous One?" If we challenge God according to His righteousness, God would reply, "I certainly am righteous." He would never say, "If I am happy, I shall be righteous, but if I am unhappy, I won't be righteous." What kind of a righteous God would this be? We must challenge God according to His righteousness because His righteousness binds Him more than His love and His grace do. God has no obligation to be loving or to show grace, but He is held responsible to be righteous. Nothing binds God as firmly as His righteousness. Every good intercessor knows that the way to bind God effectively is to challenge Him according to His righteousness. We should say, "Will the Judge of all the earth do such a thing?" And God will reply, "No, as the just One I would never do that. But you must show Me the proper number that will justify the city. If you show Me the justifying number, I'll be justified and I'll be righteous. I would never destroy that city." Proper intercession never begs God according to His love but challenges Him according to His righteous way.

I believe that many in the Lord's recovery will be brought into this kind of intercession. When God came down to visit Abraham on a human level, He was seeking one intercessor. Today God has come down to the human level once again, not to seek an individual but a corporate people. I believe that in not too long a time there will be a people on earth absolutely like Abraham, knowing the heart of God and making a challenging intercession in His presence. We may say to God, "Lord, don't You know that You have promised us definitely in the New Testament to finish the good work that You have begun?" Abraham did not cry and plead with God to spare Sodom for Lot's sake; he challenged Him. Likewise, we should not weep and beg but should challenge God. He does not want to hear our crying; He wants to hear our challenging intercession.

EXPRESSING GOD'S DESIRE

Abraham's intercession echoed the desire of God's heart concerning Lot. As he was interceding according to God's heart, his intercession spontaneously expressed God's desire. Proper intercession always expresses God's desire. This is another principle of intercession. If our intercession is initiated by our seeing of God's revelation in our intimate fellowship with Him, whatever we say to Him in our intercession will be the expression of His desire, the echo of His intention. True intercession is not to express our desire but God's desire. It is not to seek anything according to our intention but to seek the fulfillment of God's intention.

CARRYING OUT GOD'S WILL

Intercession must also carry out God's will. Although God had a will to rescue Lot, without Abraham's intercession God had no way to carry out His will. Proper intercession always paves the way for the accomplishing of God's will. It lays the tracks for the heavenly loco-motive. God desired to rescue Lot from Sodom, but He had to find a way to do this. Thus, He visited Abraham for the purpose that he might intercede on Lot's behalf. Abraham was intimately close to God's heart, and God was able to open His heart to him. Immediately Abraham echoed back to God His heart's desire in a challenging intercession. This intercession was the expression of God's desire and the carrying out of His will.

There is the urgent need of this kind of challenging intercession in the church life today. All the messages that the Lord has been giving us are for the carrying out of His will. In this life-study we do not care for mere Bible teaching. We are concerned for the release of the present word of the Lord for His recovery. After reading this mes-sage, a strong echo will resound throughout the Lord's recovery as many of the dear saints respond to His word and are brought into a full realization of genuine intercession. From now on, many of us will exercise our spirit to intercede for the church by challenging God according to His heart's desire. We know that His heart's desire is to save His people out of the wicked city, to rescue today's Lot from the condition of condemnation. If we are so close to God, fellowshipping with Him in an intimate way, we shall be able to read His heart and echo His heart's desire back to Him in a glorious intercession. In the next message we shall see that Abraham's intercession was very effective. In 19:27-29 we see that Abraham was still with God's heart. Abraham woke up early in the morning and looked at the city, being very concerned for Lot. In 19:29 we are told clearly that God remembered Abraham and "sent Lot out of the midst of the overthrow, when he overthrew the cities in the which Lot dwelt." This effective intercession will more and more be realized and practiced among us in the church life.

UNTIL THE LORD HAS FINISHED HIS SPEAKING

This chapter does not end with Abraham's speaking; it ends with God's speaking. Verse 33 says, "And the Lord went his way, as soon as he had finished speaking to Abraham" (Heb.). The record here is the record of Abraham's intercession. But it does not say that Abraham had finished his speaking; it says that the Lord had finished His speaking. Proper intercession is always God's speaking. Apparently we are speaking; actually God is speaking in our speaking.

I like the verse which says that the Lord went His way as soon as He had finished speaking to Abraham. Many times in our prayers we say, "Amen," after we have finished speaking. Our "Amen" means the same as good-bye. I can testify that hundreds of times I have said good-bye to the Lord in this way before He has finished speaking to me. I prayed for a certain length of time and then said, "Amen," meaning good-bye. But deep in my spirit I sensed that God was saying, "What are you doing? I haven't finished talking to you. Why don't you stay for another few minutes?" Many of us have had this kind of experience. Our "Amen," our good-bye, was too fast. We need to stay in the presence of God until He has finished His speaking to us. Our intercession must utter what God is speaking.   ✻

16

LIVING IN FELLOWSHIP WITH GOD A DEFEATED RIGHTEOUS MAN

Abram dwelt in the land of Canaan, and Lot dwelt
in the cities of the plain, and pitched his tent toward Sodom.

Genesis 13:12

And Lot sat in the gate of Sodom....Then the angels hastened Lot,
saying, Arise, take thy wife, and thy two daughters, which are here;
lest thou be consumed in the iniquity of the city.
And while he lingered, the men laid hold upon his hand.

Genesis 19:1, 15-16

And having reduced to ashes the cities of Sodom and Gomorrah,
condemned them to ruin, having set them as an example
to those who intend to live an ungodly life,
and rescued righteous Lot, who had been oppressed by
the licentious manner of life of the lawless.

2 Peter 2:6-7

The Bible is a marvelous book. Alongside of the record of Abraham, it gives us the negative history of Lot. For quite a long time, I did not understand why the Bible included such a negative record.

There are certain verses in Genesis 19 that, humanly speaking, I do not like to talk about. But the Lord's divine revelation is economical; not one word is wasted. Hence, every word in the Holy Bible is very important. What then is the purpose of chapter nineteen of Genesis? It is to give us a warning example. I have the strong burden that in this message so many of us, especially the young people, need to see this warning example. We need such an example because today's situation is no better than that of Sodom.

We thank the Lord that His Word gives us both a positive history of Abraham and a negative one of Lot. There is no record in the entire Bible that is as complete as the account of Abraham's life. This record shows how Abraham was called by God, how he answered God's calling, how he lived by faith in God for his existence, how he was trained to know grace for the fulfillment of God's purpose, how he was dealt with by being circumcised, and how he was brought into intimate fellowship with God, cooperating with Him on the human level. I appreciate this record of a fallen man who was saved, transformed, and brought into wonderful fellowship on the human level with the glorious and holy God. Yet alongside of this record, we have a black, negative record of Lot. In this message we must consider this record in detail, taking it as a warning for ourselves and for our children and relatives.

If we read 2 Peter 2:6-9, we see that Peter was much in favor of Lot. In verse 8 Peter referred to him as a "righteous man" whose "righteous soul" was vexed with the unlawful deeds of the people in Sodom. In verse 9 he describes Lot as godly. Thus, according to Peter's concept, Lot was both righteous and godly. Although we may find it difficult to believe this because Lot's record in Genesis is so negative, we must believe it because the Bible tells us so. If you still say that Lot was not righteous and godly, then I would ask you about yourself. Are you more righteous and godly than he? In a sense, Lot was more righteous and godly than many of us. But although he was saved, righteous, and godly, he was a defeated righteous man.

PASSIVELY BROUGHT INTO GOD'S WAY BY OTHERS

As we consider Lot's history, we see that he was passively brought into God's way by others (11:31; 12:5), having been brought into God's way by his grandfather and his uncle. His grandfather brought him from Ur of Chaldea to Haran, stopping halfway because the grandfather would not go on. When God took the grandfather away, Abraham, Lot's uncle, took him from Haran to Canaan. Although it is good in the eyes of God that there are grandfathers and uncles who can bring their grandchildren and nephews into God's way, it is not the best to be passively brought on by others. Lot had a very weak start. He did not have an active, positive beginning in spiritual things. Young people, it is not the best to be passive concerning holy things or your following of the Lord. Lot was righteous and godly, but he was defeated because he had a very weak, passive start. His passive beginning was the cause of his eventual defeat.

NEVER HAVING GOD'S APPEARING

Lot never had God's appearing. As I read through the verses about Lot again and again, I could not find a hint that God ever appeared to him. Although God and the two angels visited Abraham, only the two angels came to Lot. Does this mean that God is unfair or a respecter of persons? Of course not. God is fair and is no respecter of persons. God did not appear to Lot or reveal Himself to Lot, because Lot was passive, not actively seeking God, and was living in a wicked city. He did not follow God in a direct way but in an indirect way and did not walk in the way of God. Unlike Abraham, Lot had no direct relationship with God. God does not respect persons, but He does respect behavior, respecting whether or not we are active or passive in seeking Him. If you seek Him, He will appear to you. But if you do not seek Him, He will not waste His time. That God did not appear to Lot was not God's fault; it was Lot's. God wants to appear to you, but are you seeking Him and walking in His way? Do you have a heart to seek God positively and actively and walk in the way of God? If you do, God will not fail you. He will certainly appear to you.

NEVER TAKING THE INITIATIVE IN TAKING GOD'S WAY

Lot never took the initiative in taking God's way. I have been unable to find a verse which indicates that Lot ever took the initiative in this matter. The Bible says that Lot's grandfather took him to Haran; it does not say that Lot followed him. There is a great difference between the two. I am somewhat concerned for the young people among us. Many of them are in the church life because some-one brought them here. They did not take the initiative to come into the church life. As I look back upon the past fifty years, I can testify that those who showed initiative in taking the way of the church are still strong today. However, those who took no initiative but who were passively brought into the way of the church have gradually fallen away. I can give you a hundred names of those who were inti-mate with me and who were helped by my ministry who gradually fell away because they did not have a strong start by actively taking the initiative to follow the Lord. Lot should have said to Abraham, "Uncle Abraham, whether or not you take God's way, I will take it. Even though I am younger than you, I would be the leader in follow-ing God and would ask you to follow me." To say this is not to be proud; it is to be active.

HIS RELATIONSHIP WITH GOD
BEING UNDER THE INFLUENCE OF OTHERS

Lot's relationship with God was under the influence of others (13:1). When others were up, he was up. When they were down, he was down. Lot was like a piece of driftwood. When his spiritual leader drifted into Egypt, he drifted there after him. He was alto-gether under the influence of others. When Abraham was drifting southward toward Egypt and the world, Lot should have withstood him and said, "Abraham, if you go downward, I'll go upward." But we see no such tendency in Lot's life. I am concerned that in the church life today there is this kind of driftwood. Is your relation-ship with God under His direct appearing or under others' influence? Do not think that Lot suddenly drifted into Sodom. No, it was a gradual development starting from a very weak beginning. If as you read this message you feel that you have not had a strong beginning, be encouraged for it is still not too late to lay a solid foundation.

LEAVING OTHERS' SPIRITUAL INFLUENCE
BECAUSE OF MATERIAL SUBSTANCE

Lot left others' spiritual influence because of material substance (13:5-13). When there was only the spiritual influence, Lot kept himself under it. But when Lot was faced with the choice between spiritual influence and material substance, he chose material substance. The principle is the same today. Material substance, that is, worldliness, is a test to those who follow the spirituality of others. Like Lot, they may be righteous but still choose material substance.

The Bible does not indicate that in the strife between Lot and Abraham in chapter thirteen Abraham was wrong. However, I believe that in a very deep sense Lot's feelings were hurt. Here I would say a word to the leading brothers. It is a very difficult matter to deal with the brothers. Abraham did nothing wrong in dealing with Lot, but simply because he dealt with him, Lot would never return to him. Abraham never forgot Lot. When he heard that Lot had been captured by Chedorlaomer, he led the fight against the kings and rescued Lot. When Abraham learned that God was about to destroy Sodom, he interceded for Lot. In 19:27 and 28, Abraham rose up early in the morning and looked toward Sodom and Gomorrah because he was so concerned for Lot. Nevertheless, because of his hurt feelings, Lot would not return to Abraham, but could say, "I have nothing to do with you. Even though you brought me back from captivity, I will never return to you." When Lot was delivered from the city of Sodom, he did not consider returning to Abraham. If he had returned, his life would not have had such a pitiful ending.

I am burdened that the young brothers and sisters will see that it is dangerous to dissent with and to leave the older generation in the Lord. When as a child I was rebuked by my mother, I would turn my face away from her for several days. I was wrong and I knew that she had rebuked me in love, but simply because she rebuked me, I refused to see her face. The principle is the same in the church life. Although others may love us, we do not like to be rebuked by them. I have learned that rebuking others builds up enmity. I spoke a frank word in love to certain brothers, and my frankness offended them. This might have been the reason why Lot would not return to Abraham. There is no indication in the Word that Lot thanked Abraham for delivering him from captivity. It might have been that he would not give up his hurt feelings and humble himself. We should not insist upon holding on to such human feelings. We, unlike Lot, should humble ourselves, lose our face, and return to Abraham and remain with him. The sooner we do this and the more we do it, the better.

DRIFTING INTO A SITUATION
WHICH WAS WICKED AND SINFUL BEFORE GOD

Lot drifted into a situation which was wicked and sinful before God (13:11-12). Once you leave the source of spiritual influence, you will automatically go downhill. You will never go upward. Never forsake the proper spiritual influence, for it is your protection. If you give it up, you will lose your protection, and, like Lot, will drift downward into Sodom. In spite of the fact that Lot knew Sodom was wicked in the eyes of God, he eventually entered into that evil place and lived there.

Ur of Chaldea was a place of idols, Egypt was a place of worldly riches and pleasures, and Sodom was a city of sin. These three places form a triangular boundary around the land of Canaan. We, God's called ones, live within this triangle and must be careful lest we fall back to the city of idols, go down to the place of worldly pleasures, or drift into the city of sin. Although Lot stayed away from the land of idols and the place of worldly pleasures, he drifted, like a piece of driftwood, into the city of sin.

SOVEREIGNLY WARNED BY BEING CAPTURED

Lot was sovereignly warned by being captured (14:11-12). God was merciful to him, not allowing him to live in Sodom peacefully. As a warning and a discipline, God caused Lot to be captured.

RESCUED FROM CAPTIVITY BY THE LORD'S OVERCOMER,
BUT NOT HELPED TO COME BACK TO THE WAY OF GOD

Although Lot was rescued from captivity by the Lord's overcomer, he was not helped to come back to the way of God (14:12-16). For a long time I was troubled by Lot's not returning to the way of God. He might have been stubborn. Do not think that passive people are submissive. Nearly all the passive ones are rebellious. Lot did not learn the lesson and he did not return to God's way.

GOING BACK TO LIVE IN THE WICKED CITY
WHICH WAS CONDEMNED BY GOD
AND WAS TO BE DESTROYED BY THE JUDGMENT OF GOD

Lot went back to live in the wicked city which was condemned by

God and which was to be destroyed by the judgment of God (19:1-13). Lot did not go there to visit; he went there to live. When the two angels came to execute God's judgment over Sodom, Lot was sitting in the gate of the city, in contrast to Abraham who was sitting at his tent door. According to ancient custom, whoever sat at the gate of the city was one of the elders, for only they had the privilege of sitting there. Lot became a leader in Sodom! Suppose the Lord or His angels were to visit you. Where would they find you—sitting at your tent door, or at the gate of the wicked world? Where you are sitting determines whether or not the Lord will come to you.

The angels refused to enter Lot's house (19:2). Compare this with the visit the Lord and the angels paid Abraham in the previous chapter. When Abraham invited them to stay, they immediately agreed. But the two angels did not want to enter into Lot's house and stay there, because it was in such a wicked city. After Lot pressed upon them greatly, they went in and stayed with him (19:3).

While the angels were staying in Lot's house, the Sodomites came to indulge in their sodomitical lust, coming from every corner of the city (19:4-11). A Sodomite is a homosexual. Paul speaks of them in Romans 1:24 and 27. There are many Sodomites today and much sodomitical lust is expressed. Sodomites seem to have no spirit; they are like brutal animals.

Lot was even willing to sacrifice his two daughters to satisfy the Sodomites' lust (19:7-9). Whether he was forced to do this or not, he never should have done it. This shows that Lot's sense of morality had been drugged. We may use the smell of garlic as an illustration of this. If we were to eat garlic all day long, our sense of smell would eventually be drugged. If someone having a fresh sense of smell would come into the midst of the garlic eaters, he would immediately notice the scent of garlic. Lot and his children remained in the garlic room of Sodom for years, and their sense of morality was drugged. Lot would consider sacrificing his virgin daughters to save his two guests. How could he consider such a thing! Although he was a righteous man, he had lost his sense of morality and shame.

In order to meet such a wicked situation, the angels smote the Sodomites with blindness (19:11), indicating that all the men in Sodom were blind and in darkness. All Sodomites are blind. If a man were not blind, how could he be a Sodomite? This shows that sinfulness blinds people.

HIS CHILDREN BEING CORRUPTED

Lot's children were corrupted by living in the wicked city. The word of the angels in 19:12 indicates that Lot might have had sons as well as daughters. In chapter eighteen Abraham might have considered that there were at least ten people in Lot's family. The angels said to Lot, "Hast thou here any besides? son-in-law, and thy sons, and thy daughters, and whatsoever thou hast in the city, bring them out of this place: for we will destroy this place, because the cry of them is waxen great before the face of the Lord; and the Lord has sent us to destroy it" (19:12-13). Lot had to tell his sons-in-law and his children that God was about to judge that city. But when Lot preached the gospel to them, some would not believe the word from the Lord, thinking that he was joking. Verse 14 says, "Lot went out, and spake unto his sons-in-law, which married his daughters, and said, Up, get you out of this place; for the Lord will destroy this city. But he seemed as one that jested unto his sons-in-law" (Heb.).

Others of Lot's children had no sense of morality (19:30-35). Look at what his daughters did after they escaped from the city! After escaping from Sodom, Lot and his daughters still had wine with them (19:32). If they had not brought the wine with them, how else could they have had it in the cave where they were dwelling? How drugged they were by the sinful situation in Sodom! When I was visiting some saints in Las Vegas in 1963, they vindicated their living in that city, saying, "It is not wrong for us to stay in this gambling city, because we are here as a testimony for the Lord." I did not argue with them, but deep within myself I said, "If you stay here for some years, your children will have no sense about the wickedness of gambling." Many of the young people today have been drugged. Look at the way they dress: there is no sense of morality or feeling of shame. Many times when I am on the street I have to shut my eyes. For young ladies to be without a sense of shame is to be without protection. Throughout the whole world the sense of shame and morality has been drugged. Because most of the young people were raised in a sinful atmosphere, their senses have been drugged. But if they would come in to the church life and remain in its pure atmosphere for a few months, they would never return to the sinful world. They would be unable to stand its smell.

We live in an evil age and need protection from it. Our family and our children must be protected. We all must escape Sodom and shut our doors to its evil atmosphere. If we do not, our descendants will be drugged. How could Lot and his children have conducted themselves in the way they did after Sodom was destroyed? Because their sense of morality had fallen so low. If we remain in the fresh air, we shall immediately sense the bad smell of immorality. But if we do not discern any bad smell, it means that our sense of morality has been drugged.

HE HIMSELF BARELY SAVED
THROUGH THE OVERCOMER'S INTERCESSION

Lot himself was barely saved through the overcomer's intercession (19:15-25, 29). Even after the angels told Lot that Sodom was to be destroyed, he still lingered there. He had no willingness to escape from the city, but the angels held his hand and pulled him out. Verse 16 says, "And while he lingered, the men laid hold upon his hand, and upon the hand of his wife, and upon the hand of his two daughters; the Lord being merciful unto him: and they brought him forth, and set him without the city." Lot was not faithful, but the Lord was merciful, pulling him out of Sodom as wood plucked out of a fire.

HIS WIFE BEING SAVED FROM DESTRUCTION
BUT BECOMING A PILLAR OF SALT

Lot's wife was saved from destruction, but she became a pillar of salt (19:15-17, 26; Luke 17:32). In the form of powder, salt is useful. But when salt becomes a block, it is useless. That Lot's wife became a pillar of salt meant that she had lost her usefulness in the hand of God and had become a sign of shame. Today Christianity helps people only to take care of the matter of salvation or perdition. But the Bible reveals that besides the matter of salvation or perdition, there is the matter of glory or shame. Lot's wife was not lost; she was saved from destruction. Eventually, however, she became a shame. Hence, the Lord said in Luke 17:32, "Remember Lot's wife," warning us that, though we are saved, at the Lord's coming back we might possibly suffer shame like Lot's wife. Although we are saved, we may become ashamed at the Lord's coming back (1 John 2:28).

In Luke 17:28-33 the Lord warns us not to look back. Why did Lot's wife look back? Because some of her children, especially her daughters, were still in Sodom and because her house and her

clothing also were there. If you read Genesis 19 carefully, you will see
that she was behind Lot. As a couple, they should have gone together;
she should not have been behind her husband. But, being behind him,
she looked back and became a pillar of salt. She looked back to the
place where she loved to live and became a sign of shame for our
warning. This is not merely a story or doctrine. We see from it that in
addition to the matter of salvation, there is the matter of shame.
When the day of judgment arrives, will you share in the glory or in
the shame? We shall not suffer perdition, for our salvation is assured.
However, as this warning example indicates, we may be put to shame.

HIS LIFE ISSUING IN BRINGING FORTH
MOABITES AND AMMONITES

Lot's life issued in bringing forth Moabites and Ammonites (children of Ben-ammi), who were rejected by God even to their tenth
generation (19:36-38; Deut. 23:3). What a pitiful ending to Lot's
life! He did not bring forth an Isaac but Moabites and Ammonites
who were rejected by God. Here in the story of Lot we see the record
of a defeated righteous man. Alongside of the white record of the
victorious Abraham, we have the black record of the defeated Lot.
The record of Lot's life should be a strong warning to us all.

17

LIVING IN FELLOWSHIP WITH GOD
A PILLAR OF SALT

And when the morning arose,
then the angels hastened Lot, saying,
Arise, take thy wife, and thy two daughters,
which are here;
lest thou be consumed in the iniquity of the city....
Then the Lord rained upon Sodom and upon Gomorrah
brimstone and fire from the Lord
out of heaven;
and he overthrew those cities, and all the plain, and
all the inhabitants of the cities, and
that which grew upon the ground.
But his wife looked back from behind him, and
she became a pillar of salt.
Genesis 19:15, 24-26

Remember Lot's wife.
Luke 17:32

The previous message was on Lot, who was a defeated righteous man. In this message we come to Lot's wife, who became a pillar of salt (19:26). Genesis 19 might be the only record in human history regarding a pillar of salt, and we need to consider it very carefully.

This pillar of salt was not created by God. Lot's wife became a pillar of salt. It is very meaningful that in His heavy word recorded in Luke 17, spoken at a time when people were inquiring about the coming of the kingdom, the Lord Jesus said, "Remember Lot's wife" (Luke 17:32). In a sense, the Lord seemed to be saying to His disciples, "Don't talk about the kingdom. Rather, you must recognize what the age will be like when the kingdom comes. It will be like the days of Noah and the days of Lot. Both are prefigures of the days of My coming." Thus, in the Lord's heavy, solemn, and sobering word, three ages are mentioned: the age of Noah, the age of Lot, and the age at the time of the Lord's coming back.

When we covered Noah in some of the foregoing messages in this life-study, we pointed out that he lived in a befuddled age, and that the people of his age were befuddled, drugged, and doped by their lusts and evil pleasures. However, in Luke 17:27, when the Lord spoke of the days of Noah, marriage was mentioned. But when He spoke of the days of Lot, there was no mention of marriage, because in Sodom marriage had been completely degraded, and the people indulged in their sodomitical lust. In Luke 17:28 and 30 the Lord said, "Likewise, even as it happened in the days of Lot: they were eating, they were drinking, they were buying, they were selling, they were planting, they were building. ...It will be in the same way on the day in which the Son of Man is revealed." After saying this and immediately before telling us to remember Lot's wife, the Lord said, "In that day, he who shall be on the housetop and his goods in the house, let him not come down to take them away; and he who is in the field, likewise, let him not turn back to the things behind" (Luke 17:31). In Palestine the houses had flat roofs. The Lord was saying, "If you are on your housetop at the time of My coming, do not come down into your house to take away your stuff. If you do, you will be left. If you are working in the field, do not return home. You must forget everything except Me." Immediately after this word, the Lord said, "Remember Lot's wife."

Today, like the people in the days of Noah and in the days of Lot, many Christians are doped and befuddled, having lost the proper sense of the things of God. Some even teach that believers may be raptured while they are playing football. But according to the revelation of the Holy Word, when the Lord comes back, He would not take any of His saints who are still participating in worldly entertainments. We Christians are the crop of God growing with Christ as the life seed (Matt. 13:3-8, 18-23). No Christian who is mature in the growth of life still participates in any worldly entertainments. Since the Christians who continue to participate in worldly entertainments are not ripe, but are green and raw, the Lord would not reap them from the field. The befuddled Christians of today need to hear such a sobering word.

The record of Lot's wife becoming a pillar of salt is found in the - section on living in fellowship with God. Although this section in Genesis covering chapters eighteen through twenty-four is the record of a life that was in fellowship with God, it includes the black record of a defeated saved man, his wife, and his two daughters. Lot had more than these two daughters, but when the angels came to Sodom, they could not find the others. Genesis 19:15 says, "When the morning arose, the angels hastened Lot, saying, Arise, take thy wife, and thy two daughters, which are found; lest thou be consumed in the iniquity of the city" (Heb.). The angels seemed to be saying, "Lot, we can only find two of your children. We were sent here by God to rescue you and all your family, but only these have been found. Our commission is to destroy the city. Now you, your wife, and your daughters must escape." The next verse says that Lot lingered. According to the original, Lot not only lingered; he hesitated, being unwilling to leave the city. Since he was hesitating, the angels "laid hold upon his hand, and upon the hand of his wife, and upon the hand of his two daughters; the Lord being merciful unto him: and they brought him forth, and set him without the city." When the angels had brought the four of them outside the city, they said, "Escape for thy soul; look not behind thee" (v. 17, Heb.). But verse 26 says that Lot's wife "looked back from behind him, and she became a pillar of salt." Lot's wife was saved, for she was pulled out of the city and saved from its destruction. But although she was saved, she nevertheless became a pillar of salt. It is certain that becoming a pillar of salt is not a good thing; it is a shame.

As I have said many times, the book of Genesis contains the seeds of nearly all the divine truths. The pillar of salt in 19:26 may also be considered as a seed. The growth of this seed is in Luke 17:32, where the Lord tells us to remember Lot's wife, and in 1 John 2:28, where we are told that we might be put to shame at the Lord's appearing. The harvest is in Revelation 16:15, where the Lord says, "Behold, I come as a thief. Blessed is he who watches and keeps his garments, that he may not walk naked and they see his shame." The Lord will come as a thief, not giving any prior notification. If at that time our nakedness is exposed, we shall be put to shame. Thus, the seed of being put to shame was sown in Genesis 19, grows in Luke 17 and 1 John 2, and is reaped in Revelation 16. My burden in this message is to impress you that the book of Genesis not only has the seed of Abraham, but also the seed of Lot and of his wife, who became a pillar of salt, a sign of shame.

The basic concept of this message is that a genuine saved person faces the definite possibility of being put to shame. Do not listen to the befuddling teachings of this age. Many teachings in Christianity today drug people, and those who absorb such teachings are neither sober in their mind nor living in their spirit. In this message we need to hear a sobering word from the Lord, a word that will sober our mind and quicken our spirit.

LOT'S WIFE

As we have already pointed out, there is no doubt that Lot's wife was saved from destruction. This is so definitely and clearly revealed that no one can argue with it. But, as we have seen, she looked back from behind her husband and became a pillar of salt. That she walked behind her husband indicates that she was even less willing than her husband to leave Sodom and that she was not happy to follow him out of the city. If she had been happy to flee Sodom, she would have walked side by side with her husband. Even before she looked back and became a pillar of salt, she was already behind her husband. At this point, let me say a word to the wives. In committing sin, it is good for a wife to be reluctant to follow her husband, but concerning the things of God, it is not good for her to be slow in following him. Concerning the things of God, the best thing for a wife to do is to go along with and walk together with her husband. Wives, in the things with God, do not go behind your husbands. If you do, you, like Lot's wife, may suffer and become a pillar of salt. This is a warning to us all.

That Lot's wife became a pillar of salt signifies that she had lost her function and had become a sign of shame. When salt is in the form of powder, it is very useful. The more that salt is ground into fine powder, the better it functions. But no one uses salt in the form of a pillar. The

Lord Jesus said that we, the saved and regenerated ones, are the salt of the earth (Matt. 5:13). Our function is to kill the germs of this corrupted world. However, if we become tasteless (Luke 14:34), it means that we, like Lot's wife, have lost our function. As one of the people of God, Lot's wife should have been filled with the salty taste and been able to kill the germs of corruption around her, but she lost her taste and became functionless. She was a sign of shame.

In writing the book of Genesis, the Spirit of God was unwilling to give the name of Lot's wife. Although the name of Abraham's wife, Sarah, is mentioned many times, there is no mention of the name of Lot's wife. It is unworthy of mention. That poor saint walked behind her husband and looked back toward the city of Sodom. She might have looked back for her children, her house, and her other belongings. All her goods were left there in Sodom. Her interests, heart, desire, and soul were still there, though her body had been pulled out of that city. Hence, at her looking back to that place, the Lord caused her to become a pillar of salt as a warning example to us all.

In Luke 17, the Lord used Lot's wife as a warning example for His disciples. However, not many Christians today live under this warning. Nevertheless, we must heed the warning that a truly saved person faces the possibility of being put to shame at the Lord's appearing. I certainly do not want to become a pillar of salt. Do you? To become a pillar of salt is not a glory; it is a shame. What a shame for a believer to become a lifeless pillar of salt standing in the open air for nothing but suffering!

PEOPLE WHO ARE NOT ABSOLUTE
IN FOLLOWING THE LORD

Luke 14:25-33 speaks of absoluteness in following the Lord. We must follow the Lord in an absolute way. Although the Bible teaches us to love others, here Luke 14:26, a holy word out of the mouth of the Lord Jesus, says, "If anyone comes to Me and does not hate his father and mother and wife and children and brothers and sisters, and moreover, his own soul life also, he cannot be My disciple." It is impossible for anyone to follow the Lord in a proper way without being absolute. Our parents, wives, children, brothers, sisters, and our own soul life should all be secondary. Only the Lord Himself must be the first, and we must follow Him in an absolute way. When the Lord speaks of hating our relatives for His sake, He does not mean a real hatred but a loving hatred.

In this portion of the word out of the mouth of the Lord, we see that we must follow Him in the way of absoluteness. It is not a matter of worshipping God on Sundays nor of having a home Bible study according to our pleasure. Such a home Bible study may be another type of hobby or entertainment. In the eyes of God, your home Bible study may be no different from a basketball game. You play your Bible ball in your Bible study, using your living room as your playground. You are not absolute in following the Lord. I am not joking; I am speaking the truth. I am not only saying this to others but also to myself. The Lord can testify for me that as I was preparing for this message, the Lord asked me, "How about you? I have charged you to give this message, but are you absolute in following Me?" May the Lord have mercy on me that I would not preach to others and myself become a castaway. May He also have mercy on all His dear saints. How we need a sobering word that we would no longer be befuddled! If we believe John 3:16, we must also believe Luke 14:26-35. Many messages have been given and booklets published on John 3:16, but where are the messages and booklets on Luke 14:26-35? In the Lord's recovery we should not hide any truth from His people.

Those who are not absolute in following the Lord become useless. Tell me, how many Christians today are truly useful in the Lord's hand for God's economy? Most Christians have become useless as far as God's economy is concerned. They are like salt that is tasteless (Luke 14:34).

Such Christians are not only tasteless, but according to Luke 14:35, they are "fit neither for the soil nor for the manure pile," but to be cast out. The land here is the field which grows things for God that He might accomplish His purpose. The dunghill in the universe is the lake of fire, where every dirty thing will be piled up. Luke 14:35 mainly refers to the coming age of the kingdom. In the kingdom age there will be the earth, the land for the fulfillment of God's purpose, and there will also be the lake of fire, the dunghill. Christianity always tells people that there are only two places—heaven or hell. But in this verse the Lord Jesus speaks of the third place, saying that tasteless salt, being fit for neither the land nor for the dunghill, is cast out. Where was the pillar of salt which Lot's wife became? Was it in heaven or in Sodom? It was in neither place, but in the third place. Although you have read through the Gospel of Luke, have you ever seen that in this chapter there are three places? Where will you be—in the land, in the dung-hill, or cast out to the third place?

In Matthew 25:30 the Lord said that the unprofitable servant would be cast into outer darkness. The outer darkness must also be the third place. What this will be and where it will be, the Bible does not say. Nevertheless, the Bible does say that if you are a slothful servant, at the Lord's coming back you will be fit neither for the land because you were unprofitable, nor for the dunghill because you have been saved. Where then will you be? In the third place, a place outside both the glorious kingdom and the lake of fire. Few Christians have ever seen that in the Bible there is a third place prepared for the defeated saved ones. This is a sobering word.

We need to be deeply impressed that in the full revelation regarding man in the divine Word there are three places—a place for salvation, a place for perdition, and a place for shame. Where was Lot's wife? Although she was saved, she was in the third place, the place of shame. This is the teaching of the Lord Jesus in the Gospel of Luke. Do not try to argue with it.

BELIEVERS WHO LIVE IN THE WORLD
AS THE WORLDLY PEOPLE AND SEEK TO SAVE THEIR SOUL

Believers who live in the world as the worldly people and seek to save their soul, their soul-life, will suffer shame as did Lot's wife, and will lose their soul at the Lord's coming back (Luke 17:28-33). Most Christians are like this. Although they are believers, yet they live like worldly people, shopping and dressing in the same way as the worldly people do. Since they live and walk the same as the worldlings, there is no difference between them and the worldly people.

To save the soul means to refuse to suffer for the Lord's sake. Christians who save their soul like to have their pleasure. They say, "What's wrong with going to sporting events? It's not sinful." Although it may not be sinful, it is worldly. I am not saying that Christians should have no physical exercise for their health. We certainly need that. But once any form of exercise becomes a sport or entertainment, it is worldly. If you enjoy it and find it pleasurable, it means that you are saving your soul. To have any psychological and worldly enjoyment is to save the soul.

Today is not the time for us Christians to have psychological and worldly pleasure or enjoyment; it is the time for us to suffer in our soul, in our psychology. As long as we can maintain our existence, it is sufficient. We should not seek psychological and worldly pleasure. Since World War II, who has given such a sobering word? During the past thirty-one years, I have been watching and observing, but I have not heard a sober word or warning telling Christians that we are not on this earth for our psychological and worldly enjoyment, and that we must suffer the loss of every kind of amusement and entertainment. Your enjoyment of certain music at home may be a saving of your soul. Many Christians cannot overcome their television sets. Their watching television may be a saving of their soul. I am neither religious nor legal, but I do say that today is not the time for us to have psychological and worldly amusement; it is the time for us to suffer in our soul. This suffering in the soul is for the saving of the soul. If you are not willing to suffer in order to save your soul, you will suffer shame as Lot's wife did and lose your soul at the Lord's coming back.

It is wrong to teach that all Christians will be raptured at one time at the Lord's coming back. That teaching befuddles the spiritual sense of the Lord's people. In Luke 17:34 and 35 the Lord said, "I tell you, in that night there will be two on one couch; the one will be taken, and the other will be left. There will be two grinding at the same place; the one will be taken, but the other will be left." You may argue, saying, "The one taken is a believer, and the one left is an unbeliever." But that is your interpretation. While both are the same, doing the same thing in the same place, only the Lord knows who is genuinely for Him. If you read the context of Luke 17:22-37, you will see that this word is not given to unbelievers but to the Lord's disciples. It was a word given to them concerning the time of His coming. The "two" in verses 34 and 35 refer to two of the Lord's disciples, one of whom will be taken and the other of whom will be left. The one who will be taken will surely not be like Lot's wife. The disciple who will be left will be like Lot's wife. This is a sober word.

CHILDREN OF GOD WHO DO NOT ABIDE IN THE LORD AS THE ANOINTING TEACHES

The children of God who do not abide in the Lord as the anointing teaches will be put to shame at the Lord's coming back (1 John

2:27-28). We who are in the Lord's recovery know what is the inner teaching of the inward anointing. But do we abide in the Lord according to the teaching of the living anointing within us? First John 2:27 and 28 charge us to abide in the Lord according to the anointing. For example, if you are about to go shopping and the anointing says no, will you say, "Amen, Lord"? If you do, that is good. However, if you say, "Lord, I won't buy anything bad," the Lord may say, "I don't care whether you buy something good or bad. Don't go." We should simply say, "Amen, Lord, I'm just abiding in You according to Your teaching of the inward anointing." We all need to abide in the Lord in this way.

If we do not abide in the Lord according to the anointing, we shall "be put to shame from Him at His coming" (1 John 2:28). To feel shameful is one thing; to be put to shame is another. This verse is not saying that we shall feel shameful, but that we shall "be put to shame." Notice that, according to the Greek, it does not say, like the King James Version, "before Him" but "from Him." The Greek preposition here is *apo,* which means "away from." If we abide in the Lord according to the anointing, when He appears, we shall have confidence, assurance, boldness, and peace and not be put away from Him. Literally, the Greek words translated "at His coming" mean "in His presence." The Greek word for presence is parousia, which includes the meaning of coming. We may have His coming and yet not be in His presence. For example, the President of the United States may come to Anaheim tonight, but only a few people will enter into his presence, that is, into his parousia. The Lord Jesus will come, but will you be worthy to be in His presence? If you live in a worldly way, loving the world and making the Lord the last in your life, how could you be brought into His presence when He comes? We must abide in the Lord according to the inward anointing so that we may have confidence, boldness, and assurance before Him in His presence at His appearing and not be put to shame away from Him.

At His appearing, the Lord will deal with His believers. If His believers follow Him today in the way of abiding in Him according to the inward anointing, they will then have peace, boldness, assurance, and confidence and will be brought into His parousia, into His presence. If they do not abide in Him today, at His appearing, they will be put to shame away from Him. To be put to shame away from Him must mean to be put to the third place, the place which is neither the field for the fulfilling of God's purpose, nor the dunghill in the lake of fire. It is the place of shame outside His presence. A believer who is put to shame away from Him is not lost. He is still a saved person, but he must suffer being put to shame. That being put to shame will be for him a dealing and a discipline; it will be the chastisement exercised by the sovereign Lord over His defeated believers. This matter is quite clear and is very serious.

BELIEVERS WHO DO NOT WATCH
FOR THE LORD'S COMING BACK AND LIVE A PROPER LIFE

The believers who do not watch for the Lord's coming back and live a proper life will suffer shame (Rev. 16:15). In Revelation 16:15 the Lord tells us to keep our garments. In the Bible, a garment always signifies what we are in our walk and living. We must have a clean walk, and our spiritual garment must be pure, white, and approved by God. We must watch for the Lord's coming and keep our garments pure. If we live such a clean life, we shall have no nakedness when He comes and men will not see our shame. This verse also says that the Lord is coming as a thief. He will not come as a visitor announcing His arrival ahead of time. When we do not think that the thief will come, he comes. I have been told that thieves often come about three or four o'clock in the morning, at the time when people are deeply asleep. We need to be sober and watching. Otherwise, the Lord will come as a thief and our nakedness will be exposed. Once again, this tells us that there is the possibility that a saved person may be put to shame at the Lord's coming back.

GOD'S PEOPLE WHO DO NOT LIVE
AND WALK ACCORDING TO HIS ECONOMY

God's people who do not live and walk according to His way, that is, according to His economy, will come short of the fulfillment of His purpose and be put to shame. As we have seen, this is the significance of the pillar of salt. Do not take this merely as a Bible study, but as a warning for us all. Even we who are in the Lord's recovery cannot afford to be loose or indifferent. We must be sober and consider the situation to be quite serious. We need to have a life and walk that fulfills God's purpose. Then at the Lord's appearing we shall be in His parousia and not be cast out to the third place, the place of shame.   ※

18

LIVING IN FELLOWSHIP WITH GOD
THE SEED BY INCEST

Thus were both the daughters of Lot
with child by their father.
And the firstborn bare a son, and called his name Moab:
the same is the father of the Moabites unto this day.
And the younger, she also bare a son, and
called his name Ben-ammi:
the same is the father of the children of Ammon unto this day.

Genesis 19:36-38

An Ammonite or a Moabite shall not enter into the congregation
of Jehovah; even to the tenth generation, no descendent of theirs shall
enter the congregation of Jehovah forever.

Deuteronomy 23:3

And they took wives for themselves from among the Moabite women.
One's name was Orpah, and the second's name was Ruth....

Ruth 1:4

As I have pointed out many times, nearly all the seeds of the divine revelation are found in the book of Genesis. A seed is a primitive form of something. Although its size is small and its form is simple, once a seed has been sown into a field, it will grow. As it grows it takes on another form. First it is a sprout and later it is fully developed. Although the final form of its development is different from that of the seed, all the principles and major aspects of it are found within the seed. If we would understand Genesis 19, we must consider it as a seed which has its growth, development, and harvest in the following books of the Bible. Although the record concerning Lot and his daughters in Genesis 19:30-38 is a negative seed, concerning such an ugly thing as incest, it serves the positive purpose of giving us a strong, sobering warning.

In this message we must see the portrait of a most ugly thing—incest. Genesis 19:30-38, probably the first recorded case of incest in human history, is part of the section on living in fellowship with God. As we consider this matter, we must cover six points: the family, the father, the mother, the daughters, the seed, and the far-reaching and unsearchable mercy of God.

Firstly, we have the family, the group, and secondly, we have the father, the leader of this group. Thirdly, we have the mother who was the leader's helper. The leader of any group needs help. The proper helper in a family is the wife, and in the Bible a wife is called a help-meet. In figure, the wife in a family signifies a helper in life. This concept is according to the principles of the Bible. Consider the example of Sarah. Abraham had a family for God's purpose, for Abraham alone could do nothing for the fulfillment of God's purpose. He needed a helper in life. Although he turned to Hagar for help, she was not a helper in life but a helper in the flesh. Sarah was the unique helper, the one who had the function in life. Without her, Abraham could never have brought forth Isaac for the fulfillment of God's purpose. The church today is a spiritual family in which there also is the need of the proper function in life to bring forth "Isaac" for the fulfillment of God's purpose. As we shall see, at a certain point, Lot's family group lost its function in life because the wife became a pillar of salt. She should have been salty and maintained a good flavor, but due to her worldliness she lost the function in life. In figure, becoming a pillar of salt indicates the loss of the function in life. Although there was a group with a leader, there was no wife with the function in life, only a pillar of shame. This is true of many Christian groups today. Although these groups have leaders, they do not have the proper wife with the genuine function in life.

Because Lot's family had lost its function in life, it had improper members—the daughters. I am not happy to call the members of Lot's group daughters, for the word daughters is a good term. What kind of people were they? Were they daughters or wives or mothers? I simply do not know what to call them. If you call them daughters, you must say that they were incestuous daughters. Although they might have been mothers, they were incestuous mothers. I feel ashamed to even speak of what they did. After lying with their father, the first daughter encouraged the second to do the same thing. How shameful! These were the members of Lot's group. Many Christian groups today also have such improper members. They, like Lot's daughters, desire to have the seed but do not care for the proper means. They may say, "Let us go to win souls," but they win souls through the way of spiritual incest.

In 19:30-38 we have the group, the leader, the helper in life, the members, and the seed by incest. But praise the Lord that eventually the far-reaching and unsearchable mercy of God is seen in one of the descendants who came out of this incest. Ruth, a Moabitess, a descendant of Lot through his daughter, became the great grandmother of David and an ancestress of Christ. Is this not the far-reaching and unsearchable mercy of God? However, when we hear of this, we should not say, "Let us do evil that good may come."

THE FAMILY—THE GROUP

Let us now consider these six points in more detail. Based upon the principle that everything in the book of Genesis is a seed, we may say that Abraham's tent, in which he had intimate fellowship with God on the human level, was a miniature of the tabernacle which God commanded Abraham's descendants to build as His dwelling place on earth. Abraham's tent was the seed, and the tabernacle erected in the wilderness by the children of Israel was the growth. The temple built in the good land of Canaan was a further development of this seed. Today's church, as the real dwelling of God on earth, is the fulfillment of what has been portrayed in the Old Testament by Abraham's tent, the tabernacle, and the temple. Eventually, the New Jerusalem will be the ultimate harvest of this seed. Revelation 21:3 says that "the tabernacle of God is with men, and He shall tabernacle with them." Thus, in Genesis 18 we have the seed, and in Revelation 21 we have the harvest.

In the same principle, during the time of Abraham and Lot, God had a people on earth. His people were composed of two families, the families of Abraham and of Lot. This was a seed, a miniature, of God's people in the following ages. Firstly, the children of Israel were the development of the seed of God's people, and now the church today is the continuation of this development. Eventually, in the New Jerusalem we shall see that all the redeemed ones throughout the generations will be the full harvest of God's people on earth. Once again we have the seed, the development, and the harvest. By this we see that what is present with the seed should also be found with the development.

At the beginning, Abraham's family and Lot's family, being God's people, were one. At a certain time, however, division came in and they were divided. When they were one, they were not a group; they were the people of God, God's one people. When division came in, it produced a free group. That ancient free group was the seed and the miniature of today's free groups. The free groups among God's people today are actually a further development of this seed. The division which was sown by Lot was developed after the time of Solomon when the children of Israel were divided and a free group was produced. That free group, the nation of Israel, was never recognized by God. God only recognized Judah because Judah was on the proper ground. The principle is the same in the church age. The whole church should be God's one people. In the early days, the church was uniquely one. But division after division came in, producing many free groups. We praise the Lord that this division will not continue into the new heaven and new earth. It will be terminated by the Lord's coming back.

APART FROM GOD'S WITNESS AND TESTIMONY   ✦   We have seen that Lot's separation from Abraham was the seed both of division and of today's free groups. Who was the cause of that division? The fault was not on Abraham's side; it was on Lot's side. The members of Lot's family might have argued, "Aren't we also God's people? Why do you, the members of Abraham's family, always say that you are the people of God?" Yes, Lot's family was a part of the people of God, but they had left God's witness and testimony, which were Abraham and what he was testifying. God's witness and testimony were at the tent of Abraham by the oaks of Mamre in Hebron, not with Lot in the city of Sodom. In chapters eighteen and nineteen we see that God and the two angels were happy to stay with Abraham, enjoying dinner and intimate fellowship with him. But when the angels went to the wicked city of Sodom, God did not go with them; He remained with Abraham. While both groups were God's people, where was God's presence? Only with Abraham's family. God's presence was with Abraham's family because his family was the typical people of God and had the proper standing of God's testimony. Although Lot was one of God's people, he was not on the proper ground by the oaks of Mamre in Hebron; he was in Sodom, on the ground of division and free groups. All God's people, being His family, should dwell by the oaks of Mamre in Hebron, where God can pay them a friendly and intimate visit. Here we can see the difference between the church and the free groups: all the free groups are God's people, but the church is by the "oaks of Mamre" in "Hebron," continually enjoying God's intimate presence. What then about the free groups? As it was with the case of Lot's family, God does not meet with them. They are His people, and He cares for them and does not forget them, but His presence is not with them. After the angels left for Sodom to rescue Lot and his family, God's presence was with Abraham, His dear friend. Where are you—with Abraham's family in Hebron or with Lot's free group in Sodom?

Does not the Bible say that Lot was a righteous man? Yes, we are clearly told in 2 Peter 2:7 and 8 that Lot was righteous. Are not the people in the free groups saved? Certainly they are. But look at the situation: the people in the free groups are in a place which is under God's condemnation. This is clear in the enlightenment of the divine revelation. Suppose you were alive during the days of Abraham and Lot. With which group would you have been? Perhaps you would have said, "You say that Lot's group is a division. Isn't Abraham's group also a division? Neither Abraham's group nor Lot's group is the whole body. They both are the same. Why do you make so much of the difference between Abraham's family and Lot's family when both of them are God's people? Since both are God's people, today I will be with Lot and tomorrow I will visit Abraham." Although you might stay with Lot, God would not. This makes a great difference.

Besides the family which was on the ground where they could have intimate fellowship with God, there was a free group. Today's situation is a further development of this seed. Be honest and fair about the free groups. Is there the testimony of God among them? No, God is not expressed in the free groups. They do whatever they like, and there is no witness or testimony with them. Lot's family became such a free group because it was apart from Abraham and what he was testifying. If I had been Lot, having the light which we have today, I would have said, "Uncle Abraham, even if you force me to leave you, I would refuse to go. If you don't like me, I would still embrace and kiss you. I would stay with you because you are God's witness and because the testimony of God is with you. I will never forsake this testimony." We should have this attitude today. Although we may not be happy with the brothers in the church, we should say, "Brothers, although I don't feel happy with you and although you may mistreat me, I will never leave God's testimony." The source, the root, of the problem of the ancient free group was its departing from God's witness and testimony.

As many of us can testify, when we departed from the denominations, we were happy and felt as though we were in the heavens. But it is quite a different matter to leave the church. If you forsake the church, your joy will disappear and will not return until you return to God's testimony. I do not say this lightly. Without exception, those who have left the church have lost their joy. Once a person leaves the church, it is very difficult for him to come back. Look at Lot: although he was rescued after the slaughter of the kings, he refused to return to Abraham. Even after he had been delivered from the destruction of Sodom, he still did not go back to him. Later on, we shall see that Lot still had his self-choice. That we are joyful after leaving the denominations but joyless after leaving the church proves what is the church, which has God's presence, and what is a denomination, which does not have God's presence. Although we may not be able to discern the difference between them by our thought, we can discern it by the sense of life deep in our spirit.

DRIFTED INTO THE WICKED CITY   ✦   After Lot's group had left God's witness and testimony, they drifted into the wicked city of Sodom (13:12-13; 19:1). If you leave the church life, you will be defeated. Like a piece of driftwood that cannot control its direction but is carried along by the current, you will drift with the tide of this age and float downward until you find yourself in a wicked city.

RESCUED YET STILL HAVING SELF-PREFERENCE   ✦   After Lot was rescued from the destruction of Sodom, he still had his self-preference

(19:20-23). He begged the rescuing angels to allow him to go to a little city named Zoar. God was merciful, and the angels granted Lot his request. If you trace the history of many dissenting groups, you will see that it is the same. At first, they were in a big city, and God gave them no blessing. Then, after God intervened, they moved to a Zoar, a little city far away from God's testimony. They firstly left God's testimony and drifted into a God-condemned situation, and then, still having their own choice, went to a little place.

ISOLATED FARTHER OFF FROM GOD'S WITNESS AND TESTIMONY   ◆
Eventually Lot went to dwell in a cave (19:30). Like Lot, some free groups, after leaving a large city and going to a small one, have gone to live in a cave. They have isolated themselves from the rest of God's people, refusing to have fellowship with them. They may say, "Why do you say that you are the church and that we are not?" If they are the church, they should not dwell in a cave but come out to fellowship with God's people. But they only care for their little group in that cave. What they have is the cave life, not the church life.

THE FATHER—THE LEADER

BEING DRUNK WITH WORLDLY WINE BY THE DESIRE OF SECURING SEED   ◆   Now we come to the father, the leader. In the cave, Lot became drunk with wine (19:32-35). As I have pointed out previously, it was very strange that these escapees had wine with them in the cave. They were so addicted to wine that they must have brought it with them when they fled Sodom. Wine was the drug that befuddled them. When they were in the cave, Lot's daughters did not have proper fellowship with him, saying, "Father, our mother has become a pillar of salt, and we don't have husbands. How can we have seed? We must do something about it. May we all pray together?" If they had done this, there would have been no incest. But they did not fellowship in the spirit, nor pray to the Lord. The older daughter, the one who was more experienced with the drugs of Sodom and who had been more befuddled by them, proposed to the other that they make their father drunk with wine and lie with him that they might have seed by him. If you examine today's situation, you will find that the leader of nearly every free group has been drugged and befuddled with some wine. A proper leader must be sober. Lot should have said to the daughter who came to him with wine, "What are you doing? Throw that away." But Lot was not a sober person; he drank, and he even drank without self-control. He became drunk to such an extent that his daughters laid with him and he had no awareness of it. Most of the leaders of the free groups, being drunk with some wine, say, do, and decide things in a befuddled way. Because of the befuddled condition of so many leaders, most of the members of their groups have been drugged.

SLUMBERING AND SLEEPING   ✦   After Lot became drunk, he slumbered and slept. The same condition prevails among the free groups today. Concerning the testimony of God, the leaders are slumbering and sleeping. They may be very active in the things which they are pursuing, but they are asleep as far as God's testimony is concerned.

BEING BEFUDDLED   ✦   Furthermore, Lot was befuddled, having lost the sense of life (19:33b, 35b). When the first daughter came in to lie with him, "he perceived not when she lay down, nor when she arose." The same occurred with the second daughter the next night. What sin can surpass this? He even had no sense about his daughters' lying with him! The leaders of many free groups today have also lost the sense of life. They are not aware of the violation of some of the governing principles ordained by God.

THE MOTHER—THE HELPER IN LIFE

We have seen that the mother, who, as the wife, should have been the helper in life, became a pillar of salt because of her worldliness (19:26). When Lot's family came into the cave, there was no function of life, for there was no function of the proper wife. As a result, they turned to incest, using such a sinful thing to replace the lost function of life. This is also the situation among many so-called Christian groups. They have lost the function of the Body of Christ, the proper function of life, and use worldly methods to fill the gap. Like Lot's group, they cannot produce the proper "Isaac" for the fulfilling of God's purpose. Because they use incest to secure seed, they produce "Moabites" and "Ammonites."

THE DAUGHTERS—THE MEMBERS

We have seen that the leader was drugged and befuddled and that the function of life was lost. But the daughters, the members of this free group, still wanted to bear fruit and have the increase. Although they had neither the proper leadership nor the function of life, they had an evil way of acquiring the seed. The same is true among many free groups today. In order to bear fruit, we should live by Christ, live out Christ, pray, and help people to receive the living word of God so that they might be reborn. This is the way to bring forth the proper fruit to be the "Isaac" for the fulfilling of God's purpose. But look at today's situation: some groups use rock music, dancing, drama, movies, and games to satisfy their desire of securing the increase. In the eyes of God, this is spiritual incest. The free groups adopt these methods because the wife, being worldly, has lost her function. In the churches we need the function of life to produce seed. Once people have lost the proper wife with the function in life, they use ugly and worldly means for securing the increase. This is the way of "incest" which brings forth "Moabites" and "Ammonites."

HAVING LOST THE SENSE OF MORALITY   ✦   Lot's daughters had lost their sense of morality, having been drugged with the wicked current of the evil world. If they had had any sense of morality, they never would have considered lying with their father. The first daughter laid with her father without any sense of shame and encouraged her sister to do the same. They talked peacefully with one another about this without any feeling of guilt. When they were all in Sodom, Lot even proposed sacrificing his daughters to satisfy the Sodomites who were indulging in their sodomitical lust. How could a man with a proper sense of spiritual morality have proposed such a thing? He should have said, "Let them kill me and my guests, but I will never do this to my virgin daughters." Where was Lot's sense of morality? Lot had been drugged. The result was that his daughters had no sense of morality and that their humanity was degraded to the lowest level. Some free groups today have also been drugged with the wicked current of the evil world and only care for success, not for the means. They need the de-drugging of God's sobering word.

DESIRING TO HAVE THE SEED REGARDLESS OF THE MEANS   ✦   Lot's drugged daughters were desirous of having seed regardless of the means (19:31-35). They cared only for the goal, not for the way.

Many Christian groups are like this. They say, "What is wrong with preaching the gospel in this way as long as we bring people to Christ? We have won a great many people. How many souls have you won?" They care for soul-winning, but they do not care for the proper way of doing it.

HAVING COMMITTED INCEST   ✦   Lot's daughters committed incest, breaking the governing principle ordained by God (19:36). Here we need to refer to Matthew 7:21-23. The Lord said that when He comes back, some so-called Christian workers will say, "Lord, Lord, did we not prophesy in Your name, and in Your name cast out demons, and in Your name do many works of power?" (Matt. 7:22). If they had not done these things, they would be unable to talk like this. The Lord will not deny that they did such works. But in Matthew 7:23 the Lord said that He will "declare to them, I never knew you; depart from Me, workers of lawlessness." For the Lord to say, "I never knew you" means "I never approved of you because you are a worker of lawlessness." The runners in a race must stay in their lane. However fast they run, they are not permitted to run lawlessly outside the boundaries of their lane. Likewise, we need a governing principle for our spiritual activity. It is not a matter of prophesying, casting out demons, or working miracles. It is a matter of the Father's will (Matt. 7:21). Our spiritual activities must be the doing of the Father's will. Our preaching, loving one another, and all we do must be the Father's will. If we lack the assurance deep in our spirit that what we are doing is the Father's will, we should not do it. If we do things without this assurance, we shall break the governing principle and commit spiritual incest. This is lawlessness in the eyes of God. The Lord will never approve of such lawless workers.

THE SEED BY INCEST

The daughters of Lot produced seed by incest. The names of their two sons are very meaningful. The first, Moab, means "from father" (19:37). When the first sister named her boy "from father," she was saying, "I have a child from my father." She even gave her child a name to remind her of this. The second daughter gave birth to a boy named Ben-ammi, which means "son of my kin" (19:38). As far as these daughters were concerned, as long as they had seed for their race, everything was all right. If they had had no seed, their free group would have been terminated. Today's situation is absolutely the same. Many free groups only care for the continuation of their kin, that is, of their group. They do not care for God's will nor for the proper way, but bring forth seed by incestuous activities.

The seed produced by incest became a great damage to the people of God through fornication (Num. 25:1-5). As God's people were wandering in the wilderness, the Moabites came in. Firstly, they hired the Gentile prophet Balaam to curse God's people (Num. 22:2-7), but God turned that curse into blessing (Num. 23:11; 24:10). Secondly, Balaam counseled the Moabites to seduce the children of Israel to worship idols and commit fornication (Num. 31:16). Idolatry always brings in fornication, for these two evil "sisters" go together. In Christianity today there are the teachings of Balaam mentioned in Revelation 2:14. The Lord told the church in Pergamos, a degraded, worldly church, that some among them held the teachings of Balaam, the teachings which damaged God's people through idolatry and fornication.

God severely judged the Israelites for their idolatry and fornication with the Moabites, telling Moses to "take all the heads of the people, and hang them up before the Lord against the sun, that the fierce anger of the Lord may be turned away from Israel" (Num. 25:4). Furthermore, God rejected the Moabites and the Ammonites with a holy and divine hatred, commanding the Israelites not to "seek their peace nor their prosperity all thy days forever" and declaring that no "Ammonite or Moabite shall enter into the congregation of the Lord; even to their tenth generation shall they not enter into the congregation of the Lord for ever" (Deut. 23:3-6). Everything relating to the Moabites and Ammonites was under God's condemnation, and the children of Israel were forbidden to seek their peace or prosperity.

In Genesis 16 through 21, there are three kinds of births: the birth of Ishmael, the birth of Moab and Ben-ammi, and the birth of Isaac. The birth of Ishmael was by fleshly effort, and the birth of Moab and Ben-ammi was by incest. But the birth of Isaac was by the grace of God. Ishmael, brought forth by fleshly effort, was rejected by God. Moab and Ben-ammi, brought forth by incest, were a shame in history. Only Isaac, brought forth by God's grace, was used to fulfill the purpose of God. We all must test ourselves to see what kind of seed we are bringing forth—Ishmael, Moab, or Isaac. We may have some increase, some fruit, but are they Ishmaelites, Moabites, or Isaacs?

THE FAR-REACHING AND UNSEARCHABLE MERCY OF GOD

Although the Moabites were rejected to the tenth generation, in the case of Ruth we see the far-reaching and unsearchable mercy of God (Ruth 1:2, 4-5, 8, 15-19, 22; 4:13, 17). Elimelech, the husband of Naomi, brought his family from Judah to seek the peace and prosperity of the Moabites. After Elimelech died, his two sons "took them wives of the women of Moab" (Ruth 1:4). When the two sons died, Naomi was left in Moab with her two daughters-in-law. As Naomi was returning to Judah, Ruth, refusing to depart from her, said, "Entreat me not to leave thee, or to return from following after thee: for whither thou goest, I will go; and where thou lodgest, I will lodge: thy people shall be my people, and thy God my God" (Ruth 1:16). Through seeking God absolutely, Ruth, a widow Moabitess, entered into the holy congregation of God's people, married Boaz, and became the great grandmother of King David. Eventually, she not only entered into the holy congregation of God's people, but also entered into the genealogy of Christ, becoming an ancestress of Christ and having a part in His incarnation (Matt. 1:1, 5). This is the far-reaching and unsearchable mercy of God. God's mercy is waiting for us to seek Him and His people. Do not stay in Moab—come to Judah. God's congregation and Christ's incarnation are with His people in Judah. The right standing means a great deal. You must change your standing and your ground. If you would be in the holy congregation and have a part in the incarnation of Christ, you must come out of Moab and be with the people of God in Judah.

Lot, who was one of God's people, and his family left God's witness and testimony. The issue of his life was the bringing forth of Moabites and Ammonites. Ruth, a widow Moabitess who was seeking after God, came to God's people and God's testimony. The issue of her life was the bringing forth of Christ. What a wonderful mercy of God is available to His seekers! Even a descendant of Moab, a man born through incest, could participate, through redemption, in the incarnation of Christ.   ❊

19

LIVING IN FELLOWSHIP WITH GOD
THE HIDDEN WEAKNESS AND A SHAMEFUL INTERCESSION

And Abraham journeyed from thence
toward the south country.

Genesis 20:1

Beautiful in elevation,
 The joy of the whole earth,
Is Mount Zion, the sides of the north,
 The city of the great King.

Psalm 48:2

So Abraham prayed unto God: and God healed Abimelech,
and his wife, and his maidservants; and
they bare children.

Genesis 20:17

The Bible is an honest book. After Genesis 18 and 19, in which we see Abraham's high attainment in his experience of God, there is a record of his weakness in Genesis 20. Can you believe that after having such intimate fellowship with God and after making such a glorious intercession,

Abraham could have the experience recorded in chapter twenty? It is difficult to believe and understand how Abraham could have shown such weakness. Once again we see that the Bible is not man-made. If it were of human manufacture, the writer would not have included this record of Abraham's weakness and shortcomings. But the Bible is honest and it has Genesis 20 as part of the divine record.

When I was young, I appreciated chapters eighteen, twenty-one, twenty-two, and twenty-four, but I had no interest in chapter twenty. In this chapter two main things are recorded: the hidden weakness and a shameful intercession. Abraham, a man of God, had a weakness hidden deep within him. While in chapter eighteen he made a glorious intercession, in chapter twenty we find the record of a shameful one.

THE HIDDEN WEAKNESS

JOURNEYING TOWARD THE SOUTH   ✦   Let us first consider Abraham's hidden weakness (20:1-16). In verse 1 we are told that "Abraham journeyed from thence toward the south country." Abraham's journeying toward the south meant that he had left the standing of fellowship at the oaks of Mamre in Hebron. He should have remained in Hebron because there he had intimate fellowship with God. Nothing is better than this. It was not too long after he had intimate fellowship with God that he left Hebron and journeyed southward. Between the time the Lord spoke to Abraham regarding the birth of Isaac in 17:21 and 18:14 and the time of Isaac's birth in chapter twenty-one, there could not have been more than a year. Why did Abraham suddenly leave Hebron and journey toward the south during that year? In figure, south signifies easiness and north hardships. The south is warm and the north is cold, but God dwells in the north (Psa. 48:2; 75:6-7; Ezek. 1:4). In the north we have hardships with God's presence. In the south we have easiness, but without God's presence. There is no hint in Genesis 20 that God told Abraham to journey southward. In making this journey, Abraham acted on his own.

Abraham might have wanted to have a change and take a vacation. Although you may be enjoying the church life in Anaheim, one day you may feel that you need a change and desire to journey southward to Mexico City. The church life is marvelous and we all enjoy it very much. But some may become a little bored and want to take a trip to Las Vegas. If you go to Las Vegas and meet someone there who asks about what you do at home, you will find it difficult to give him an honest answer. On two occasions, when Abraham was in such a situation, he was not truthful (cf. 12:9-12). In chapter twelve Abraham journeyed southward because there was a famine in the land. That famine gave him an excuse for going southward to Egypt. But in this chapter Abraham had no excuse. He and his wife might have been bored and wanted a vacation. If they had remained by the oaks of Mamre in Hebron, Abraham would have had no need to lie. His lying was due to his wrong position. We see by this that the proper standing means a great deal. I do not believe that any brother can pray-read or give a living testimony in a casino in Las Vegas. He would not have the standing there to do such a thing. In order to do anything for God, we must have the proper standing. When Abraham left the standing of intimate fellowship with God and journeyed southward, he lost God's presence. The Bible does not say that in the south country God appeared to Abraham, nor that Abraham erected an altar and called on the name of the Lord. He had altogether lost the proper standing on which he could have fellowship with God. Young people, you must see that you need to stay in the right position. If you stay in the church, you will be kept and preserved. But if you journey southward, you will forsake the proper standing and lose God's presence. Spontaneously, your old man will return.

Before chapter twenty Abraham was circumcised. In chapter twenty, he should have been a circumcised person, not a natural person, for he had truly been dealt with by God. Some Christians claim that once they have experienced a certain blessing, they can no longer be in the flesh. But look at the example of Abraham. Although he had been circumcised both physically and spiritually, when he left the proper standing of fellowship with God, he was in the flesh again. After having such a high attainment in his experience with God, Abraham, the father of faith, acted the same as he did in Genesis 12, more than twenty years before. By this we see that as long as we are still in the old creation we are capable of doing anything in the flesh. If we do not remain in fellowship with God, we can do the same things that the worldly people do. Do not say that because you have been regenerated, have experienced the baptism of the Spirit, or have had a second blessing, you can no longer be in the flesh. However many are the blessings that you have received from God, if you do not remain in fellowship with Him, you will be in the flesh. Your experience proves that this is true.

We should never have any confidence in our self. The self is absolutely untrustworthy. We must put our trust in the presence of the Lord, telling Him, "Lord, if You take Your presence away from me, I am just a dog. But I praise You that in Your presence I'm a saint, one of the people of God." How much God's presence means to us! When Abraham was bringing God on His way in chapter eighteen, he was a wonderful saint, a man who could stand before God and talk face to face with Him as with an intimate friend. But in chapter twenty this wonderful person became very mean. After he had left the standing of fellowship with God, he could lie at the sacrifice of his wife. It seems unbelievable, but he did it. If we consider our past experience, we shall find that at least a few times we have done the same kind of thing. This shows us the importance of remaining in the presence of God. Our protection is not our self; it is His presence.

REPEATING THE OLD FAILURE   ✦   After Abraham had left God's presence and had journeyed toward the south, he repeated an old failure—lying by sacrificing his wife (20:2; cf. 12:11-13). To lie is one thing, and to sacrifice our wife is another. Although many brothers may lie, perhaps none of them would sacrifice his wife. But Abraham did it. I admire Sarah for being such a good wife. She did not complain but was agreeable with her husband's lie.

THE HIDDEN WEAKNESS EXPOSED   ✦   In 20:8-13 we see Abraham's hidden weakness exposed. Abraham did not lie accidentally; it was planned from the day he first began to follow the way of God. Abraham told Abimelech, "It came to pass, when God caused me to wander from my father's house, that I said unto her, This is thy kindness which thou shalt shew unto me; at every place whither we shall come, say of me, He is my brother" (v. 13). This hidden weakness was kept within Abraham even after he had been circumcised. In principle, most of us are the same today. On the one hand, we are following the Lord in the church; on the other hand, we have a reserve. In case a certain thing happens, we have a reserve plan to deal with it. Do you mean to be absolute with the Lord? If you do, ask Him whether you still hold on to some hidden reserve. Although you may not believe that you have a reserve, when you take a vacation from the church life, it will be exposed. Many young sisters who are following the Lord in the church have a reserve deep within them. They say to themselves, "Maybe some day a certain thing will happen. If it does, I know just what I will do about it." This is the reserve planned from the time they first began to follow the Lord. Yes, we are living by faith in the church life. But what do we do when our faith fails? We use our reserve. Perhaps after a short while your weakness will be exposed. This will prove that in spite of your claim to be absolute, you are still not one hundred percent absolute.

I believe that the purpose of this record in chapter twenty is to show us that sooner or later our hidden reserve will be exposed. The Bible is different from any worldly book, for it is a genuine and honest record of a God-seeking people. However much we seek after God, we still have a reserve. I fear and tremble that perhaps there is still deep within me a hidden reserve that one day will be exposed.

PRESERVED BY GOD'S SOVEREIGN CARE   ✦   In the Bible, Abraham, in figure, stands for faith and Sarah stands for grace. In other words, in the presence of God, a man always stands for faith and the wife always stands for God's grace. Abraham was the father of faith, and his life was a life of faith. Since Sarah is the figure of God's grace, for Isaac to be born of her meant that he was born of grace. Ishmael, on the contrary, was born of Hagar, of the law, of bondage. In figure, whenever faith becomes a failure, grace is damaged. This means that when faith fails on our side, grace suffers on the Lord's side. Each time Abraham failed, Sarah suffered, and when Sarah suffered, grace suffered.

Furthermore, grace and testimony go together. Whenever we have grace, we have the testimony. When Abraham lied, he did not have the enjoyment of grace. Therefore, he lost his testimony. Whenever faith fails, grace suffers, and the testimony of grace is lost.

God came in to rescue Sarah and to restore her. In figure, this means that God came in to take care of His grace and His testimony. God knows how to sovereignly protect His grace and preserve His testimony. We do not know how many times we have been in danger of damaging grace and losing the testimony because we have left the proper standing. But at a certain juncture, God came in to deal with the circumstances so that the testimony of His grace might be preserved. If this had been clear to Abraham, he would not have lied;

he would have believed that God would care for His grace and His testimony.

Although Abraham's faith failed, God still preserved him by His sovereign care (vv. 3-7, 14-16). Because Abraham's experience had become abnormal, God did not appear to him. In chapters eighteen and nineteen, God appeared to Abraham but not to Lot. Here in chapter twenty, He did not appear to Abraham; He appeared to Abimelech in a dream (v. 3). In a sense, Abraham's standing in chapter twenty was nearly the same as Lot's in chapter nineteen. Therefore, God appeared to Abimelech, a Gentile king, telling him that the one who had lied to him was His prophet. Abimelech was surprised to hear that one of God's prophets had lied to him at the sacrifice of his wife. In this chapter, we see God's wisdom, sovereignty, fairness, and care. Leaving Abraham, the one who had lied, God spoke to Abimelech, the one who had been cheated, saying, "Behold, thou art but a dead man, for the woman which thou hast taken; for she is a man's wife" (v. 3). Abimelech was shocked. Then God told him that he must restore Abraham's wife and that Abraham would pray for him (v. 7). God did not inspire Abraham to pray for Abimelech; rather, He indicated to Abimelech that Abraham was a prophet and had the position to pray for the king and his family. In doing this, God did not rebuke Abraham.

Although Abraham was outside God's presence, God still preserved His testimony and gave Abraham many riches (vv. 14-16). When Abraham defeated Chedorlaomer and the other kings and rescued Lot, he refused to accept anything from the king of Sodom because he had the Most High God (14:21-24). However, when Abimelech gave Abraham sheep, oxen, servants, and silver, Abraham did not dare to say, "I don't need your help. I have the Most High God." He did not have the position to say this, and his mouth was shut. I do not believe that Abraham thanked Abimelech for his gifts or was happy to receive them. When he received all those gifts from Abimelech in front of Sarah, he must have been ashamed. God wisely and sovereignly restored Sarah, taking care of His grace and His testimony, and at the same time He disciplined Abraham.

A SHAMEFUL INTERCESSION

After receiving the gifts from Abimelech, Abraham prayed for him (vv. 17-18). Abimelech needed Abraham's intercession because the Lord had closed up all the wombs of the house of Abimelech. Do you think that you would be able to pray in such a shameful situation? Abimelech might have said to Abraham, "Why did you, a prophet of God, lie to me? Look at what has happened! Now that everything has been settled and I have returned your wife, I want you to pray for me." Many times, after we have failed the Lord, we are unable to pray for days, even though no one knows about our failure. How much more difficult it was for Abraham to pray in the presence of Abimelech! Nevertheless, Abraham prayed, and "God healed Abimelech, and his wife, and his maidservants; and they bare children" (v. 17).

In order to intercede for Abimelech, Abraham had to overcome two things: his memory of his failure before Abimelech and his consideration of his wife's barrenness. He had to forget his failure before Abimelech and not consider his wife's barrenness. If I had been Abraham, I would have said, "I'm sorry, Abimelech, but I have failed the Lord and now I don't have the faith to pray for you." We all must learn that interceding for others does not depend upon our success; it depends upon the need. Once a need has been designated by God, we must intercede for it. Abraham might have said to the Lord, "I have failed. I lied to Abimelech and he has rebuked me. How can I intercede for him?" When we intercede for others, we must forget about ourselves, our surroundings, and our circumstances and intercede as if there were no one on earth except us and God. In spite of our failures, we must exercise our spirit and pray with boldness.

Although God was forced to leave Abraham and go to Abimelech, Abraham was higher than Abimelech. Although he had failed, Abimelech was far below him. The Bible says that the greater always blesses the lesser (Heb. 7:7). Because Abraham was higher than Abimelech, he could intercede for him.

Furthermore, we should not think that because God has not answered our prayers for our own needs we cannot pray for others. If I had been Abraham, I might have said, "Abimelech, you ask me to pray for you. I have been praying for my wife for years without receiving an answer. Because of this, I'm not sure that God will answer my prayer for you and I don't have the boldness to pray." We need to forget about our unanswered prayers and pray for others. If we would not pray for others, God will probably not answer our prayers for our own needs. Do not say that since your own need has not been met, you cannot pray for others. When Abraham forgot his need and interceded for Abimelech and his house, not only were their needs met but also his. If you forget your need and pray for the needs of others, God will not only answer your prayer for them but also your prayer for yourself. He will take care of your needs.

Abraham's intercession for Abimelech was a shameful one. In such a shameful situation it is difficult for anyone to intercede. The Bible does not give us a full record of Abraham's intercession for Abimelech like it does of his intercession for Lot. Perhaps Abraham was not bold or strong in spirit. Nevertheless, he interceded for Abimelech and his prayer was answered. By this we see that although we may not be bold in our spirit, as long as we intercede for others according to God's designation, our intercession will be answered. I can testify to this from my experience. A number of times I was in difficulty and prayed about it. But I received no answer. Suddenly people came to me who had the same difficulty and asked me to pray for them. After I prayed for them, God not only answered my prayer for their need but also my prayer for my own situation.

We all must learn not to pray according to our victory. It is easy to pray after we have been victorious, but not after we have failed. Although I do not encourage anyone to fail, I do say that we should not be bothered by our failures. God does not count on our failures; He counts on what we are. In the presence of God, we are the new man. This is what we are, and we must pray according to it. Because we are still in this old creation, we may fall back and fail. But we can forget that failure in the old creation and stand upon our position in the new creation. When Abraham stood on his position of being God's prophet, he could pray for Abimelech.

Genesis 20 is a very dear chapter, and we need to spend time to consider all its main points: the hidden weakness of God's seeking one; the way he was rebuked by Abimelech and was temporarily set aside by God; his intercession for Abimelech and his family; and the way God answered his prayer. If you dwell on this chapter for a few hours, your spirit will be richly nourished. As I consider this chapter today, I find it more needful than chapter eighteen. Although chapter eighteen is sweet, chapter twenty is precious, teaching us some precious lessons.

It teaches us that interceding for others does not depend upon our condition. It depends upon our standing. It depends upon who we are. We are the prophet of God, the new creation, the members of the Body of Christ. Being in the church life as a member of the Body of Christ gives us the standing to intercede for others. Forget about your environment and your failures. If you hold on to your feelings, your mouth will be shut, Satan will be victorious over you, and you will be deadened for days. This is very serious. We must forget our failures and our needs and take the proper standing to intercede for others according to God's designation and believe in God for others.

We also must learn to know ourselves. Do not think that if you have attainments as high as those recorded in Genesis 18 and 19, you will have no problems. We cannot afford to take a vacation from our fellowship with God. Do not have any confidence in your old self. Although your old self has been dealt with by God, it is still untrustworthy, even if it has been fully circumcised. Whether we are aware of it or not, deep within us there is a certain reservation in following the Lord. One day this reservation, this reserve of our natural weakness, will be exposed. Do not be surprised when it happens. Be prepared to take grace, forget your failures and your needs, and intercede for others. Stand on your position as a member of the Body of Christ, as a part of the new man, and as a saint in the Lord's recovery and pray, even if you pray with a sense of shame. Your intercession may be shameful and there may be no glory in it, but God will still answer it. Along with His answer to your shameful intercession, He will also answer your previously unanswered prayers for your own needs. How wonderful this is!

When, as God's prophet, Abraham lied to others, they became deadened. But when he forgot his failure before them and interceded for them, they received life and he himself was revived. Likewise, if we forget our failures and intercede for the needs of those before whom we have failed, we shall not only minister life to them but also to ourselves. May we all learn the lessons contained in this chapter.

20

LIVING IN FELLOWSHIP
WITH GOD
THE BIRTH AND GROWTH
OF ISAAC

And Abraham called the name of his son that was born unto him,
whom Sarah bare to him, Isaac....
And Sarah saw the son of Hagar the Egyptian,
which she had borne unto Abraham, mocking.
Genesis 21:3, 9

And Abraham planted a grove in Beer-sheba, and called there
on the name of the Lord, the everlasting God.
Genesis 21:33

But just as at that time he who was born according to the flesh
persecuted him who was born according to the Spirit, so also it is now.
But what does the Scripture say?
"Cast out the maidservant and her son, for the son of the maidservant
shall by no means inherit with the son of the free woman."
Galatians 4:29-30

In the foregoing messages we have covered nearly ten chapters in
Genesis regarding Abraham's experience with God. In those chapters
we saw that Abraham, God's called one, had come to many stations

and had passed through many stages. Now in Genesis 21 Abraham comes to a wonderful and marvelous station. Here Isaac is born.

The goal of God's calling of Abraham was to bring forth a seed. This matter of the seed was first mentioned in 12:7 and is referred to many times in the following chapters. In nearly every chapter God touched Abraham concerning the seed. Why was it so difficult for Abraham to have a seed? He was called, at the latest, at the age of seventy-five, but twenty-five years later he still did not have the seed, although God had called him for that very purpose. Because he had difficulty producing the seed, Abraham first relied upon Eliezer, whom God rejected. Then, hearkening to his wife's proposal, Abraham produced Ishmael by Hagar. However, God also rejected Ishmael, saying that He did not want a seed out of an Egyptian maid but out of Sarah. God seemed to say to Abraham, "Yes, you have produced a seed, but it is out of the wrong source. I will never approve that source. I have nothing to do with it. You may love Ishmael and care for him, but I do not." After the birth of Ishmael, God came in to tell Abraham that he had to be circumcised. At that time, God also strengthened and confirmed His promise to Abraham. After his circumcision, Abraham had intimate fellowship with God, enjoying the highest experience with God of anyone in history up to that time.

When, at the time of chapter twenty, the seed still had not come, even such a giant of faith as Abraham could not stand the test. As we saw in the last message, he was apparently bored in his experience of God and took a vacation. Abraham might have said to God, "God, You have promised again and again to give me a seed. You have dealt with me about this and that until I have nothing left. You have said no to everything I have done. Now I am bored and would like a change. I want to take a vacation." Abraham journeyed southward, that is, downward. Like everyone who takes a vacation after working hard, Abraham was seeking easiness. Because of this, he repeated an old failure. But God preserved him, creating a situation in which, in spite of his failure, circumstances, and environment, he had to intercede for Abimelech and his house. Not one thing was an encouragement to Abraham in this matter. Yet, being the giant of faith, he interceded, not with boldness or the release of the spirit, but in a shameful way. Nevertheless, his shameful intercession was answered. Not only did Abimelech's wife and maidservants bear children, but Sarah also gave birth to Isaac. One prayer of intercession received two answers.

When we come to Genesis 21 we see that Abraham has returned from his vacation and is back in business again. In chapter twenty he tried to take a vacation and stay away from his divine job, but he did not succeed and God forced him to make an intercession. That intercession brought him back from vacation to his divine employment. Now, in chapter twenty-one, Abraham is back in his "office."

Genesis 21 has two sections. The first section, verses 1 through 13, is thoroughly covered by the Apostle Paul in Galatians 4:22-31, where he allegorizes this portion of Genesis. By means of Paul's allegorization, seeking Christians throughout the centuries have been able to learn the true significance of the first part of Genesis 21. I wish that Paul had allegorized the remainder of that chapter, but he kept silent about it. Most Christians only consider 21:14-34 as a story of Ishmael's dwelling in the wilderness and becoming an archer and of Abraham's dealing with Abimelech over the well at Beer-sheba, not thinking that this portion of the Word has much spiritual significance. But if the first section of Genesis 21 has a spiritual significance, then the second section must also have a spiritual significance. In this message we need to cover the significance of both sections.

ISAAC BORN—CHRIST BROUGHT FORTH THROUGH US

In the first section we see the birth of Isaac (vv. 1-7). Isaac, whose name means "laughter" or "he will laugh" (vv. 3, 6), was born according to God's promise (v. 1) at the appointed time, the time of life (v. 2; 17:21; 18:10, 14). As far as Abraham and Sarah were concerned, the birth of Isaac was a great matter. What is the spiritual significance of Isaac's birth? This is easy to see from Paul's allegory in Galatians 4. As Abraham was called by God, so we are God's called ones today. In God's calling us there is a goal, the same goal as there was with His calling Abraham—to bring forth the seed. God has called us to bring forth Christ. If you consider the experience of Abraham as recorded in chapters eleven through twenty and compare it with your own, you may be surprised to see that his experience is the same as yours and that his life is your biography. Our biography was written long before we were born. Whatever our age or generation may be, we all have the same biography. As Abraham was called to bring forth Isaac, so we have been called to bring forth Christ. We have not been called to produce good behavior. God's goal is that we bring forth Christ.

All the difficulties Abraham encountered in bringing forth Isaac were on his side, not on Isaac's. In like manner, it is easy for Christ to come through and out of us, but we have many problems. In fact, we ourselves are the problem. We simply are not the right persons to bring forth Christ. Although we can produce many things and have done so ever since we were saved, it is very difficult for us to bring forth Christ. I was a Christian for many years and still did not know how to bring forth Christ. I did not even know what it meant to bring Him forth. I am concerned that so many of us do not have the thought of bringing forth Christ. Some might even ask, "Hasn't Christ been brought forth already? Why must we bring Him forth again?" Yes, Christ has been brought forth, but every saved person must still bring Him forth.

In order to bring Christ forth, we must be circumcised. Our natural life and strength and our self must be terminated. This termination opens the way for the very El-Shaddai, the all-sufficient One, to come into our being as the all-sufficient grace to bring forth Christ. Abraham experienced this. In Genesis 21, Abraham reached his goal and Isaac was born, having been brought forth through Abraham. Today Christ, the real Isaac, needs us to bring Him forth. Both the Christian life and the church life are simply the bringing forth of Christ. We must bring Christ forth in our meetings, daily life, home life, and on our jobs.

Isaac's birth was not by Abraham's natural strength nor according to Abraham's time. It was by God's work of grace and it was according to God's time, the time of life appointed by God. Abraham was tested by this. His natural strength went ahead of God, trying to bring forth the seed God had promised. According to his natural strength, he had a time of expectation. But all that his natural strength produced was rejected by God. Before Abraham's natural strength was dealt with and terminated, God would not and could not do anything to bring forth through him the very seed He desired to have for the fulfillment of His purpose. Hence, God had to wait. While God was waiting, Abraham was tested. It is the same with us in the matter of bringing forth Christ. Our natural strength always causes God to wait. God's way and His timing are always a hard test to our natural life. God's grace will never do anything to help our natural life to bring forth Christ. He must wait until our natural life has been dealt with and terminated. Then, according to His timing, He will come in as the strength of grace to bring forth through us what He desires to have. If we would fulfill the divine purpose of God's calling, we all must learn this basic lesson. Never try to fulfill God's purpose by your natural strength and according to the time of your expectation. God has His way and His time. Only by His way and at His time can we bring forth Christ for the fulfilling of His purpose.

ISAAC GROWN UP—CHRIST FORMED IN US

After the birth, there is the need of growth. Verse 8 says that "the child grew, and was weaned: and Abraham made a great feast the same day that Isaac was weaned." It is not sufficient simply to bring Christ forth. The very Christ whom we have brought forth must grow. In the past few years, many of us have brought forth Christ, but I wonder whether this Christ has grown up. Has there been the time of weaning? Isaac grew up and was weaned away from his mother's nourishment, meaning that he was no longer a young child but had become a young boy. On the day of his weaning, Abraham made a great feast. We can understand the significance of this according to our experience. When in the church life we see that Christ has grown up in certain brothers and sisters, we all will be happy and have a great feast, a great enjoyment.

It is not easy to have either the birth of Isaac or his growth. Likewise, it is not easy to have Christ brought forth, nor to have Him grown up. In the church life we need to have both the bringing forth and the growth of Christ. I thank God that Christ has been brought forth among us, but I hesitate to say that we have had much of the growth of Christ. It is wonderful to see that Christ has been brought forth in a particular young brother, but we are still waiting to see in him the growth of Christ. We want to see that the Christ in him has been weaned and is no longer a baby. Although the Christ in that brother may not yet be a full-grown man, we want to see Him as a strong boy. Christ must be formed not only in us but also among us (Gal. 4:19). In both our daily life and the church life we need the expression of a formed Christ. Then we may have a great feast for the enjoyment of God's grace.

ISHMAEL'S MOCKING OF ISAAC

According to Genesis 21, it was not the birth of Isaac that stirred up trouble; it was his growth. When Isaac was born, Hagar and her son Ishmael were not bothered very much. But after Isaac had grown up, Ishmael began to mock him (v. 9). In the biblical sense, this means that Ishmael was persecuting Isaac. God even counted Ishmael's persecution of Isaac as the beginning of the four-hundred-year persecution of His people (15:13; Acts 7:6). Ishmael's mocking was a serious thing because Isaac was God's ordained seed and Ishmael was the counterfeit. The counterfeit always hates the ordained. We, the ordained seed, are hated by the counterfeit. As Paul says in Galatians 4:29, "But as then he that was born according to flesh persecuted him that was born according to Spirit, so also it is now." The growth of Isaac stirred up that persecution.

HAGAR AND ISHMAEL CAST OUT

Sarah, the one who represented grace, would not tolerate Ishmael's mocking of Isaac and said, "Cast out this bondwoman and her son: for the son of this bondwoman shall not be heir with my son, even with Isaac" (v. 10). When I read this verse as a youth, I did not agree with Sarah, thinking that she was jealous and unfair. It was she who proposed to Abraham that he have a son by Hagar and now she tells him to cast Hagar and Ishmael out. According to my youthful understanding, I would have cast Sarah out. But one day, as I was thinking in this way, God rebuked me. That day I was arguing in favor of Hagar and Ishmael and sympathizing with Abraham, for "the thing was very grievous in Abraham's sight because of his son" (v. 11). Although I thought that Abraham should have answered Sarah, telling her that she was cruel, he said nothing to her. Rather, God came in and told Abraham, "Let it not be grievous in thy sight because of the lad, and because of thy bondwoman; in all that Sarah hath said unto thee, hearken unto her voice; for in Isaac shall thy seed be called" (v. 12). The heavenly Judge made the final decision, telling him to do what Sarah requested. Only Isaac, not Ishmael, was to be counted as the seed. Although Abraham had failed God in chapter twenty, he was quick to obey Him in chapter twenty-one. Verse 14 says that Abraham rose up early in the morning and sent Hagar and Ishmael on their way.

We need to see the spiritual significance of the casting out of Hagar and Ishmael. Like all Christians, you have been trying to do good since the day you were saved. But God has dealt with you, and many times you have been disciplined and cut. If you are a married brother, God has undoubtedly used your wife as the knife to cut your natural life. Every wife is such a sharp knife in the divine hand. Many Christian husbands can only be thoroughly dealt with and disciplined by the cutting of the wife-knife. No husband can escape it. I am happy to see that in the local churches God has used the wife-knives to deal with the natural life of the brothers. In this way, we brothers learn the lesson of hating our natural life and all the good things we can produce out of ourselves.

Although we may hate our natural life and all that it produces, we do not hate it absolutely. Deep within, we still appreciate it and say, "This Ishmael whom I have produced is quite good. He was born of me." Such a concept always delays Isaac's birth. It was only after Abraham had undergone dealing after dealing and failure after failure that Isaac finally came forth.

Christ has been born in our Christian life, but we still keep our Ishmael, hesitating to give up our good behavior. Many of us still boast in our natural goodness, saying, "I am not as proud as some of the brothers and sisters are. I thank God that I was born humble." The sisters might criticize others, saying, "I would never gossip the way Sister So-and-so does. I was not born that way." Even some elders and so-called ministers of the Word cannot keep from boasting of their natural attributes. Perhaps they say to themselves, "Brother So-and-so is so quick to lose his temper. But I thank God that my natural birth is much better than his." Although you may not utter this, it is nevertheless hidden deep within you.

When the Christ who has been born in our Christian life has begun to grow up, our natural goodness will mock Him. Then the grace within us will say, "Cast out the law! Cast out the bondwoman and what you have produced with her by your fleshly effort." Will you do this? You may do it apparently, but secretly you still hold on to Hagar and Ishmael, to the law and to your natural attributes and goodness. Not many Christians today have the boldness to say as Sarah did, "Cast out this bondwoman and her son." Not many would say, "Cast out the law, the effort of the flesh, and all the success of my effort." Rather, we cling to our success and hold on to our natural goodness.

But sooner or later God will force us to abandon the law, our self-effort, and all we have produced. The brothers and sisters will then begin to rise up and say, "From now on there will be no more Hagar and Ishmael. They must go." Like Abraham, they will send them away with only bread and water (v. 14). Sooner or later we all must do this. We must rise up one morning, give the law a skin of water, and say, "Law, go your way, and take with you the one you helped me to produce. Don't leave him with me, because I don't want him anymore. I loved Ishmael in the past, but now I give him up." The law and the result of the effort of the flesh must be fully abandoned.

TWO WELLS—TWO SOURCES OF LIVING

In the first section of this chapter, we have two seeds, two kinds of persons, and two lives. Without the second section, however, we can see neither the source nor the result of their living. In the second section we have two wells, one for Ishmael (vv. 14-21) and one for Isaac (vv. 22-34). Since the Bible does not waste any words, this record of two wells for two kinds of lives must be very meaningful and full of spiritual significance.

THE WELL FOR ISHMAEL   ✦   *In the wilderness close to Egypt*   ✦
Ishmael's well, the source of his living, was in the wilderness close to Egypt (vv. 19-21; 25:12, 18). In the Bible, the wilderness always represents a place rejected by God. God never accepts the wilderness. As long as we are in the wilderness, we are rejected by Him. The best illustration of this is the wandering in the wilderness by the children of Israel. In figure, the wilderness also signifies our soul. If we live in our soul, we are straying in the wilderness that is rejected by God. The wilderness where Ishmael's well was located was close to Egypt. He could easily drift from there into Egypt. This means that when we are in our soul, in our natural being, we are wandering in the wilderness and can easily drift into the world.

Making Ishmael an archer   ✦   Ishmael's source of living made him an archer (v. 20). The difference between an archer and a planter is that a planter grows life and an archer kills it. An archer is a wild hunter like Nimrod in 10:8-12, a killer in the wilderness. This section of the Word even uses the word "bowshot" to describe the distance between the place where Hagar was sitting and the place where she had cast her child (vv. 15-16). Thus, in this portion of the Word, it is revealed that if we stay in the wilderness of our soul and drink water out of the well for Ishmael, the source of his living, we shall be made an archer using the bow to kill life for building up our own kingdom, not a planter growing life for the building up of God's kingdom.

Leading to the joining to Egypt   ✦   Ishmael's source of living eventually joined him to Egypt, that is, to the world (v. 21). When Hagar took a wife for Ishmael, she took a wife from Egypt, from her own source. Being an Egyptian, she desired to have an Egyptian woman as her daughter-in-law. By taking a wife out of the land of Egypt for Ishmael, Hagar sealed him with the things of Egypt. We see from all this that there is a well, a source of living, which can make us a wild hunter who kills life and can join us to the world.

THE WELL FOR ISAAC   ✦   Praise the Lord that there is another well—the well for Isaac (vv. 22-34). Many verses in the Bible speak of this positive well. Psalm 36:8 says, "Thou shalt make them drink of the river of thy pleasures." The Lord likes to make us drink of His river of pleasures. In John 4:14 the Lord Jesus said, "Whoever drinks of the water that I shall give him shall by no means thirst forever; but the water that I shall give him shall become in him a spring of water welling up into eternal life." This means that God Himself will be our life. In John 7:37 and 38 the Lord Jesus also spoke of drinking: "If anyone thirst, let him come to Me and drink. He who believes in Me, as the Scripture said, out of his innermost being shall flow rivers of living water." Moreover, in 1 Corinthians 12:13, the Apostle Paul says that we have all been made to drink of one Spirit, that is, of one well of water. Even the last chapter of the Bible contains a word about drinking: "And the Spirit and the bride say, Come!...Let him who is thirsty also come; he who wills, let him take the water of life freely" (Rev. 22:17). This divine well must be the source of our living.

Although Christ has been brought forth and has grown up, in the church life we still must learn that there are two sources or two kinds of living. What kind of living do you have—the living of Ishmael or the living of Isaac? It is insufficient merely to say that you have the living of Isaac. You must examine the kind of water you are drinking day by day. Are you drinking of the well for Ishmael? If you are, that well will make you an Ishmael and will cause you to drift into the world. Are you drinking of the well for Isaac, the well which signifies the divine well, the well of Christ, the well of the Spirit? If you are drinking of this well, the divine water which flows out of it will accomplish a great deal.

In Beer-sheba close to the land of the Philistines   ✦   The well for Isaac was in Beer-sheba, close to the land of the Philistines (vv. 25-32). This well, unlike the well for Ishmael, is not near Egypt but at the border of the land of the Philistines and the good land of Canaan. Beer-sheba was in the land of the Philistines and later became the southernmost part of the Holy Land. When describing the geography of the Holy Land, the Bible even uses the phrase "from Dan to Beer-sheba" (1 Sam. 3:20), because the distance from Dan in the north to Beer-sheba in the south includes the whole land of Canaan. In the Bible the land of the Philistines has a peculiar significance. It is not a place which rejects God absolutely; it is a place which accepts God but handles the things of God according to human cleverness, not according to God's economy. Consider as an illustration the way in which the Philistines handled the ark (1 Sam. 6:1-9). They did not reject it; they received it, but they handled it in a natural way according to their cleverness. Likewise, in Genesis 20 and 21 we see that Abimelech, the king of the Philistines, did not reject God but accepted Him in his own clever way. Abraham took God according to His economy; Abimelech took Him according to the way of human cleverness. This is the significance of the land of the Philistines.

At the cost of seven ewe lambs—Christ's complete redemption   ✦
The well for Isaac was a redeemed well (vv. 28-30). This well, which Abraham had dug, was lost, having been violently taken away by Abimelech's servants (v. 25). Then Abraham redeemed it at the cost of seven ewe lambs. In typology, these lambs signify the full redemption of Christ, indicating that the divine living water has been redeemed, bought back, by Christ's full redemption. Today, while the whole human race is living by a source which is without redemption, we are living by a redeemed source. The living water which we are drinking today is not natural; it has been redeemed at the cost of Christ's complete redemption.

By a covenant—the new covenant   ✦   The well for Isaac also needed a covenant (vv. 31-32). The covenant here is a seed of the new covenant. Our living water today is not only redeemed water but also covenanted water. Ishmael drank of wild water, water that was without redemption and covenant. But all the water which Isaac drank was redeemed water, the water of the covenant. Since we have begun to know Christ, the source of our living has also been the redeemed and covenanted water.

For planting   ✦   In Beer-sheba Abraham planted a tamarisk tree (v. 33, Heb.). A tamarisk, a type of willow tree, has very fine leaves, often grows near water, and gives the impression of the flowing of the riches of life. That Abraham planted a tamarisk after making the covenant for the well at Beer-sheba indicates that the water of which he drank was flowing in a rich way. The Lord Jesus said that whoever believes in Him will have rivers of living water flowing out of his innermost being.

The church life today is by the well in Beer-sheba. When you drink of this well and live by it, you will be like a tamarisk flowing with the riches of life. Whenever people come to you, they will never sense dryness but will be refreshed by the water of life. Beer-sheba, which means "the well of an oath," is the place where the church should be. The church should be at the well of an oath with a covenant, and should also be full of tamarisk trees. We all need to be a flowing tamarisk. If you look at the branches of a tamarisk tree, they will remind you of the flowing of the riches of life. Praise the Lord that there are some real tamarisks in the local churches!

Here, at Beer-sheba, there is the planting, but with Ishmael in the wilderness there is wildness. Many Christian groups today are like a wilderness. They only make people wild. But the proper church life causes people to be planted. Have you been planted? Once you have been planted, you can no longer be wild.

In this section of the Word it is clearly revealed that there are two sources of living. One is the natural source in the wilderness of our soul, whereas the other is the redeemed source in the garden of our spirit. At Beer-sheba, Abraham was contending for the well which had been so violently taken away. Today we also need to fight for the divine well that we may have it for both the Christian life and the proper church life.

With the calling on the name of Jehovah, the Eternal Mighty One   ✦
Verse 33, which tells us that Abraham planted a tamarisk tree in Beer-sheba, also says that he "called there on the name of the Lord,

the Eternal God" (Heb.). Here we see another special title of God—Jehovah, El Olam. In chapter seventeen we saw El-Shaddai, the all-sufficient Mighty One. Here we see El Olam. The Hebrew word olam means eternity or eternal. However, the root of this Hebrew word means to conceal, hide, or veil from sight. Anything which is veiled spontaneously becomes secret. Abraham eventually experienced God as the Eternal One, as the secret and mysterious One. We cannot see or touch Him, yet He is so real. His existence is eternal, for He has neither beginning nor ending. He is the Eternal God (Psa. 90:2; Isa. 40:28).

Here we find another seed which is developed in the New Testament. The God whom Abraham experienced in chapter twenty-one is the same as the One revealed in John 1:1, 4: "In the beginning was the Word...and the Word was God...in Him was life." This life is the very El Olam. The mysterious God in eternity is our eternal life. Eternal life is a divine Person who is so concealed, veiled, hidden, mysterious, secret, and yet so real, ever-existing, and ever-living, without beginning or ending. The title El Olam implies eternal life. Here God was not revealed to Abraham but was experienced by him as the ever-living, secret, mysterious One who is the eternal life. In other words, in Genesis 21 Abraham experienced God as the eternal life. By the tamarisk tree in Beer-sheba, Abraham could testify to the whole universe that he was experiencing the hidden, ever-living One as his mysterious life. There, at Beer-sheba, he called on the name of Jehovah, El Olam. In chapter twelve he only called upon the name of Jehovah, not yet experiencing Him as the God who is the mysterious, ever-living One. But here in chapter twenty-one, after having so much experience, with Isaac at Beer-sheba under the tamarisk tree he experienced the ever-living, mysterious One as his inner life and called, "O Jehovah, El Olam!" Although no one could see this mysterious One, He was real to Abraham in his experience. The One we have within us today is the very El Olam, the hidden, secret, concealed, mysterious, ever-living One. He is our life. We may have the same enjoyment Abraham had simply by calling, "O Lord Jesus."

While Abraham was sojourning in Beer-sheba, he must have done many things. But here the Scripture only tells us of one thing—that Abraham planted a tamarisk tree at Beer-sheba and called on the name of Jehovah, El Olam. By this brief record we can see two things. One is that the planting of the tamarisk tree must have been very significant; the other is that this planting of the tamarisk tree is connected with calling on the name of Jehovah, El Olam. As we have pointed out, Genesis 1 and 2 are not merely a record of God's creation but a record of life, with the tree of life as its center. Likewise this section of the Word is not merely a record of Abraham's history; it also is a record of life, showing by what source Abraham was living. He lived by calling on Jehovah, El Olam, by experiencing the eternal, hidden God as his life. In New Testament terms, he was experiencing the eternal life flowing with all its riches like a tamarisk tree which expresses the riches of the well by which it lives. As the tree of life is the center of the record in chapters one and two, the tamarisk tree is the center of the record here. We may say that the tamarisk tree is the tree of life experienced by us. It is the expression of the tree of life. Our Christian life and the proper church life are both a tamarisk tree, expressing the tree of life by which we live. This goes together with the calling on the Lord who is our eternal life, our Jehovah, El Olam.

Making Isaac a burnt offering   ✦   This source of living water makes Isaac a burnt offering (22:2, 9). The source from which Ishmael drank made him an archer, one who lived wildly for himself. But Isaac's source of living made him a burnt offering, one who was offered to God for His satisfaction.

Leading to the offering to God on the mountain in Moriah   ✦ This source of living led Isaac up to Moriah, not down to Egypt (22:2). Ishmael's source of living leads people downward, but Isaac's source leads people upward to the mountain in Moriah where Jerusalem was later built. This going up to Moriah kept God's people from the Philistines. We also need to go up from Beer-sheba to Jerusalem, not only having the church life at Beer-sheba but also in Jerusalem. Ultimately, this proper source of life will make all of us Isaacs and will lead us to the New Jerusalem.

Here we have another seed of the divine revelation. Ishmael lived in the wilderness and was joined to Egypt, but Isaac lived in a planted place and was led to Moriah. The mountain in Moriah eventually became Mount Zion upon which God's temple was built (2 Chron. 3:1), thus becoming the center of the good land which God gave to Abraham and his descendants. After his descendants followed the way of Ishmael and went down to Egypt, God brought them out of that land with the intention of bringing them into the good land of Canaan. But their unbelief kept them wandering in the wilderness where Ishmael lived. Eventually, God brought their children into the good land and chose Jerusalem, which was built on Mount Moriah, as the unique center for them to worship Him. As a result of this, all the children of Israel were brought, three times every year, to the very mountain in Moriah to which Isaac was brought. Thus, Isaac's being brought to Mount Moriah was a seed which was developed in the going up to Mount Zion of all the children of Israel.

Out of Abraham two kinds of people came into existence. One is represented by Ishmael who lived in the wilderness and who was joined to Egypt; the other is represented by Isaac who lived at Beer-sheba and who was brought to Mount Moriah. Today there are also two kinds of Christians. One kind is like Ishmael, living for themselves in the wilderness of their soul and being joined to the world. The other kind is like Isaac, living for God in their spirit and in the church and being brought to Zion. Even we, the real Christians, may be like Ishmael, living in and for ourselves and being joined to the world, unless, as typified by Isaac, we live in our spirit and in the church that we might reach God's goal.

21

LIVING IN FELLOWSHIP WITH GOD
THE OFFERING OF ISAAC (1)

And he said, Take now thy son, thine only son Isaac,
whom thou lovest,
and get thee into the land of Moriah;
and offer him there for a burnt offering
upon one of the mountains which I will tell thee of.

Genesis 22:2

By faith Abraham,
being tested, offered up Isaac;
indeed he who gladly received the promises was
offering up his only begotten, of whom it was said,
"In Isaac shall your seed be called"; counting that God
was able to raise men even from the dead, from which
he also received him back in figure.

Hebrews 11:17-19

In this message we come to Genesis 22, where we see the climax of Abraham's experience with God. This chapter is the continuation of chapter twenty-one. These two chapters, giving the record of the birth and offering of Isaac, cover a period of at least twenty years. Some scholars believe that when Isaac was offered he was at least twenty years old. Thus, he was a full-grown man by then.

Everything recorded in these two chapters is very meaningful. As we pointed out in the last message, in 21:33, "Abraham planted a tamarisk tree in Beer-sheba, and called there on the name of the Lord, the Eternal God" (Heb.). This planting of the tamarisk tree was not an insignificant thing. Although Abraham must have done many things while he was living in Beer-sheba, the Bible only records that he contended for the well, bought it back at a cost, planted a tamarisk tree, and called on the name of the Lord, the Eternal God. If these were insignificant things, the biblical record, which is very economical, would not have included them as part of the divine revelation. The fact that the divine revelation excludes many other things but includes the record of the planting of a tamarisk tree shows its importance.

The center of the revelation in Genesis 2 is the tree of life. Likewise, the center of the revelation in the second part of Genesis 21 is the tamarisk tree. If we have the spiritual realization with the divine light, we shall see that the tamarisk tree here is the tree of life experienced and expressed. When the tree of life is not experienced or expressed by us, it is simply the tree of life. But once we experience and express it, it becomes a tamarisk tree. A tamarisk tree has slender branches and very fine leaves showing the flow of the riches of life. Thus, the tamarisk tree planted by the well of an oath in Beer-sheba pictures the flow of the riches of life, the issue of the experience of the tree of life. Is the tree of life a tamarisk tree in your experience? Whenever we come to the meetings, the tree of life must become a tamarisk tree.

With Ishmael there was not a tree flowing with the riches of life; there was a bow. While the sign of Ishmael's life was a life-killing bow, the sign of Isaac's life was a life-flowing tree. As a Christian, a child of God and a descendant of Abraham, what is your sign—a bow or a tamarisk tree? Are you killing life, or is life with all its riches flowing in you?

If the tree of life in Genesis 2 is important, then the tamarisk tree in Genesis 21 must also be important. Very few Christians, if any, have seen the importance of the tamarisk tree at Beer-sheba. Although some have paid a little attention to the tree of life, they have not paid attention to the tamarisk tree. In the past we did see the tree of life, but we did not see the tamarisk tree. Thank the Lord that in these days He has given us the vision of the tamarisk tree. One day, the inward stirring told me that I had to know the significance of the tamarisk tree in chapter twenty-one. Although this chapter does not waste a word, ignoring the other things that Abraham must have done, it specifically says that he planted a tamarisk tree in Beer-sheba. According to our opinion, the planting of a tamarisk tree may be insignificant, perhaps being only an ancient type of landscaping. But the Bible connects the planting of the tamarisk tree with calling on a new title of the Lord, the Eternal God. Notice how the conjunction "and" is used to connect these two items in 21:33. Abraham planted a tamarisk tree and there called on the name of Jehovah, El Olam. According to our human thought, planting a tree is unrelated to calling on the name of the Lord, especially to such a new and recently revealed title. But in the Bible here it gives us the ground for the proper calling on the Lord. If we would call on the name of the Lord, we need a tamarisk tree. If we do not have this tamarisk tree experience, we can only call on the old title of God, Jehovah, not on His newly unveiled title, El Olam.

In chapter twenty-one, Abraham called on a new title of God— El Olam, the mysterious, hidden, secret, yet so real, living, and ever-existing God. This title of God implies the term eternal life, for the eternal God means the eternal life. Abraham experienced the eternal life, but he did not have this term. The people in ancient times ate vitamins, but they had no scientific knowledge of them nor scientific terms to describe them. Because we were born after the writing of the New Testament, we have the term eternal life. But Abraham, who lived in ancient times, did not have such a divine term. Nevertheless, when he called on the name of Jehovah, El Olam, it is implied that he experienced God as the ever-existing and ever-living life, as the One who is real and living, yet so mysterious and secret.

We need to consider our own experience. Whenever we have had the flow of the riches of the divine life, that was the time when we called on the name of the Lord Jesus with a new realization. We called on the same Lord, but in our calling we had a fresh sense. Do you think that if you held the life-killing bow in your hand you would be able to call on the Lord's name? No, rather you would go to find an Egyptian wife.

ABRAHAM TESTED BY GOD

In the original text of the Bible, there are no chapters, verses, or paragraphs. Chapter twenty-two is the immediate continuation of chapter twenty-one. After the mention of Abraham's planting a tamarisk tree and calling on the name of the Lord, God came in to test him (v. 1, Heb.). God, unlike Satan, never tempts anyone. But He does test us like He tested Abraham. I say again that after Abraham redeemed the well in Beer-sheba, he undoubtedly did many things, but, except for the planting of the tamarisk and calling on the name of the Lord, the Bible does not mention them. Rather, it immediately speaks of God's testing Abraham.

TO OFFER TO GOD WHAT GOD HAS GIVEN HIM IN GRACE   ◆   Often after we have had the best enjoyment of the Lord, He will not ask us to do something for Him; rather, He will tell us to offer back to Him what He has given us. At such a time the Lord may say, "You have received a gift from and of Me. Now I ask you to return it." We always expect that after having a good time with the Lord He will command us to do something for Him. We never imagine that He may ask us to give back to Him that which He has given us. As Abraham was enjoying intimate fellowship with God, he was not commanded to work for Him. He received the highest demand from God—to give back to God what God had given him. From the very beginning, God never accepted anything that Abraham had. He did not care for Lot, rejected Eliezer, and told him to cast out Ishmael. Now, after Eliezer, Lot, and Ishmael had all been rejected, Abraham had acquired Isaac, the seed promised by God, and was at peace. Everything concerning Isaac was of God and by God. Never again would God say no to what Abraham had. But suddenly God came in and seemed to say, "I would never refuse Isaac. He was born of and from Me. But, Abraham, now you must give him back to Me."

Abraham was marvelous. If I had been he, I would have said, "Lord, what are You doing? You did not care for Lot, and You have refused Eliezer and Ishmael. Now You want Isaac, the one who was of You, to be given back to You. Will You rob me to such an extent?" If I had been Abraham, I would not have offered Isaac. I would have shook my head and said, "No, this certainly is not of the Lord. It would have been logical for Him to want Eliezer, and reasonable to demand Ishmael. But how could God want me to give Isaac back to Him? God is not purposeless. He promised to give me a seed, and His promise has been confirmed and fulfilled. Why would He now waste all that He has been doing with me?" Yes, God is a God of purpose, and He certainly had a purpose in asking Abraham to give Isaac back to Him.

Many Christians, including some Christian workers, have never learned the lesson of offering back to God what He has given them. Have you received a gift? Do not hold on to it. Sooner or later God will come in and say, "Offer back to Me the gift which I have given you." Has God given you a successful work? At a certain time, God may say, "This work is the Isaac which I have given to you. Now I want you to offer it back to Me." However, many Christian workers will not take their hands off the work which God has given them. Nevertheless, all that God has given us, even what He has wrought in and through us, must be offered back to Him.

TO OFFER TO GOD HIS ONLY SON WHOM HE LOVES ✦ In verse 2 God said to Abraham, "Take now thy son, thine only son Isaac, whom thou lovest, and get thee into the land of Moriah; and offer him there for a burnt offering upon one of the mountains which I will tell thee of." God told Abraham to offer Isaac, his only son whom he loved. How hard it must have been for Abraham to do this! If we had been he, we would have said, "Lord, I am more than a hundred twenty years of age, and Sarah is about to die. How can You ask me to offer back to You what You have given me?" If you have not had this experience, you will have it some day. We can testify that quite a number of times in the past God asked us to give back to Him what He had given us. The gifts, power, work, and success which He gives us must be offered back to Him. This is a real test. It would have been easy for Abraham to give up Lot or Eliezer. Even casting out Ishmael was not that difficult. But for him to offer his only son whom he loved was a very difficult thing. One day, after our having a good enjoyment of the Lord, He will ask us to give back to Him the gift, work, or success He has given us. He may say, "Now is the time for Me to ask you for something. I don't ask you to work for Me or to go to the mission field. I ask you to offer back what I have given you." This is the way we all must take today.

A life grown up by the well of the oath with the calling on the name of the Eternal God ✦ God did not tell Abraham to offer up a baby or even a little boy, but a full-grown man. Isaac's life was a life grown up by the well of the oath with the calling on the name of the Eternal God (21:33-34). Genesis 21:34, the last verse of chapter twenty-one, says, "Abraham sojourned in the Philistines' land many days." This means that Abraham remained there for a good number of years. During that time, Isaac grew up by the well of Beer-sheba, growing up by a life of planting and calling on the name of the Lord, the Eternal God. The one whom Abraham was told to offer up was a grown-up son, one who had lived with him in a life of planting and calling. The life in Beer-sheba built Isaac up to be a burnt offering, not an archer.

Offered to God on Mount Moriah where God's temple was built   ✦
When God told Abraham to offer Isaac, He told him to go to the land of Moriah and to offer him upon one of the mountains there (v. 2). The land of Moriah was a two-day journey from Beer-sheba. The mountain on which Isaac was offered was later called Mount Moriah, eventually becoming Mount Zion, the place where the temple was built (2 Chron. 3:1).

When I read 22:2 as a youth, I was bothered. I wondered why God was so troublesome, saying, "Lord, You gave Abraham a son and asked him to offer his son back to You. That was all right, but it was not reasonable for him to go to such a far-off place. Aren't You omnipresent? Were You not there in Beer-sheba? Why did You ask Abraham to journey to a mountain so far away?" At first, God did not even tell Abraham on which mountain he was to offer Isaac, saying only that it would be "one of the mountains which I will tell thee of." In asking Abraham to journey far away for the offering of Isaac, God was not being troublesome. He is never troublesome; He is always meaningful. Eventually Mount Moriah became the center of the good land, and Abraham's descendants had to go to that mountain three times a year to offer the burnt offering to God (Deut. 16:16; Psa. 132:13). Thus, we see that chapter twenty-two of Genesis is a seed.

We cannot and should not offer to God the burnt offering which He desires in the place of our choosing. We must leave our place and go to the place of God's choice. Ishmael, the archer, the bowman, went southward toward Egypt and married an Egyptian woman. But Isaac, the burnt offering, was a different kind of person. He did not go downward to Egypt; he went upward to Moriah. If you consult a map, you will see that Moriah is north from Beer-sheba. Here we have a picture of two types of persons—an archer and a burnt offering. Which will you be?

For a burnt offering for God's satisfaction   ✦   The picture in
Genesis 22 is very vivid. In his hand Abraham held the fire and the
knife. Isaac, who was carrying the wood for the burnt offering, said,
"Behold the fire and the wood: but where is the lamb for a burnt
offering?" He did not know that he himself was to be the offering.

Do you know that your destiny is to be a burnt offering? To be
a burnt offering is to be killed and burned. The growing, living, and
calling on the name of El Olam at Beer-sheba are all for the building
up of a burnt offering that we might be burned on the altar on Mount
Moriah. The water at Beer-sheba is for the fire on Mount Moriah. The
more we drink the water from the well of Beer-sheba, the more we
shall grow, and the more we grow, the more we shall be prepared for
the fire on Mount Moriah. Because of this, the Lord's recovery will
never be a mass movement; it is a narrow way. At the time of
Genesis 22, Isaac was the only person living and walking in this
narrow way. Do not expect that many will take the way of the church.
Many are happy to be a bowman, for that is a sport. But living at
Beer-sheba and calling on the name of the Lord may seem, in a sense,
to be boring. Eventually, after we enjoy a good time with the Lord, He
will ask us to offer our Isaac to Him. He will not allow us to offer Isaac
at Beer-sheba. We shall have to travel a long distance and climb
Mount Moriah. The proper church life does not produce bowmen; it
produces burnt offerings. We all must become a burnt offering.
Although this is a narrow way, it is prevailing.

Although it is a long journey from Beer-sheba to Mount Moriah
and it is a journey which causes some suffering, it results in blessing.
In the following message we shall see the blessing which comes from
the life that grows up by the well of Beer-sheba and is offered to God
on Mount Moriah. I know of a good number of very brilliant young
brothers who came into the church life with an honest heart.
Although their heart was honest, they expected that one day, after
having all the necessary experiences and receiving all the visions, they
would become something in the Lord's recovery. In other words, they
expected to be spiritual giants. Gradually, as the years went by, I
learned what was on their heart, for they came to me and told me
their story. One brother said, "When I came into the church life, I
came in honestly, but I expected that one day, after I had been perfected, equipped, qualified, experienced, and had seen all the visions,
I would be so useful in the Lord's hand. But now the Lord has told me

that He intends to burn me up." Do you expect that someday you will become a strong bowman? If you do, one day the Lord will say to you, "I don't want an Ishmael, a bowman. I want an Isaac, a burnt offering. Don't try to do anything for Me. I can do anything I want. I just want you to be a burnt offering." The life at Beer-sheba only produces a burnt offering. The more we stay in the church life, the more it will bring us from Beer-sheba to Moriah, from the growing water to the burning fire. Are you growing? Thank God for this. But your growth is a preparation for your being burned. One day we all must pass through the process of being burned as a burnt offering.

In Hebrew the burnt offering means the ascending offering. After the burnt offering has been burned, its sweet odor ascends to God for His satisfaction. It is ascending and not spreading. As a burnt offering, we must not be spreading but ascending to God by being burned.

The experience of Genesis 22 cannot come immediately after that of Genesis 12. There must be a long journey from Genesis 12 through Genesis 21. When many of us came into the church life, that was our chapter twelve, not our chapter twenty-two. Abraham had to pass through the separation of Lot, the rejection of Eliezer, the casting out of Ishmael, and the birth of Isaac. Although God had promised Abraham a seed, He did not give it to him until Abraham had made a thorough clearance of Lot, Eliezer, and Ishmael. Only then was Isaac born. But not even Isaac's birth was the end. Isaac needed to grow and be offered.

As we have seen, Isaac did not grow up in the wilderness but in Beer-sheba, properly growing by the life of calling on the Lord. At a certain point, God came in and asked Abraham to offer Isaac. It seemed that God was being somewhat troublesome. However, God would never have troubled Abraham in that way if Abraham had not been qualified. When God comes to trouble you like this, it is an honor, because it testifies that you are qualified. God did not ask Abraham to offer Lot as a burnt offering. Neither did He request that Abraham offer Eliezer or Ishmael. Rather, God told Abraham to cast Ishmael out. Only the seed who was promised, confirmed, and brought into being by God was the right person. He was the one who grew up by the well of Beer-sheba and who called on the name of the Lord. God seemed to say to Abraham, "You love Isaac, and I love him too. Now you must give him to Me." Eventually, Isaac became the forefather of the entire chosen race. He also became a forefather of Christ. God's eternal purpose can never be fulfilled by anyone other than Isaac, the one who was brought up under the care of Abraham and offered to God.

Returned in resurrection for the fulfillment of God's eternal purpose ✦ After Isaac was offered, he was returned in resurrection for the fulfillment of God's eternal purpose (vv. 4, 12-13, 16, 18). After being returned in resurrection, Isaac was another person. He was no longer the natural Isaac, but the resurrected Isaac. This is very encouraging. After we have offered to God what we have received of Him, He will then return it to us in resurrection. Every gift, spiritual blessing, work, and success we have received of God must undergo the test of death. Eventually, it will come back to us in resurrection. The Lord Jesus said, "Truly, truly, I say to you, unless a grain of wheat falls into the ground and dies, it abides alone; but if it dies, it bears much fruit" (John 12:24). Suppose God gives you a certain natural gift. That is one grain of wheat. If you keep this natural gift, never offering it to God, it will remain as one grain. But if you offer it back to God, after it has passed through death, it will be returned to you in resurrection and become a blessing. It does not depend on what we can do or intend to do for God. It all depends on our growing up to be offered to God as a burnt offering and then being raised up from the dead to be a resurrected gift. It is not a matter of being useful to God but of being under His blessing. God's blessing always comes in resurrection. For one grain to be multiplied into a hundred grains is God's blessing. If you offer your one grain to God and allow Him to put it into death, it will be returned to you in resurrection. Then you will see multiplication and great blessing. This is God's way.

ABRAHAM'S OBEDIENCE BY FAITH

In Genesis 22 we see Abraham's obedience by faith. When I read this chapter as a young man, I could not understand how Abraham as a human being and a father could have been so bold. When God asked him to offer to Him his beloved son Isaac, he did it immediately. In this chapter there is no mention of Abraham's wife. According to the record here, we are not told that Abraham talked with his wife about offering Isaac. We are only shown that he responded quickly and boldly to God's command, rising up early in the morning and going to the place of which God had spoken.

BELIEVING IN THE RESURRECTING GOD   ✦   In the Old Testament we cannot see why Abraham obeyed God so quickly and boldly. But in the New Testament we see that Abraham believed in the resurrecting God (Heb. 11:17-19; James 2:21-22). He had the faith which counted on God to raise up the very Isaac whom he was about to slay. He had received the firm and even confirmed promise that God's covenant would be established with Isaac and that he would become a great nation (17:19-21). If Abraham had offered Isaac on the altar, slaying him and burning him as an offering to God, and God did not raise him from the dead, then God's word would have been in vain. Abraham's faith was based upon God's confirmed promise. Abraham could have said, "If God wants Isaac, I will just slay him. God will raise him up for the fulfillment of His promise."

Romans 4:17, speaking of Abraham, says that the God in whom he believed is the One who "gives life to the dead and calls the things not being as being." Here we see that Abraham believed in God for two things: for giving life to the dead and for calling things not being as being. The birth of Isaac was related to God's calling things not being as being, and his being returned was related to God's giving life to the dead. Because Abraham had such faith, he obeyed God's commandment immediately. Hebrews 11:17-19 says that when Abraham was tried, he offered up Isaac by faith, "counting that God was able to raise him even from among the dead, from whence he also received him back in a figure."

ACTING ACCORDING TO GOD'S REVELATION   ✦   In obeying God by faith, Abraham acted according to God's revelation (vv. 3-4, 9-10). Everything Abraham did in this chapter was absolutely of God. Abraham did not initiate anything nor do anything according to his concept. Nothing was done by his desire or understanding. God told Abraham what to do, how to do it, and where to do it. In every aspect of his action in offering Isaac, Abraham acted according to God's revelation and instructions.

Going to Mount Moriah, the place of God's choice   ✦   Abraham went to Mount Moriah, the place of God's choice. In verse 2 God told Abraham to go into the land of Moriah and offer Isaac on one of the mountains of which He would tell him. In the next verse we are told that Abraham "rose up and went to the place of which God had told him." Before Abraham began his journey, God must have told him which mountain He had chosen. In verse 4 we are told that "on the third day Abraham lifted up his eyes, and saw the place afar off." Abraham did nothing according to his concept or choice; he did everything according to God's revelation.

What Abraham did in Genesis 22 is an important seed in the Bible. As I have already pointed out, Abraham's descendants, the children of Israel, were commanded by God to go three times a year to Mount Moriah to worship God and there to offer to Him their burnt offerings. We have seen that Mount Moriah became Mount Zion, the very center of the good land. Abraham was the first to worship God with the burnt offering on Mount Zion. Eventually, we all shall be on Mount Zion worshipping God. On the one hand, in the church life today, as true descendants of Abraham, we are on Mount Zion; on the other hand, we are on our way there. What Abraham did in chapter twenty-two was the seed. His descendants, the Israelites, were the development of this seed, and we today are the further development of the seed. We all, including Abraham, shall be in the harvest of the seed. Perhaps one day we shall shake hands with Abraham on the eternal Mount Zion and say to him, "You were on the ancient Mount Zion, we were on the new testament Mount Zion, and now we are all together here on the eternal Mount Zion."

Traveling for three days ✦ Verse 4 indicates that Abraham traveled for three days, for we are told that on the third day he saw the appointed place afar off. In the eyes of God and according to Abraham's feeling, Isaac had been killed for three days. On the third day Abraham not only offered Isaac; he also received him back. Hence, the third day is surely a sign of resurrection. It is very meaningful that the Bible does not call it the second or fourth day. If you look at a map, you will see that the distance between Beer-sheba and Moriah is approximately fifty-five miles. According to the ancient method of travel, it would have taken two days to journey from Beer-sheba to Moriah. On the third day Abraham put Isaac on the altar, and then what he offered to God was given back to him in resurrection. This is marvelous. We all must see the seed here. Praise the Lord that today we are Isaacs, not Ishmaels. We are not journeying southward toward Egypt; we are traveling northward to Mount Zion.

In order to see this, we must have the life at Beer-sheba, because only this life builds us up and qualifies us to be the burnt offering for

God's satisfaction and to receive the vision. The name Moriah means "the vision of Jah," that is, the vision of Jehovah, the vision of the Lord. This has two meanings—that we see the Lord and that the Lord sees us. On Mount Moriah Abraham undoubtedly saw God and God saw him. Likewise, on today's Mount Zion we have a vision. There is no cloud here. We are not in darkness; we are in the vision. The church life is a vision in which we see God and God sees us.

The translators are troubled about how to render verse 14, uncertain whether it should be "in the mount of the Lord it shall be seen" or "it shall be provided." According to the King James Version, verse 14 says, "And Abraham called the name of that place Jehovah-jireh: as it is said to this day, In the mount of the Lord it shall be seen." Other versions say, "In the mount of the Lord it shall be provided." Some versions even say, "On the mount of the Lord he will see." Although this verse is difficult to translate, it is easy to understand according to our experience. God's provision is always His vision. Whenever we participate in and enjoy God's provision, we have a vision. We see God and He sees us. Because we are in His provision and have the vision, everything is clear, nothing is opaque, and there is no separation between us and Him.

Where is God's provision today? It is in the church life on Mount Zion. We all can testify what a provision there is in the church life. As we are enjoying the provision, what a vision we have! We see God. We see eternity. Here in the church life everything is crystal clear and transparent in God's eyes and in ours, and nothing is opaque. We did not have this experience in Christianity. When we were there, we were in a low dungeon that was opaque on every side. But today in the church life on Mount Zion we have the full provision with the full vision. We see God and are seen by Him; God sees us and is seen by us. In God's provision, everything is transparent.

Building an altar and offering Isaac　✦　Abraham went to a primitive region, built an altar on a mountain, and there offered his only son Isaac (vv. 9-10). To build an altar there was not easy, and to offer his only son by killing him was even more difficult. But he did this. He truly meant business with the Lord. We also must build an altar and offer what God demands. This surely will cost us something.

We have seen the record of Abraham's obedience by faith. The faith with which he was thoroughly infused by God gave him this obedience. It was this infused faith that brought him to Mount Moriah where he enjoyed God's provision and had a thoroughly transparent vision from God. At that time there was no one on earth nor in the whole universe who was as clear about divine things as Abraham was. There, on Mount Moriah, Abraham experienced God's provision and received a clear vision. Everything was clear in his eyes. We must not read Genesis 22 merely as a story. We must receive divine light from it and see that Abraham's experience is being repeated in us today. Praise the Lord that we have today's Beer-sheba and Moriah. We are not going downward to Egypt; we are traveling upward to Mount Moriah, where we shall enjoy God's provision and have a transparent vision.

22

LIVING IN FELLOWSHIP WITH GOD THE OFFERING OF ISAAC (2)

And Abraham took the wood
of the burnt offering, and
laid it upon Isaac his son; and he took the fire
in his hand, and a knife; and they went both of them together.
And Isaac spake unto Abraham his father, and said,
My father:
and he said, Here am I, my son. And he said,
Behold the fire and the wood:
but where is the lamb for a burnt offering?
And Abraham said, My son, God will provide himself a lamb
for a burnt offering: so they went both of them together.

Genesis 22:6-8

For God so loved the world that He gave His only begotten Son....

John 3:16

In the last message we saw how Abraham offered his son Isaac according to God's demand. That story, recorded in Genesis 22, is not only a meaningful history but also has an implied significance, for it is a vivid picture of Christ in several aspects. Although we cannot find the title of Christ nor the name of Jesus in this chapter, many aspects of Christ are signified in the way of implication. In this message we need to see the aspects of Christ depicted in this chapter.

ISAAC TYPIFYING CHRIST

Isaac typified Christ. We have seen that Abraham answered God's call to go to Mount Moriah to offer Isaac. This is history. However, if we view this matter from the perspective of God's revelation, we shall see that what Abraham did to Isaac is a vivid picture of what the Father did to His beloved Son. When Abraham journeyed to Mount Moriah with Isaac, two young servants accompanied him. On the third day, Abraham put the two servants aside, saying, "I and the lad will go yonder and worship, and come again to you" (v. 5). From that point on, the story was different. It was no longer a story of four people—the father, the son, and the two servants; it was now a story of Abraham and his son Isaac. Abraham took the wood for the burnt offering and laid it upon Isaac, who bore it to the top of Mount Moriah. Compare this with John 19:17, which says, "And bearing the cross Himself, He went out to the place called the Place of a Skull, which is called in Hebrew, Golgotha." Isaac walked the same path on the way to Mount Moriah that the Lord Jesus later walked on the way to Golgotha. Before Christ bore the cross and walked to Calvary, Golgotha, Isaac bore the wood for the burnt offering and walked along the same way. And Jesus was crucified on the same mount where Isaac was laid on the altar. Thus, we see that Abraham was a type of the Father, and Isaac, with the wood upon him, was a type of the Only Begotten Son of God. Isaac was brought as a lamb to the altar. Jesus was also "brought as a lamb to the slaughter" (Isa. 53:7).

As Abraham and Isaac were climbing Mount Moriah, Isaac said, "Behold the fire and the wood: but where is the lamb for a burnt offering?" (v. 7). Abraham replied, "My son, God will provide himself a lamb for a burnt offering" (v. 8). Here we see that the son fellowshipped with the father. Do you not believe that while Jesus was bearing the cross on the way to Calvary He fellowshipped with the Father? And do you not believe that the Father talked with His Son? I do. If you say that the Bible does not tell us of this, I would say that Genesis 22 tells us so. We need to have the sight and the listening ear to hear the heavenly conversation on the way to Mount Moriah. Abraham and Isaac typified the Father and the Son, and their fellowship on the way to Mount Moriah was a vivid picture depicting how Jesus the Son fellowshipped with the Father as He was bearing the cross to Calvary. Although we do not have a clear explanation of this in plain words in the New Testament, we do have the picture in the Old Testament, and a picture is better than a thousand words. The picture in Genesis 22 portrays something which words cannot explain. Although the writers of the New Testament did not describe the loving fellowship between the Father and the Son on the way to Calvary, it is clearly portrayed in the picture in Genesis 22. How we all need to see this picture. As we shall see, nearly every point regarding the type in Genesis 22 is covered in John 1.

Let us consider now some details of Isaac as a type of Christ. Isaac was Abraham's only son (vv. 2, 12, 16). This typifies Christ as God's only Son (John 3:16). Isaac was Abraham's beloved son (v. 2), and Christ was the Father's beloved Son in whom He delighted (Matt. 3:17). In 22:5 we see that Isaac took his father's will, and in Matthew 26:39 we see that Christ chose the Father's will. In the picture in Genesis 22, we see that Isaac, a full-grown man, was obedient unto death (vv. 9-10). According to the record of this chapter, in the matter of offering Isaac, Abraham consulted neither with his wife Sarah nor with his son Isaac. Abraham took his son, put the wood upon him, led him up the mountain, bound him, and laid him on the altar. He did not give Isaac the opportunity to say anything. But Isaac took his father's will and was obedient to death. Likewise, when the Lord Jesus was about to die, He said, "Not as I will, but as You will" (Matt. 26:39). In Philippians 2:8 we are told that Christ was obedient unto death. Look again at the picture: Isaac was obedient unto the altar. He not only followed the father to the foot of the mount; he also obeyed him in taking up the wood and in being bound. He did not resist. Even when the father laid him on the altar, took the knife, and stretched out his hand to slay him, he did not rebel. He was obedient unto death. If we consider all these aspects of Isaac as a type of Christ as portrayed in the Old Testament, we shall see that they were sovereignly arranged, matching the clear word of the New Testament revelation.

In God's eyes, Isaac was killed. Just as Abraham was about to slay his son, the angel of the Lord intervened from heaven, saying, "Lay not thine hand upon the lad, neither do thou any thing unto him." The angel of the Lord here is actually God Himself. This is proved by verse 12 in which the angel of the Lord said to Abraham, "I know that thou fearest God, seeing thou hast not withheld thy son, thine only son from me." The "me" here is God Himself. Notice that the angel of the Lord did not say "from him," but "from me." Abraham, the father, put his son to death, but the angel of the Lord raised him up from the dead. In like manner, Acts 2:24 says that God has raised up Christ from the dead.

ISAAC REPLACED BY A RAM

Isaac was replaced by a ram, that is, by a lamb. Verse 13 says, "Abraham lifted up his eyes, and looked, and behold behind him a ram caught in a thicket by his horns: and Abraham went and took the ram, and offered him up for a burnt offering in the stead of his son." Here we see that the son was not killed, but the ram, the lamb, was. Who was killed on the cross—the Son of God or the Lamb of God? It was the Lamb of God who was killed. Christ is the Son of God, but when He was killed on the cross, He was replaced by the Lamb of God. John 1:14, speaking of the Son of God, says, "We beheld His glory, glory as of an only begotten from a father." But John 1:29 says, "Behold, the Lamb of God who takes away the sin of the world!" Here we see that the Son of God was replaced by the Lamb of God. The Lamb of God, not the Son of God, was crucified. In crucifixion, the Son was replaced by a ram.

In 22:8 Abraham prophesied that God would provide a lamb for a burnt offering. The eternal Lamb was ordained by God from eternity (1 Pet. 1:19-20). In 22:13 we see "a ram caught in a thicket by his horns." In the Bible horns signify fighting power. Christ has the fighting power, but it was caught by a thicket. The thicket signifies humanity. We are the thicket, and Christ, the Lamb of God, has been caught in us and cannot escape. He has been caught by His human nature that He might be offered as our substitute. Christ as the Lamb of God was willing to have His horns caught by humanity. When we see this clear picture, we all must say, "Lord, thank You. You were willing to be caught by us."

The Son of God was replaced on the cross by the Lamb of God. In a positive, divine sense, the Son of God was never crucified. The Lamb of God was crucified. No one could crucify the Son of God. Praise Him that He was willing to be a little lamb putting His horns among human beings and being caught by us. Thus, we see that not only did this Son of God become the Lamb of God, but that He was replaced by the Lamb of God. Although we do not have such a picture in the New Testament, we see it in the Old Testament. Along with the clear words in the four Gospels, we need the pictures in the Old Testament.

PROVIDED BY JEHOVAH-JIREH   ✦   The ram who replaced the son on the altar was provided by Jehovah-jireh (v. 14). The title Jehovah-jireh has two meanings: Jehovah will provide and Jehovah will see. There is not only a provision but also a vision. Within the provision, we have the vision. Look at the cross: what provision and vision we have there. I can testify that at the cross I have received both the provision and the vision. Before the cross, I was lacking, but at the cross I obtained the divine provision. Before the cross, I was blind, having no vision, but at the cross, through the provision, I can see. Now my sight is so clear. I have not only been provided for but also enlightened. Even many of the young people can testify that before they came to the cross, they were poor and blind. But one day they came to the cross and found the provision and the vision. May the Spirit of wisdom help us to realize the depth of the significance that is in the fact that the Son of God was replaced by the Lamb of God whose horns were caught by humanity.

TYPIFYING CHRIST AS OUR SUBSTITUTE   ✦   The Lamb of God who replaced the Son of God was our substitute (1 Pet. 3:18). As the ram was killed instead of Isaac, so the Lamb of God suffered crucifixion for us. When as a boy I heard the preaching of the gospel in which we were told that Christ suffered death on our behalf, I could not understand it fully. Only when I saw the clear picture in Genesis 22 was I able to understand how Christ was our substitute. The ram was killed for Isaac. This is a picture showing that Christ, the Lamb of God, was crucified on the cross for us. We all should have gone to the cross, but God replaced us with the Lamb of God. To this we all must say, "Praise the Lord! The Lamb of God, who is the Son of God, was our substitute."

Because the Lamb of God became our substitute, He became great and significant. In Revelation the unique title of Christ is the Lamb. When in Revelation 5 the Apostle John saw the scroll which no one in heaven or on earth was worthy to open, he wept. Then one of the elders said to him, "Do not weep; behold, the Lion of the tribe of

Judah, the Root of David, has overcome to open the scroll and its seven seals." Immediately after this, John saw the Lamb: "I saw in the midst of the throne and of the four living creatures, and in the midst of the elders, a Lamb standing." In Genesis 22 we have the seed of that Lamb. This seed grew up in John 1:29 and is harvested in the book of Revelation. Eventually, the throne of God becomes the throne of God and of the Lamb out of which proceeds the river of water of life with the tree of life growing in it (Rev. 22:1-2). All this proves that the Bible is not a manmade book. It certainly is the divine revelation. What a picture of Christ is revealed in Genesis 22!

ABRAHAM BLESSED BY GOD

WITH THE SEED MULTIPLIED   ✦   Abraham was blessed by God. The blessing here is not that of material things. Many of us have had the wrong impression in the past, saying that receiving a good job or material benefit means that the Lord has blessed us. We have all been told to count our blessings one by one, counting such things as our degree, promotion, wife, house, and children. Although I do not say that such things are not blessings, I do say that they are not golden blessings, but muddy blessings. In Genesis 22, God did not bless Abraham in this way. Rather, He blessed him with the multiplied seed, saying, "In blessing I will bless thee, and in multiplying I will multiply thy seed as the stars of the heaven, and as the sand which is upon the seashore" (v. 17). I do not care for material blessing. I care for multiplication. I would firstly like to see fifty churches in the United States, then a hundred, and then a thousand. I would also like to see that from the United States the multiplication would spread to Africa, Australasia, Europe, and even back to Jerusalem. This is the blessing I want to see.

Abraham was blessed with two categories of people, one likened to the stars of the heaven (v. 17; 15:5) and the other to the sand upon the seashore (v. 17), which is also likened to the dust of the earth (13:16). If you know history and the prophecies regarding Abraham's descendants, you will see that they are of two categories, one heavenly and the other earthly. We, the Christians, are the stars, the heavenly descendants of Abraham; and the genuine Jews, God's earthly people, are the sand, the dust. Eventually, the Jewish people will be God's priests on earth and will teach all the nations. This is prophesied clearly in Zechariah 8:20-23. Why are the Jews described both as the sand and as the dust? The sea signifies the world corrupted by Satan, and the dust is of the earth created by God. The Jews have been restored to God's creation. Hence, they are signified by the sand which is the dust beside the sea. Although they are an earthly people, they are not the dust under the sea, but the dust, the sand, by the seashore. They are separated from the corrupted sea, Satan's corrupted world. However, the stars are not only separated from the corrupted world but are also heavenly.

According to Revelation 20:8 and 9, at the end of the millennium Gog and Magog will fight against the camp of the saints and the beloved city. The camp of the saints is the camp of all the heavenly stars, and the beloved city, Jerusalem, is the city of the separated sand. The two categories of Abraham's descendants, who at that time will be caring for God's interests in the universe, will be attacked by Gog and Magog under Satan's instigation. That will be the last war in the universe, a war between the devilish people and Abraham's descendants.

The star is sown as a seed in Genesis 22 and will be harvested in Revelation 20 and 21. The New Jerusalem is composed of the twelve tribes of Israel, representing the Old Testament saints, and the twelve Apostles, representing the New Testament believers. Those represented by the Apostles are the heavenly stars, and those represented by the twelve tribes are the sand of the seashore. These two peoples eventually will be built together into the eternal New Jerusalem. Hence, the eternal New Jerusalem will be the ultimate consummation of Abraham's seed. This is God's blessing to Abraham.

After seeing this, we need to say, "Praise the Lord, God's blessing is not a good house, car, degree, promotion, wife, or child. It is the multiplication of the saints in God's recovery and the multiplication of the churches." I hope that one day a part of the New Jerusalem will be our multiplication as God's blessing to us. At that time, all the cars and houses will be gone. Only the multiplication in God's blessing will remain forever. We shall see the blessing in God's multiplication in the New Jerusalem for eternity.

Here in Genesis 22 we see a basic principle, that is, whatever God gives us will be multiplied. God gave Abraham one Isaac, and Abraham offered him back to God. Then this one Isaac was multiplied into numberless stars and sand. If Abraham would not have offered Isaac back to God, he might have had only one Isaac. But having been offered back to God by Abraham, Isaac was multiplied into the New Jerusalem. This is the way to have God's gift multiplied in us—offer back to God what He has given us.

WITH CHRIST AS HIS UNIQUE SEED   ✦   God's blessing of Abraham eventually issues in Christ as the unique seed in whom all the nations of the earth shall be blessed (v. 18; Gal. 3:16). In Galatians 3:16 Paul speaks of only one seed—Christ. We all are included in this one seed. Are we not all in Christ? Do you know the true significance of the short phrase "in Christ"? This phrase is used many times in the New Testament. In Christ we have been justified. In Christ we are sanctified. In Christ we have the sonship. Everything concerning us is in Christ. Hallelujah, we are in Christ! We are actually a part of Christ. Ultimately, all the heavenly stars and the earthly sand will be in Christ. As we have pointed out in the past, the New Jerusalem will be a great, corporate Christ. In the four Gospels we have the individual Christ, but at the end of Revelation we have the corporate Christ including all true believers.

In this one seed, Christ, all the nations of the earth shall be blessed. Have not the United States, Germany, Japan, China, and Great Britain been blessed? This is God's blessing. May we all expect that the blessing which we shall receive of God will be the multiplication that will issue in Christ, the unique seed. The multiplication that will spread to Europe, Africa, and throughout the earth must simply be Christ. All the churches on earth will just be the multiplication of Christ.

CHRIST REVEALED IN THREE WAYS

In Genesis 22 Christ is revealed in three ways: as the angel of the Lord (vv. 11-12, 15-18; Exo. 3:2-6), as the ram (v. 13; John 1:29), and as the seed of Abraham (v. 18; Gal. 3:16). When Abraham stretched forth his hand to kill Isaac, the angel of the Lord prevented him. Then Abraham saw a ram and killed it, offering it in Isaac's place. Afterward, it became a blessing in multiplication. This multiplication issues in Christ as the unique seed. Here we see the angel of the Lord stopping, the ram replacing, and the seed bringing the blessing. All three are Christ. This is too mysterious because Christ is everything. Christ was the One who told Abraham not to kill his son.

Then He immediately became the ram caught in a thicket to replace his son. After the crucifixion, He became his unique seed in God's blessing. The angel of the Lord, who was Christ, provided the ram, a type of Christ, which eventually issued in the seed, who is also Christ. Christ is everything. We do not have a small, limited Christ. We have a great and unlimited Christ who is everything. Praise the Lord!

23

Living in Fellowship with God
The Death and Burial of Sarah

Abraham came to mourn
for Sarah, and to weep for her.
And Abraham stood up from before his dead, and spake unto
the sons of Heth, saying, I am a stranger and a sojourner with you:
give me a possession of a buryingplace with you....

Genesis 23:2-4

By faith Abraham...dwelt as a foreigner in the land of promise
as in a foreign land, making his home
in tents with Isaac and Jacob,
the fellow heirs of the same promise;
for he eagerly waited for the city which has the foundations,
whose Architect and Builder is God....
But as it is, they long after a better country, that is, a heavenly one.
Therefore God is not ashamed of them, to be called their God,
for He has prepared a city for them.

Hebrews 11:8-10, 16

In this message we come to Genesis 23, a chapter which records
the death and burial of Sarah. When I was young, I did not see why

this chapter was included in the book of Genesis. I could not understand why, when Abraham must have done many great things which are not recorded, twenty verses were used to describe how he spent his time, energy, money, and even his politeness to acquire a burying place. But the Bible does not waste any words. Since every word of the Bible is God's breath, Genesis 23 must be very significant. If we consider Genesis 1 and 2 as being important, we must also consider Genesis 23 as being important. Every Christian appreciates Genesis 1 because it gives a record of God's creation. We appreciate Genesis 1 not merely as a record of creation but also as a record of life. It speaks of God's image and dominion as related to the man created by God. We also appreciate Genesis 2 because it tells us of the tree of life. However, few of us appreciate a sepulcher. But Genesis 23 is focused on the matter of a burying place and gives us a detailed account of the purchase of a sepulcher. More details are included in this story than in any other record in the book of Genesis. While every other record is quite brief, this one gives a full and clear account of where the tomb was located, who owned it, how it was purchased, and the amount Abraham paid for it. This sepulcher is mentioned in a very significant way, for we are told that not only was Sarah buried there, but that Abraham, Isaac, Rebekah, Jacob, and Leah were buried there also. It is very significant that the names of Abraham, Isaac, and Jacob are the components of the divine title of God who is the God of resurrection (Matt. 22:32).

Genesis 23 is a window through which we can see the New Jerusalem. The New Jerusalem is not found in this chapter, but it can be seen through it. This chapter is like a telescope: through it we can see the eternal tabernacle that is far off in the future.

Genesis 21 gives us the record of the birth of Isaac. This was certainly worth mentioning. Following this, in the same chapter we are told that Abraham redeemed a well, planted a tamarisk tree, and called on the name of Jehovah, El Olam. As we have seen, in chapter twenty-two we have the offering of Isaac. Then, in chapter twenty-three, we have the death and burial of Sarah. These three chapters cover at least thirty-seven years. Although a great many things must have happened with Abraham during these thirty-seven years, only four things are mentioned: the birth of Isaac, the living in Beersheba, the offering of Isaac, and the death and burial of Sarah. These three chapters exclude many things which, according to our human concept, are important, but include a detailed record of the death and burial of Sarah. Because of this, we must pay close attention to Genesis 23.

IN HEBRON—
THE PLACE OF FELLOWSHIP WITH GOD

At the end of chapter twenty-two, Abraham, Sarah, and Isaac were dwelling at Beer-sheba, undoubtedly living near the covenanted well and the tamarisk tree. This was a miniature of the church life, for the church life is always by a well of living water and a tamarisk tree. Suddenly, at the beginning of chapter twenty-three we are told of Sarah's death. Although Abraham, Sarah, and Isaac were living at Beer-sheba, she died and was buried in Hebron, the place of fellowship with God. Sarah went on from Beer-sheba to Hebron. In like manner, if the Lord delays His coming back, I would like to live in the church life and die in the fellowship with God.

According to the map, Hebron is between Beer-sheba on the south and Jerusalem on the north. It is on the way from Beer-sheba to Moriah, where Jerusalem is. If the Lord delays His coming back, I would like to be buried in a place which is on the way to the New Jerusalem. Where are you living today? We all must answer that we are living in Beer-sheba, in the church by the well of living water and the tamarisk tree. Our church life is today's Beer-sheba. Before the Lord comes back, some of the older ones may leave Beer-sheba, the church life, die in Hebron, and wait there for the New Jerusalem. Hebron is not only a place of fellowship with God; it is also a way to Jerusalem. The cave of Machpelah in Hebron is the gateway to the New Jerusalem. Perhaps some day we shall hear Sarah testify, "When I entered into the cave of Machpelah, I entered into the gate which leads into the New Jerusalem." Sarah was not simply buried in the cave of Machpelah; she is now sleeping there, waiting for the day when she will wake up and find herself in the New Jerusalem.

SARAH'S EARLY DEATH

Sarah died at the age of one hundred twenty-seven (vv. 1-2). Although this may seem to be very old today, at that time it was an early age to die. Abraham lived one hundred seventy-five years (25:7), living thirty-eight years after Sarah died. Sarah should not have died at such an early age. Her death, thirty-seven years after Isaac's birth (17:1, 17; 21:5), was abnormal.

ABRAHAM'S SUFFERING

Abraham and Sarah were the best couple in the whole universe. They truly loved one another, never having any consideration of divorce or separation. When Abraham was robbed of his wife, it was a great loss to both Abraham and Isaac. Isaac was a dear son to his mother, and she undoubtedly loved him very much. At the age of thirty-seven, he was still unmarried and lived with his mother. When he did marry at the age of forty (25:20), the Bible even tells us that Isaac was married in his mother's tent (24:67). Suddenly, the love between Abraham and Sarah and between Sarah and Isaac was broken, for Sarah, the wife and mother, was taken away by an abnormal death. Because of this, Abraham suffered greatly.

If you read Abraham's history, you will see that God was always taking things away from him. Lot separated from him, Eliezer was rejected, Ishmael was cast out, and Isaac was offered to God on the altar. Then his dear wife was taken away in death. What trials and sufferings Abraham passed through! According to our natural concept, Abraham, one who was so good with God, should not have suffered all these things. In chapter twenty-two Isaac was offered to God and returned to Abraham in resurrection. Suddenly, while Abraham was enjoying a happy life with his wife Sarah and his son Isaac, Sarah, the factor of his happiness, was taken away. The happiness in this family was dependent upon Sarah, the wife and the mother. When Sarah died, the atmosphere, life, and happiness of this family were all taken away, and the family itself was gone. What a suffering that was to Abraham!

As God's called ones, we should not expect to have a happy life here on earth. We must follow the steps of Abraham looking for a better country, for a city with foundations (Heb. 11:10, 16). Our temporary life on earth is the life of a traveler. Due to this, Abraham paid little attention to his dwelling place and simply erected a tent. He was a sojourner, a stranger, who was looking for a permanent dwelling place.

Abraham lived for thirty-eight years without Sarah's help (25:8). In the Bible, the number thirty-eight is the number of sufferings, trials, and tests. The children of Israel suffered trials and tests in the wilderness for a period of thirty-eight years. As we have seen, Isaac was forty years old when he married. In the Bible, the number forty also means trials, temptations, and tests. We also have another number in this chapter—four hundred—which is ten times forty. The first time the number four hundred is used in the Bible is in Genesis 15:13, where Abraham was told that his descendants would suffer affliction for four hundred years. Here in 23:16 we read that Abraham bought the sepulcher at the cost of four hundred shekels of silver. This indicates that it was a test, trial, and suffering.

As you read this chapter in the past, perhaps you did not have the feeling that Abraham was suffering. But notice two words in verse 2—"mourn" and "weep." Abraham mourned and wept for Sarah because he had lost his happiness and his family life. The Hebrew words translated "mourn" and "weep" indicate much more than just mourning and weeping. Abraham suffered intensely at losing his wife in his old age; he was deeply hurt. His great suffering is indicated by the numbers thirty-eight, forty, and four hundred.

ABRAHAM'S TESTIMONY

Abraham, one who had suffered the loss of his dear wife, had a very strong testimony. The Hittites addressed him as lord and called him "a mighty prince" (v. 6). The Hebrew words translated "mighty prince" may also be rendered "a prince of God." In Hebrew, the word for "mighty" is the word for God. Abraham expressed God as a prince of God and was respectable as a mighty prince. In his own eyes, he was a stranger, but in the eyes of the people, he was a mighty prince and a prince of God. He was truly a weighty man.

We all need to be weighty and have the same kind of testimony that Abraham had. In our neighborhoods, occupations, and schools, we must not be light and allow others to look down on us. We must be weighty, and others must estimate us very highly. Although we should not estimate ourselves so highly, we must be high in the eyes of others. I hope that the teachers in the junior high schools will say that the young brothers from the church who are students in their class are mighty princes. Young brothers, do not just pray boldly in the meetings. You must also be weighty in school. Simply having good behavior does not mean very much. We must have weight. Gold and diamonds are weighty, but popcorn and cotton candy are light. If you are gold or diamond, you will have weight. As God's called ones, we Christians should be so weighty that people are surprised and say, "Why is this young man so weighty? He is neither common nor abnormal. Although he is a normal young man, there is no lightness with him. He must be a prince."

We are weighty because we have God in us. The called ones need to call on the name of Jehovah, El Olam. The more Abraham called on this title of the divine Being, the more weighty he became. God is gold. If we call on Him, we shall become golden. The more we call on the golden God, the more of His golden element will be infused into our being. Consider the difference between wood and petrified wood. Wood is light, but petrified wood is weighty. It is even more weighty than stone, because weighty minerals have been wrought into it. We all were born light, but we have been reborn to be weighty. In addition to our rebirth, we have the process of transformation. The way in which wood becomes petrified is through the continuous flow of water. This flow of water carries away the element of wood and adds in its place the element of various minerals, transforming the wood into a weighty, precious stone.

It is insufficient for us merely to be good neighbors. We must be weighty children of God. As God's called ones, we are now under His infusion. We must be so strong and weighty that people will say that we are a mighty prince, a prince of God.

As a mighty prince, Abraham was respectable (v. 6). He respected others and received their respect in return. He was also wise (vv. 3-13). In this chapter we see that Abraham had a wise way of communing with people, speaking to them in a very tasteful and wise manner. Furthermore, Abraham was honest and did not take advantage of anyone (vv. 14-16). His intention was to purchase the sepulcher. When it was politely offered to him as a gift, Abraham, after learning that its value was four hundred shekels of silver, agreed to pay the full amount. He did not seize the opportunity to take advantage of others, and he did not bargain about the price. He gave Ephron the price he asked, paying the full amount, the full money. Likewise, we should not impress people with our scarcity; we must show our riches. This is our testimony. I feel badly about the low level of morality in today's Christianity. What a poor standard of behavior there is! We must express God showing that we, as the children of God, are weighty, respectable, and honest. We should be willing to suffer loss, but not to take advantage of others. Whether we lose or gain means nothing. If we lose, we shall still live; if we gain, we cannot live any longer. How we must learn to be honest and respectable, expressing God in a weighty manner.

A SEPULCHER OF CHOICE

Verse 6 speaks of the "choice" sepulcher, referring to the best sepulcher. When the Lord Jesus was on earth, He did not have a good dwelling place. But after He died, He was put into a very good burying place (Matt. 27:57-60). He lived in a poor home, but He was buried in a rich tomb. In the Bible, this is a principle. We should not live in a good home, but we should prepare the best tomb. Abraham paid more attention to the sepulcher than to the tent. Genesis does not say a word regarding how Abraham put up his tent, how much he paid for it, or exactly where he erected it. He pitched his tent like someone who goes camping in the mountains for a few days. Abraham, a true camper, was camping throughout his entire life. Although he did not care very much about the tent, he was very concerned for the sepulcher. In this chapter we find a full description in detail of the cave of Machpelah in the field of Ephron. Not even the Old Testament city of Jerusalem is described in such a detailed way.

Let us now consider the meaning of this. In the light of the New Testament, we can see that Abraham was called by God and realized that he was a stranger, a sojourner, looking for a permanent city and a better country (Heb. 11:9-10, 16). As he was looking for this better country, his dear wife suddenly died. But Abraham did not give up his faith. Neither did he say to Isaac, "Isaac, your mother and I have been looking for a city with foundations and for the better country which God has promised us. We have always had this expectation. Now your mother is dead. How will she ever get there? What should we do? Probably our God is not trustworthy and we should not believe in Him anymore." Abraham did not speak in this way. As we examine the record in Hebrews, we see that Abraham was not disappointed and did not lose his faith. Rather, he had strong faith in the God of resurrection, believing that his dear wife would be in that city and in that better country. This belief implies resurrection.

Genesis 23 is not a chapter on resurrection; it is a chapter on the gate into resurrection. In Genesis 23 Sarah did not enter into resurrection; she entered into the gate. According to Abraham's realization, Sarah's death was the entering into the gate of resurrection. Abraham did not take this matter lightly. Although he might have been somewhat light with his tent, he was not light concerning the burying place of his wife. His intention in purchasing the cave of Machpelah was not only to bury Sarah there, but also to bury himself there. The word Machpelah in Hebrew means double or doubling. Everyone who was buried in this cave was buried as one of a couple: Abraham and Sarah, Isaac and Rebekah, Jacob and Leah (v. 19; 25:9; 49:29-32; 50:13). Deep within, Abraham was filled with the expectation that one day his wife would be in the city of foundations. This implies resurrection. Shortly before his death, Jacob charged his sons to bury him in the cave of Machpelah. Although in ancient times it was not a small thing to take Jacob from Egypt to Canaan to be buried, Jacob's sons did it for him (50:13). By this we can realize that, as he was about to die, Jacob did not consider death as a termination but as a station, as the gate into the better country.

Abraham was filled with the hope of resurrection. He might have even loved the dead body of his wife more than he loved Sarah when she was living. If Sarah could have spoken to Abraham, she might have said, "Abraham, why are you so good to me after I have died? When I was living you never prepared a good tent for me. Now that I am dead, you have paid so much money to buy a cave in which to bury me. Why did you buy a cave with a field and trees? What are you doing?" Abraham might have said, "Sarah, you must realize that you are not being buried here. You will just rest here. I have prepared the best bedroom for you in which you may rest as you wait for that day. If that day is far off, I will come to be one with you and we shall rest together. This is why I have purchased the field as well as the cave. Look at the life in the field. It is not a place of death—it is a place of life."

In the Bible, a field signifies the growth of life, that is, resurrection. This is true even today. If you do not believe in resurrection, I would ask you to consider a wheat field. Not long after the grains of wheat are planted, they rise up again. In 1936, I was preaching the gospel to a group of students at Ching-Hua University in China. One evening, after I had preached, a young student came up to me and, wanting me to explain the matter of resurrection, said, "I have no problem with Christianity, but I cannot believe in the resurrection. How can we, in our modern, scientific age, believe in such a superstitious thing as resurrection? How can a dead person be resurrected? Yet, this is one of the main teachings in the Bible." I said to him that this was easy to explain. Through the window of the room in which we were sitting we could see wheat fields. I said, "Look at the wheat fields. Do you see the wheat that is growing there? Can't you see resurrection in these fields? The seed is sown into the soil, dies, and eventually the wheat comes forth. This is resurrection." This simple illustration convinced him, and he was saved. Now he is one of the leading co-workers on the island of Taiwan.

A growing field signifies resurrection, but driftwood signifies death. Abraham did not put Sarah into a place of death, but into a place of life, a place full of resurrection. The cave in which she was buried was in the end of the field (v. 9), and there were many trees nearby (v. 17). Suppose the cave of Machpelah was surrounded by piles of driftwood. Whenever anyone saw this, he would immediately have had the sense that it was a place of death, a place of termination. But the cave of Machpelah is not the place of termination; it is a place full of the expectation of resurrection. It is on the way to resurrection. In this place, Sarah could restfully sleep as she waited for that day to come. If she could speak, she might say, "I am not waiting in a place of death. I am in a living place. Look at the field and the trees. Someday, I'll be in resurrection." Sarah's death did not disappoint Abraham in his search for a better country and for a city with foundations. On the contrary, it stirred up his expectation of the coming day. Therefore, he devoted much attention and spent a large amount of money to purchase the burying place for Sarah, himself, and his descendants. If we have the light from the New Testament, we shall realize that this indicates the expectation of resurrection. Once again I say that the sepulcher is the passageway, the gateway, into the expected city, the New Jerusalem. Hallelujah, the cave of Machpelah is on the way to Jerusalem!

We know that Genesis 23 indicates the expectation of resurrection because the Lord Jesus said that the God of Abraham, the God of Isaac, and the God of Jacob is not the God of the dead but of the living (Matt. 22:31-32). In our eyes, Abraham, Isaac, and Jacob are dead, but in God's eyes, they are living.

Our forefather, Abraham, God's called one, did not care very much for the present, but he did pay attention to the future. The choice sepulcher was for the future. In principle, we also should not prepare a better home for the present but a gateway for the future. We are not here for today but for tomorrow. If the Lord delays His coming back, we all shall enter into this gateway. We should not pay too much attention to the present but rather to the future. We should live in a tent looking for the city which has foundations. ✖

24

LIVING IN FELLOWSHIP WITH GOD
THE MARRIAGE OF ISAAC
A PRACTICAL LIVING IN ONENESS WITH THE LORD

And Abraham
said unto his eldest servant of his house,
that ruled over all that he had,
Put, I pray thee, thy hand under my thigh:
and I will make thee swear by the Lord,
the God of heaven, and the God of the earth,
that thou shalt not take a wife
unto my son of the daughters of the Canaanites,
among whom I dwell: but thou shalt go unto my country,
and to my kindred, and take a wife
unto my son Isaac.

Genesis 24:2-4

The Bible reveals that God's eternal purpose is to express Himself through a corporate Body and that this purpose is fulfilled by the divine life. If we would probe into the depths of the book of Genesis, we must see these two things. In Genesis 1:26 we see that man was made in God's image. The man here is not an individual man but a corporate man. We may say that it is mankind, a corporate Body that can express God's image. In Genesis 2 we see that for the fulfillment of God's purpose we must have the divine life signified by the tree of life. In these two chapters we have two crucial words—image and life. Image reveals God's eternal purpose, and life unfolds God's way of fulfilling His purpose. Never consider Genesis as merely the record of God's creation and the history of some patriarchs. This view is too superficial. When we plunge into the depths of this book, we see that it is not merely a record of creation and history, but that it is a revelation of God's eternal purpose and His way of fulfilling it.

With these two points in mind, let us now come to Genesis 24. Everyone who reads Genesis thinks of this chapter as the record of a marriage. However, the important thing here is not the marriage but what the marriage indicates, implies, and typifies. When we were on Genesis 1 and 2, we saw that those chapters are not only a record of God's creation but a record of life. Everything found in those chapters is related to life. Anything that is not related to life is excluded. If you read those chapters carefully, you will see that many aspects of God's creation are omitted because they are not related to life. In the same principle, only those aspects of Abraham's history which are related to life are recorded in chapters twenty-one through twenty-four.

The entire book of Genesis, a book of only fifty chapters, covers over twenty-three hundred years, the first twenty-three centuries of human history. If Genesis were a record of history, it would need hundreds of chapters to cover this span of time. The fact that such a long period is covered in just fifty chapters proves that Genesis is not a record of history. I say again that although Genesis apparently is a record of history, it actually is a record showing God's eternal purpose and the way of fulfilling it by life. Anything which is not related to God's purpose and its fulfillment by life is not recorded in this book.

Chapters twenty-one through twenty-four, covering forty years (25:20), mention five main things: the birth of Isaac, the growth of Isaac, the offering of Isaac, the death and burial of Sarah, and the marriage of Isaac. Although this record is brief, it is very meaningful. Here we see a proper birth and the proper growth. This birth and growth produced a burnt offering for God's satisfaction. After the birth and growth in chapter twenty-one, we have the burnt offering in chapter twenty-two. Then, as we have seen, in chapter twenty-three we have the death of Sarah and a detailed account of her burial. Following this, in chapter twenty-four, we see a wonderful marriage. But this chapter is not merely the record of a marriage; it is a story which has a deep meaning and significance in life.

According to the common understanding of most Christians, the main point of this chapter is that Isaac is a type of Christ as the Bridegroom and that Rebekah is a type of the church as the bride. However, this is not the main point. The primary point is the practical living in oneness with the Lord for the fulfilling of God's purpose. We should not understand the Bible according to our common knowledge or tradition, but come back to the pure Word. Whenever we read any portion of the Scriptures, we must forget all we have learned in the past and look to the Lord for something new. Fifty years ago I read Genesis 24 carefully, doing my best to remember every point. Nevertheless, when I come to this chapter now, I do not care for what I had in the past. I like to come to this portion of the Word as if I were reading it for the first time. I can testify that just recently I have seen something new in this chapter.

Have you ever realized that in Genesis 24 we can see a practical living in oneness with the Lord? As we have seen, God has a purpose, and the way to fulfill His purpose is by life. These are the two governing points in understanding the Bible. If we would understand Genesis 24, we must apply these two governing points. Why does Genesis 24 give us such a record of Isaac's marriage? If we only read chapter twenty-four we cannot see the purpose of this record. In order to answer this question we must read the three foregoing chapters. Genesis 21:12 says, "In Isaac shall thy seed be called." God called Abraham with a purpose. For the fulfillment of this purpose, God promised to give Abraham the good land and the seed which would inherit the land. God's eternal purpose is to express Himself in a corporate way. In order to have this corporate expression, God must have a people. This people is the seed of Abraham. Furthermore, in order to have the people to express God corporately there is the need of the land. What then is the purpose of the marriage in Genesis 24? Is it simply that a single man might have a happy, comfortable life? No. If you consider the Bible as a whole, you will see that Isaac's marriage was altogether for the fulfillment of God's eternal purpose. Without marriage, how could Isaac have brought forth the seed? If this single man was to have seed for the fulfillment of God's eternal purpose, he had to get married. After Abraham had been tested in chapter twenty-two, God said, "In blessing I will bless thee, and in multiplying I will multiply thy seed as the stars of the heaven, and as the sand which is upon the sea shore; and thy seed shall possess the gate of his enemies; and in thy seed shall all the nations of the earth be blessed" (22:17-18). Here we also have the seed for the fulfillment of God's purpose. Thus, Isaac's marriage was not common nor merely for his human living; it was for the fulfillment of God's eternal purpose.

ABRAHAM

Abraham's living was a practical living in oneness with the Lord. Abraham did not suddenly have a vision in which God told him that He had a high purpose to carry out on earth, that He needed him, and that Isaac had to be married in order for God's purpose to be fulfilled. There is no such vision in chapter twenty-four. Rather, the record in Genesis is common and human. According to this record, a man had a son in his old age. When this son was thirty-seven years old, the wife and mother died, and the father buried her in a very meaningful way. The father and the son, both of whom were now unmarried, were left alone, living together in that sad condition for three years. The son might have said, "Father, where is my mother?" and the father might have replied, "Son, where is your wife?" The father was burdened to take care of his son. Perhaps he said, "I have lost my wife, and my son is now forty years of age. This surely is the right time for him to get married. But we are surrounded by Canaanites, none of whom would ever be accepted by God." There is no record that God said, "Abraham, let Me charge you to send someone to your own country to get a wife for Isaac. I will never allow you to take a Canaanite woman as a wife for your son." Although there is no record of God's saying this, Abraham did have this understanding. From where did he derive it? It came from his living in accordance with God's concept.

Abraham was a man who lived in oneness with God. If I live in oneness with a certain brother day after day, there will be no need for him to tell me of many things. I will already know what he likes and what he does not like, what pleases him and what offends him. If I love him and live in oneness with him, whatever I say and do will be in accordance with his likes or dislikes. I am sorry to say that many Christians do not live in oneness with God. When important matters arise, they kneel down and pray, "O Lord, what is Your will?" Eventually, they do not follow God's will but their own concept. We do not know God's will by praying in such a way. If we would know God's will, we must live in oneness with Him. If we live in oneness with Him, He will not need to tell us what He desires, because we shall already know it by being one with Him.

Although Abraham was desperate to take care of his son's marriage, he would not accept a Canaanite as Isaac's wife. If we had been Abraham, we might have taken the easy way and said, "There are many girls here in the land of Canaan. Why can't I choose one of them as the wife for my son? There may be one very nearby." Abraham did not think this way, but sent his oldest servant far away, back to the country from where he came, to find a wife for Isaac. Although God never told Abraham to do this, what Abraham did was according to God's inner will and concept. As we have seen, Abraham knew God's will and mind because he was living in practical oneness with Him.

Abraham was not the only person who had such a living. All those mentioned in this chapter were living in an atmosphere of oneness with God. Abraham, the oldest servant, Rebekah, Laban, Bethuel, and Isaac were all living in oneness with God. I hope that everyone in the churches will see that we need such a living for the fulfillment of God's purpose today. We do not need to pray and seek after God's will; we need to live in oneness with God. When we live in oneness with Him, we shall share His concept, and whatever we think and do will be in accordance with His feeling. God will not need to say anything, for we shall sense what He senses, knowing His inner feeling because we live in oneness with Him.

MOVING IN ACCORDANCE WITH GOD'S ECONOMY ✦ Abraham moved in accordance with God's economy (vv. 3-8). What he did in obtaining a wife for Isaac was for the fulfillment of God's eternal purpose. We long to see that all the marriages in the churches will be for the fulfillment of God's purpose. This kind of marriage requires a daily living in oneness with God. Young brothers, if everything you do is in accordance with God's economy, even your marriage will be the carrying out of His economy. You need to say, "Lord, what I am doing here today must be in accordance with Your economy. I am single now, but one day I will be married. May my marriage be for Your economy." This is the main revelation in Genesis 24. The primary thing in this chapter is not that Isaac is a type of Christ as the Bridegroom and that Rebekah is a type of the church as the bride. I say again that the primary thing revealed here is the practical living in accordance with God's economy for the carrying out of His eternal purpose. We need a life which resembles that of Abraham. His motive, action, and everything he did were in accordance with God's economy.

I doubt that Abraham was as clear about God's economy as we are today. Nevertheless, he told his servant that God had called him, had promised to give the land to his seed, and that the servant had to go to his country to find a wife for Isaac. In the light of the whole Bible, we can see that this was the carrying out of God's economy. How we need such a life today! Our motive, action, and all we do must be the carrying out of God's economy. This does not simply require that we know God's will and then do certain things. No, we need a daily living that is in oneness with God. We must be this kind of person. If we are such a person, whatever we say will be God's expression, and whatever we do will be for the fulfillment of His purpose. This is the life that we need for the church life today. Do not say, "Oh, I don't know the Lord's will concerning my marriage or my schooling. I must fast and pray for three days and nights." Let me tell you honestly that although I tried this for years, it never worked very well.

Consider the example of Abraham, the first of God's called ones. Since he was the first called one, we see in his case the principle of the first mention. Abraham did not act in today's traditional, religious way, fasting and praying to seek the Lord's will. He did not suddenly have a dream in which he saw Rebekah in the land of Chaldea waiting for Abraham's servant. As verse 40 indicates, Abraham walked before the Lord. As a person walking in the presence of the Lord, he did not need to fast or pray in order to know God's will. Since he walked in the Lord's presence, whatever he did was God's will and according to God's economy.

CHARGING HIS SERVANT WITH THE LORD   ✦   Abraham did not charge his servant to be faithful, honest, or to do a good work; he charged him with and by the Lord (vv. 2-3, 9, 40-41). Here we see that the atmosphere in which Abraham lived was the Lord Himself. By charging his servant with the Lord, he brought him deep into the Lord. Likewise, we should not charge people with our wisdom or even with our love, but with the Lord.

BELIEVING IN THE SOVEREIGN LORD ✦ Abraham believed in the sovereign Lord, telling his servant that the Lord would send His angel with him and prosper his way (v. 40). Abraham seemed to be saying, "God will send His angel before you. Although I am sending you to do the job, I believe in God. In a sense, I don't believe that you can accomplish this work, but I trust in the living God. You don't need to be burdened or to worry. Just go and do the job, for my God will send His angel to do the work for you." What a life Abraham had! If we had been Abraham, we might have said, "My servant, you must realize that I have passed through many experiences. Let me now give you a map and tell you of the people and their customs." Abraham did not do this. Rather, he only charged his servant to serve by the Lord, assuring him that God would send His angel before him and prosper his way. Here we see Abraham's living faith.

THE OLDEST SERVANT

FAITHFUL IN RESPONSIBILITY ✦ Abraham's oldest servant was faithful in responsibility (vv. 5, 9, 33, 54, 56). He followed Abraham's footsteps in being faithful. I believe that he was infused by and with Abraham's life, seeing how Abraham did everything by trusting in the Lord. As a result, the servant also trusted in Him.

TRUSTING IN THE LORD FOR HIS RESPONSIBILITY ✦ Abraham's servant trusted in the Lord for his responsibility (vv. 12, 21, 42). He prayed to the Lord in a clear, humble, yet simple way. Everyone who truly believes in God is simple. When he came to the well near the city of Nahor, he prayed, saying, "O Lord God of my master Abraham, I pray thee, send me good success this day, and shew kindness unto my master Abraham. Behold, I stand here by the well of water; and the daughters of the men of the city come out to draw water: and let it come to pass, that the damsel to whom I shall say, Let down thy pitcher, I pray thee, that I may drink; and she shall say, Drink, and I will give thy camels drink also; let the same be she that thou hast appointed for thy servant Isaac; and thereby shall I know that thou hast shewed kindness unto my master" (vv. 12-14, Heb.). His prayer was answered immediately. Before he had even finished speaking, Rebekah came with her pitcher upon her shoulder. When he asked her for a drink, she not only gave him a drink but also drew water for all his camels. After she had done this, the servant was clear that Rebekah was the one and he gave her a ring and two bracelets.

LOOKING FOR THE LORD'S LEADING IN THE ENVIRONMENT   ✦   The servant knew the Lord's will by looking for His leading in the environment (vv. 13-21, 26-27, 48-49). We also can see God's sovereignty in our environment. No one told the servant to go to the city of Nahor, the city of Abraham's brother. He just went there and at the well he met Rebekah, Nahor's granddaughter. Nothing was accidental; everything was ordained before the foundation of the world and was carried out through Abraham's servant, a man who trusted in God.

REBEKAH

CHASTE, KIND, AND DILIGENT   ✦   In verse 16 we are told that Rebekah was "very fair to look upon, a virgin." Rebekah was chaste and pure. She was also kind and diligent (vv. 18-20). When Abraham's servant asked for a drink, she immediately gave it to him. She also drew water for his camels. It was hard work for a young woman to draw water out of the well and pour it into the trough for ten camels to drink, but she did it. If the young sisters want to be under God's sovereignty, especially with respect to their marriage, they need to be kind and diligent. Any young woman who is unkind and sloppy should remain single. When people ask you to do one thing, you must do two things for them. And the second thing should far surpass the first thing. You should not only give a man water to drink, but should also draw water for his ten camels. If you do this, you will be qualified to obtain your husband, your Isaac. This is some advice to all the young single sisters.

ABSOLUTE   ✦   Rebekah was absolute (vv. 57-58, 61). Although Rebekah had never seen Isaac, she was willing to go to him without hesitation. She did not say to her mother, "Mother, I have never seen Isaac. Perhaps I should correspond with him first and afterward have

him pay us a visit. Then I could decide whether or not to marry him."
Rebekah did not talk in this way. Although her brother and mother
were hesitating, wanting her to stay for at least ten days, she said, "I
will go." She was absolute.

During the past forty years, I have seen a number of young sisters
who developed mental problems as a result of considering marriage.
Some spent days, weeks, months, and even years considering
whether a particular brother was the one whom God had prepared
for them. When such sisters came to me, I said, with a rebuking
tone, "If you feel he is the brother, marry him blindly. But if he is
not the one, forget about him and don't talk about it. The more you
consider, the more you bother God, yourself, and me. How can I tell
you yes or no? If I say yes, you will say that I do not know him well.
If I say no, you will feel unhappy because you have already fallen in
love with him. Don't think about it anymore. Either marry him or
forget about him." I was serious in telling them this. Young sisters, if
you want to be married, you must learn to be kind, diligent, and
absolute.

SUBMISSIVE ✦ Rebekah was also submissive (vv. 64-65). When
she saw Isaac and realized who he was, "she took a veil, and covered
herself." Sisters, do not put a piece of cloth on your head as a decora-
tion or ornament. It must be a sign of your submission. Once you are
married, you are no longer your own head. Your husband is your
head, and your head must be covered. This is the true meaning of
marriage.

LABAN AND BETHUEL

Laban and Bethuel were in the fear of the Lord (vv. 29-31). They
were also very hospitable (vv. 31-33). Hospitality often brings in the
greatest blessing. For Rebekah, the daughter of Bethuel and the sister
of Laban, to become Isaac's wife was a great blessing. That blessing
was secured by their being hospitable. If they had not been hospitable
but rather had rejected Abraham's servant, that wonderful marriage
would never have taken place. Furthermore, they accepted the Lord's
sovereignty, saying, "The thing proceedeth from the Lord: we cannot
speak unto thee bad or good" (vv. 50-51, 55-60). Laban and Bethuel
recognized that this was the Lord's doing and that they had no right

to say anything about it. Here we see the atmosphere of their life, a life in oneness with God.

ISAAC

Isaac was not a man of activity, for he did not do anything. He simply dwelt by a well, by a place of living water. Verse 63 says, "Isaac went out to meditate in the field at the eventide." Translators of the Bible are bothered about the rendering of the Hebrew in this verse. Some versions interpret it as meaning that Isaac went to the field to pray, and others say that he went to the field to worship. It might have been that Isaac was meditating in the presence of the Lord, possibly considering his marriage. He had lost his mother, did not have a wife, and the most trustworthy servant had gone on a journey. Isaac did not know if the servant would ever come back. The family had no safety or security, and he was in a desperate situation. Hence, he went out to the field to seek the Lord and meditate before God. While he was meditating, Rebekah came. After the servant had told Isaac all that had happened, Isaac took what his father had done for him and married Rebekah (vv. 66-67). His marriage was an inheritance, not a strife. He did not strive for a wife; he inherited what his father had done for him. He did not do a thing to get a wife. He only took what the father had secured for him. Acting in this way, he was one with the Lord that the purpose of God might be fulfilled in him. He had a real and solid marriage without a wedding ceremony.

FULFILLING THE PURPOSE OF GOD

Isaac's marriage eventually fulfilled the purpose of God (21:12b; 22:17-18). The life of those in this chapter was not merely for their own human living; it was a life that issued in the fulfillment of God's eternal purpose, a life which brought forth Christ and produced the kingdom of God for God's economy.

25

LIVING IN FELLOWSHIP WITH GOD
THE MARRIAGE OF ISAAC
A TYPE OF CHRIST
MARRYING THE CHURCH

*And Isaac
went out to meditate
in the field at the eventide:
and he lifted up his eyes, and saw, and,
behold, the camels were coming.
And Rebekah lifted up her eyes, and when she saw Isaac,
she lighted off the camel.*

Genesis 24:63-64

*Let us rejoice and exult,
and let us give the glory to Him,
for the marriage of the Lamb has come, and His wife
has made herself ready.*

Revelation 19:7

The Bible is a divine book composed with the divine concepts. Because of this, it contains many wonderful records, of which

Genesis 24 is one. This chapter not only unfolds a living in oneness with God; it also implies something deeper than human living. This is the reason that it is difficult for the human mind to fathom the depths of the Bible. On the surface of Genesis 24, we have a record of human living, but in its depths there lies something divine. Although it is easy to view the surface, it is difficult to probe into the depths.

In Genesis 24 we see a marriage which is a type of Christ marrying the church. In the New Testament we cannot find a verse which says that this marriage is a type of Christ marrying the church. However, the New Testament clearly reveals that Isaac, the son of Abraham, was a type of Christ being Abraham's unique seed (Gal. 3:16). Based upon the fact that Isaac was a type of Christ, we may infer that Isaac's marriage was a type of the marriage of Christ.

Because the Bible is a divine book composed with the divine concepts, we can see these concepts in the various biblical records. For example, we are all familiar with the story of Joseph. Although there is no word in the New Testament saying that Joseph was a type of Christ, any reader of the Bible can recognize that Joseph's story closely resembles that of Christ. Some Bible teachers say that we should not allegorize anything in the Scriptures unless the New Testament indicates that it is an allegory or a type of certain spiritual things. But we should not insist on this, for although the New Testament does not say that Joseph was a type of Christ, every Bible teacher recognizes that Joseph was an excellent type of Christ. As we read the story of Joseph, we see that it depicts the life of Christ. Many incidents in Joseph's life, such as his betrayal, are similar to those in the life of Christ. In the same principle, because Isaac is a type of Christ and because the marriage of Isaac resembles the marriage of Christ, we may say that the marriage recorded in Genesis 24 is a type of the marriage of Christ.

In Genesis 24 we have four main persons: the father, the son, the servant, and the bride. This is very meaningful. As we come to the New Testament, we see that the Triune God is working together to obtain a bride for the Son. What is the subject of the New Testament? If you say that the subject of the New Testament is just Jesus as our Savior, I would say that this is good, but that it is not all-inclusive. The subject of the New Testament is the Triune God, the Father, the Son, and the Spirit, working together to obtain the bride for the Son. The Father made the plan, the Spirit carries out the Father's plan, and the Son enjoys what the Father has planned and what the Spirit carries out. Who is the bride? The bride is a part of the human race which will marry the Son and become His counterpart. Matthew 28:19 speaks of the Father, the Son, and the Spirit. In the Acts and Epistles we see how the Spirit works according to the Father's plan to obtain the bride for the Son. At the end of the New Testament, in the book of Revelation, we see the bride. Revelation 19:7 says, "The marriage of the Lamb is come, and His wife has made herself ready." Ultimately, the whole New Jerusalem, a city-lady, will be the bride (Rev. 21:2, 9-10). Although such a term as city-lady may sound strange, there is nothing wrong with using it, because the New Jerusalem will be a female, the wife of the Lamb, the counterpart of the Son of God. The entire New Testament is simply a record of the Triune God working together to gain a part of the human race to be the bride, the counterpart, of the Son.

THE FATHER'S PLAN

Firstly, we have the Father's plan. According to the King James Version, Ephesians 3:11 speaks of "the eternal purpose which he purposed in Christ Jesus our Lord." The word purpose is an archaic term for the modern word plan. When we speak of God's plan we are referring to God's purpose. In eternity past God made a plan, a plan to have the church for Christ (Eph. 3:8-11). God's plan is not just to have a group of sinners, nor to have a group of redeemed ones. Such a concept is too low. God's plan is to have a bride for His Son.

We have heard time and time again that Christ came to save sinners. But have you ever heard a message telling you that Christ came to have the bride? John 3:29 says, "He who has the bride is the bridegroom." In the four Gospels the Lord Jesus told His disciples that He was the Bridegroom (Matt. 9:15). He came not only to save sinners but to have the bride. Are we still sinners? No, we are the bride! Praise the Lord that we are no longer sinners—we are the bride! Should we still come to God confessing our sins in a begging way? No, we must come to Him joyfully, saying, "Praise the Lord! I am so happy that I am no longer a sinner. I'm a part of the bride!" Christ came not merely to be our Savior and Redeemer; He also came to be the Bridegroom. God did not plan to save a group of poor sinners and bring them all into heaven. God planned to take a part of the human race and make them the counterpart of His dear Son. Eventually, in the new heaven and the new earth, we shall not have a group of pitiful sinners; we shall have the bride, the New Jerusalem, the wife of the Lamb.

As we have seen, God the Father planned to take a bride for His Son out of the human race. Abraham, a type of the Father, charged his servant, a type of the Holy Spirit, not to take a wife for his son from the daughters of the Canaanites but from Abraham's kindred (24:4, 7). In typology, this indicates that the counterpart of Christ must come from Christ's race, not from the angels nor from any other creatures. Since Christ was incarnated as a man, humanity has become His race. Do not always think of humanity as being so poor. Humanity is not poor. Because humanity is the race of Christ, it is dear and precious to God. Only out of humanity can God obtain the counterpart for His Son. Therefore, we all must be proud of being a part of humanity and must say, "Praise the Lord that I am a man! Thank Him that I was not created as a part of the angelic race but as part of the human race."

In Genesis 2 we see that God brought the living creatures to Adam to be named by him. Adam said, "This is a dog, and this is a cat. This is a monkey, and this is a donkey." As he looked at all those creatures, he did not find his counterpart among them. Thus, God caused a deep sleep to fall upon Adam, took one of his ribs, and built it into a woman as his counterpart (2:21-22). Hence, Adam and Eve were of the same race. This indicates that Christ's counterpart must come from His race, the human race. We all have been created as the human race, and as a part of the human race we all have been reborn. Only the human race is qualified to be the counterpart of Christ.

THE SPIRIT'S ERRAND

While the father had a plan, the servant received a commission, an errand (v. 33). Abraham commissioned him to go to his race and take a wife for his son. This signifies that God the Father has commissioned God the Spirit. The New Testament reveals such a divine commission.

TO REACH THE CHOSEN BRIDE   ✦   As Abraham commissioned his servant to reach the chosen bride (vv. 10-21), so God the Father commissioned God the Spirit to reach the human race. We all can testify that at a certain time the Spirit of God came to us. Perhaps you would say, "I didn't realize that God the Spirit came to me. I only know that someone preached the gospel to me." As that person was preaching the gospel to you, you were attracted by what he said and were willing to receive it. Although you did not understand everything he was saying, something deep within you was responding. In our mentality, many of us said, "I don't like this," but deep within our spirit we said, "This is very good." In my early ministry in China I did a great deal of gospel preaching. When the learned Chinese, who thought of Christianity as a foreign religion, heard our preaching, they said in their mentality, "This is a foreign religion; I don't like it." But, as many of them later testified, while they were saying this, something deep within them said, "This is what I need." What was it that caused them to respond in this way deep within? It was the Holy Spirit reaching them.

Rebekah never dreamed that she would be selected to be Isaac's wife. According to the custom of the time, she simply went to draw water late in the afternoon. But on this day something special happened. Before she came to the well, Abraham's servant was already there. This indicates the Spirit's coming to the human race (v. 10). Before we ever heard the preaching of the gospel or came to a gospel meeting, the Holy Spirit was already there waiting.

In Genesis 24, Abraham's servant, who had come to a well (v. 11), asked a woman to give him a drink of water (v. 17). In John 4, the Lord Jesus, who had come to Jacob's well (John 4:6), also asked a woman for a drink. Preachers often say that we are thirsty and need the living water to quench our thirst. But have you ever heard that the Holy Spirit is thirsty and needs you to quench His thirst? In Genesis 24 we see a servant who was thirsty after his long journey, and in John 4 we see a Savior who was thirsty after His tiring journey. Who was more thirsty in Genesis 24, the servant or Rebekah? The servant was. Likewise, who was more thirsty in John 4, the Lord Jesus or the Samaritan woman? The Lord Jesus was. Hence, as we preach the gospel, we must tell people that the Father, Son, and Spirit are thirsty for them.

Rebekah did not have the sense that she was thirsty; neither did she feel the need for a husband. It was the servant who was thirsty. By the time he had reached the city of Nahor, he was thirsty both physically and spiritually, thirsting for the woman who would be the proper wife for his master's son. In John 4, the Lord Jesus also was thirsty both physically and spiritually. As you are reading this message, the Holy Spirit is even now thirsty for you. Will you give Him a drink and quench His thirst?

When we heard the preaching of the gospel in the past, we did not realize that the Holy Spirit was thirsty for us. We might have thought, "Why is this preacher so ambitious to convince me?" But that was not the ambition of the preacher; it was the thirst of the Spirit. As you were listening to the preaching of the gospel, did you not sense that someone was desirous of having you? At the time you were saved, you felt that someone was chasing you. On the one hand, you said, "I don't like this"; on the other hand, something deep within you said, "You cannot run away."

As Rebekah went to draw water from the well that day, she was completely innocent, having no idea of what was to happen to her. She did not realize that by giving a man a drink of water and by drawing water for his camels she would be caught. But the father far away had made a plan to take a woman from her race as the wife for his son and had commissioned his servant to carry out this plan. Thus, the servant came to the city of Nahor and purposely waited there by the well. He was a real hunter hunting for a wife for Isaac. If Rebekah had never spoken to the servant, she would not have been caught. But, as we have seen, what happened did not depend on her. The servant had already prayed that the Lord would give him success, saying, "Let it come to pass, that the damsel to whom I shall say, Let down thy pitcher, I pray thee, that I may drink; and she shall say, Drink, and I will give thy camels drink also: let the same be she that thou hast appointed for thy servant Isaac; and thereby shall I know that thou hast showed kindness unto my master" (v. 14). While he was still speaking in this way, Rebekah came. When he asked her for a drink of water, she not only gave him a drink, but said, "I will draw water for thy camels also, until they have done drinking" (vv. 18-19). Although Rebekah did not realize it, in doing this, she was caught.

Many of us can testify that, at the beginning, we did not think well of Christ. But at a certain time something deep within began to love Him. When I was a youth, I did not understand very much about Christ, but I did love Him. Although I could not explain it then, I simply began to love Him. But now I know the reason: in eternity, the Father had planned to catch me. Although I am just a little man, I am more than worthy of being caught by God. We all have been caught by Him according to His plan. Let me ask you, did you desire to be saved or to be a Christian? None of us did. But one day we heard the name of Jesus and responded to it in love. This is the sign that we have been chosen. Who brought the servant to the city of Nahor where Rebekah dwelt? And who brought Rebekah to the well where the servant was waiting? Undoubtedly, it was the Spirit of God. Our being saved did not depend on us. It was the result of the Father's plan and the Spirit's commission.

Abraham's servant eventually reached Rebekah through the satisfying water (v. 14). God's chosen ones are the satisfying water to the Holy Spirit. Today the Holy Spirit comes to seek God's chosen ones as Christ did at the well of Sychar (John 4:7). If anyone responds to Him and satisfies His desire, this is a sign that he is one of those chosen for Christ and that he will be gained by the Holy Spirit for Christ.

TO BRING THE RICHES OF CHRIST TO THE BRIDE   ✦   The Spirit also brings the riches of Christ to the bride (vv. 10, 22, 47, 53). After the camels had finished drinking, the servant put a golden ring on Rebekah's nose and two bracelets upon her hands (v. 22, Heb.). The best way to catch a person is to catch his nose. That Rebekah had a ring on her nose and bracelets upon her hands meant that she had been caught. After giving her these things, the servant asked her, "Whose daughter art thou? tell me, I pray thee: is there room in thy father's house for us to lodge in?" (v. 23). Once the servant was brought into Rebekah's home, he testified of Isaac's riches. After Rebekah's brother Laban and father Bethuel accepted the servant's proposal, he gave Rebekah more of Isaac's riches, articles of silver, articles of gold, and raiment (v. 53). He also gave precious things to her brother and her mother. This is exactly what John 16:13-15 reveals concerning the Spirit. In these verses, the Lord Jesus said that the Spirit will not speak of Himself, but that He will glorify the Son. All that the Father has is His, and the Spirit receives of His and discloses it to the disciples. Suppose Abraham's servant had said to Laban, "It is difficult for Abraham to earn a living in Canaan, and his son Isaac is not healthy. I have been sent to get a helper for him." Do you think that after hearing such a thing Rebekah would have said, "I will go"? No, she would have run away instead. But the testimony of Abraham's servant was not poor; rather, it was very rich. The servant said that the Lord had blessed his master Abraham, that he had become great, that he had given all things to his son Isaac, and that his master had charged him to find a wife for his son. As Rebekah was listening to this testimony, she was attracted to Isaac and was willing to go to him.

This is a picture of how the Holy Spirit comes to us testifying of the riches of Christ. Today Christ is the One appointed to inherit all the riches of the Father. We know this because the Spirit has told us of it through the Scriptures. Because of the Spirit's testimony, we have all been attracted to Christ. Every saved one who loves and seeks the Lord has been attracted in this way. We do not care for the things that the worldlings are seeking. We enjoy coming to the church meetings and telling the Lord Jesus how much we love Him. Oh, we love Him, we seek Him, and we praise Him! Over and over we say, "Lord Jesus, I love You."

Rebekah realized the riches of Isaac through the gifts which Abraham's servant brought forth to her. Today we realize the riches of Christ, which He has received of the Father, through the gifts that the Spirit has dispensed to us. Before Rebekah met Isaac in the good land, she had participated in and enjoyed Isaac's inheritance. It is the same with us in partaking of Christ's inheritance. Before we meet Him, we enjoy the gifts of the Spirit as a foretaste of the full taste of His riches.

To CONVINCE THE BRIDE ✦ The Spirit also convinces the bride (vv. 54-58). After the servant, typifying the Spirit, brought Rebekah the riches, she was convinced and was willing to marry Isaac. Although her relatives wanted her to linger, Rebekah, upon hearing the servant's testimony of Isaac, said, "I will go" (v. 58). She was willing to go to Isaac in the land of Canaan. Likewise, we are willing to go to Christ. Although we have never seen Him, we have been attracted by Him and we love Him (1 Pet. 1:8). Although Rebekah had never met Isaac, she loved him. When she heard about him, she simply loved him and wanted to go to a land far off to be with him. As long as we have the willingness to go to Christ, it is a sign that we are the chosen Rebekah. As I have watched the young people loving Jesus, I have said, "What are all these young people doing here? Why don't they seek the things of the world?" But deep within, I know the reason. We have all been convinced that Christ is the wonderful One. He is the most lovable One in the whole universe. How we love Him! As Rebekah was riding on the camel to be with Isaac, she must have said many times, "Isaac, I love you! Isaac, I want to see you and be with you!" It is the same with us today. As we are traveling on our long journey, we say over and over again, "Jesus, I love You. Jesus, I long to meet You and be in Your presence."

To bring the bride to Christ   ✦   Eventually, the servant brought Rebekah to Isaac (vv. 51, 61-67). Although it was a long journey, he brought her through and presented her to Isaac as his bride. The Holy Spirit has convinced us and now He is bringing us to Christ. Although it is a long journey, eventually He will bring us through and present us to Christ as His lovely bride.

THE CHURCH'S RESPONSE

Now we must see the church's response. As we have seen, Rebekah responded immediately, being willing to go with the servant to Isaac. Although there is within our old, fallen nature a reluctance to follow the Lord immediately, we cannot deny that there is also within us the willingness to follow Him. Although we are still in this old nature, it is nevertheless easy for us to follow the Lord. It is much easier to follow Him than not to follow Him. Do not believe the lie of the enemy that you can easily be frustrated in following the Lord. Tell the enemy, "Nothing can frustrate my desire to follow the Lord. Deep within me there is the longing to follow Him." Satan is a liar. Sometimes he even lies to us through preachers who speak negative things and tell us that we cannot love the Lord Jesus. Do not believe the lies, but declare, "No! I can and I do love the Lord Jesus!" We may even lie to ourselves, saying, "I'm so weak. I just can't follow the Lord. I'd better turn around and go back." We must reject this lie and say, "I will never go back. I will follow the Lord Jesus." Never believe the lie that you do not love the Lord. Tell the enemy, "I love the Lord Jesus. My loving Him does not depend upon my ability to love. It depends on His being so lovable. Because He is lovable, I cannot help loving Him." If I gave you a pair of old shoes, you would reject them, saying, "I don't care for those!" But if I gave you some diamonds, you would easily love them, not because you have the ability to love but because the diamonds are lovable. Likewise, we do not love the Lord Jesus because we are able to love; we love Him because He is so lovable. In Genesis 24, it was not Rebekah who was able to love Isaac and respond to him; it was Isaac who was lovable.

DOING WHAT THE SPIRIT EXPECTS   ✦   Our response to the Holy Spirit is that we always do what He expects. Abraham's servant expected that Rebekah would give him a drink of water and then draw water for his ten camels, and Rebekah did exactly what he expected (vv. 18-20), satisfying the servant's thirst. Often we have unconsciously done what the Holy Spirit expected, satisfying His desire, doing it without knowing what He expected. Our doing this was a sign that we were under the moving of the Spirit.

RECEIVING THE GIFTS   ✦   After doing what the servant expected, Rebekah received the gifts. Firstly, the servant put a golden ring on her nose. Although ladies today like to put rings on their ears, here the ring is put on Rebekah's nose. In reading the Song of Songs, I was surprised to see that the Lord does not appraise the ears of the seeking one. Instead, He appraises her nose, saying, "Thy nose is as the tower of Lebanon which looketh toward Damascus," and, "The smell of thy nose like apples" (7:4, 8). In Song of Songs 2:3, the seeker says, "As the apple tree among the trees of the wood, so is my beloved among the sons. I sat under his shadow with great delight, and his fruit was sweet to my taste." Because she had been enjoying the apples, her nose had the smell of apples. What is the significance of this? The function of the nose is to smell. Putting a golden ring on Rebekah's nose meant that her smelling function had been caught by the divine nature. Once we have this ring on our nose, we have the divine smell and taste. As the book of Hebrews says, we have tasted of the heavenly gift, the good word of God, and the works of power of the coming age (Heb. 6:4-6). Before I was saved, I had a particular taste. However, after I received the Lord, my taste changed. I had received the divine taste. Is there a golden ring on your nose? Is your nose like the high tower of Lebanon? According to Leviticus 21:18, no one with a flat nose could serve as a priest. We all must have a high nose, not a flat one.

We, the saved ones, have the divine smelling function with the divine taste. Since we have this taste, there are many things in the department stores which we cannot buy. What tells us not to buy these things? The golden ring on our nose. By our nose with the golden ring we smell that something is wrong with certain items in the stores. Because we have such a nose, we do not need others to tell us what to do or what not to do. The function of our smelling and tasting organ tells us what matches God's taste and what does not. We must have a high-tower nose and a nose with the smell of apples. Our spiritual nose must be a high tower in the Spirit. Our spiritual nose must be with the smell of Christ. The more we enjoy Christ as the apple tree, the more we have a nose full of His apple smell.

The servant also put two bracelets on Rebekah's hands (vv. 22, 47). In a sense, she was handcuffed. According to the New Testament concept, this means that we have received the divine function (Rom. 12:4). The more we are handcuffed by the Spirit, the more gift we receive of Him. We have not only received the divine taste; we have also acquired the divine function. The two bracelets given to Rebekah were ten shekels in weight and thus could fulfill the requirements of God's commandments. The weight of the golden ring on her nose, on the contrary, was just a half shekel. This half shekel signifies the first taste, the foretaste. The half we have tasted indicates that another half, the full taste, is coming. While the taste is only in part, the functions are in full. Do not say that you have only half a function. No, your function, your talent, is complete. Everyone has at least one full talent. The taste which we have received of the Holy Spirit is only partial, but the divine function which we have received of Him is complete.

Rebekah also received articles of silver, articles of gold, and raiment (v. 53), all of which indicate the riches of Christ. At first, Rebekah received a golden ring on her nose and two bracelets on her hands. After the acceptance of the servant's errand, more riches were brought forth. Likewise, after we came into the church life and accepted the Spirit's commission, the riches of Christ, the articles of silver, the articles of gold, and the raiment, were brought forth for our enjoyment.

By all these details we can realize that the record in Genesis 24 is altogether divine and implies the divine concept. This is not my allegorization; it is recorded in this way. Why was the golden ring just half a shekel and not three quarters of a shekel? Why were the bracelets ten shekels and not nine or eleven shekels? Why did the servant not bring forth all the other riches until his errand had been accepted?

All this matches the revelation in the New Testament. Today we are not only enjoying the golden ring on our nose and the bracelets on our hands; we are also enjoying the articles of silver and of gold and the raiment. In the church life all the riches of Christ are ours.

FOLLOWING THE SPIRIT   ✦   After receiving and enjoying all these riches, Rebekah followed the servant, traveling through the desert on a camel until she met Isaac (vv. 58, 61-65). Likewise, we are following the Spirit, traveling a long journey on a "camel." When we meet Christ, we shall dismount from our "camel." All the modern conveniences, such as telephones, automobiles, etc., are our "camels" today. Rebekah traveled through the desert on top of a camel, and we are traveling through the desert on today's modern "camels." According to Leviticus 11, a camel is unclean; yet it is useful. Many of today's conveniences are not clean in the eyes of God. Nevertheless, they enable us to travel through the desert. When we meet Him, we shall leave the "camels."

THE SON'S MARRIAGE

In a good sense, the son, Isaac, did nothing. This indicates that everything is planned by the Father and carried out by the Spirit. All the Son does is receive the bride.

Isaac received Rebekah at eventide (vv. 63-64). This implies that the marriage of Christ will be at the eventide of the age. At the close of this age, Christ will come to meet His bride.

Isaac brought Rebekah into his mother Sarah's tent and loved her (v. 67). As we have seen, Sarah typifies grace. Hence, this means that Christ will meet us in grace as well as in love.

This chapter ends with the words, "Isaac was comforted after his mother's death." If I had been the writer, I would have said that Rebekah was comforted after her long journey. But the Bible does not say this. Do not consider your comfort, your satisfaction; rather, consider Christ's comfort, Christ's satisfaction. If Christ has no comfort and satisfaction, we cannot have any comfort and satisfaction either. Our satisfaction depends on His. Our comfort is His comfort, and His satisfaction is ours. Christ is now waiting for His comfort. When will He have it? On the day of His marriage. That day will come.   ※

26

Having No Maturity in Life

*Now Sarai, Abram's wife, bare him no children: and she had
a handmaid, an Egyptian, whose name was Hagar.
And Sarai said unto Abram, Behold now, the Lord hath restrained me
from bearing: I pray thee, go in unto my maid; it may be that I may
obtain children by her. And Abram hearkened to the voice
of Sarai....And Hagar bare Abram a son: and Abram called
his son's name, which Hagar bare, Ishmael.*

Genesis 16:1-2, 15

*And the Lord visited Sarah as he had said, and the Lord did
unto Sarah as he had spoken. For Sarah conceived, and bare Abraham
a son in his old age, at the set time of which God had spoken to him.
And Abraham called the name of his son that was born unto him,
whom Sarah bare to him, Isaac.*

Genesis 21:1-3

*Then again Abraham took a wife, and her name was Keturah.
And she bare him Zimran, and Jokshan, and Medan, and Midian,
and Ishbak, and Shuah.*

Genesis 25:1-2

The Bible is a complete revelation. The content of this revelation
is God's eternal purpose. As we have pointed out many times, God's
eternal purpose is to work Himself into a corporate man so that
He may have a corporate expression in the universe. If we would

understand any portion of the Bible in a proper way, we must keep this matter in mind.

In this message we come to Genesis 25. Many years ago, I did not like the first part of this chapter. But since there are no wasted words in the Bible, this portion of Genesis 25 must be very significant. If we do not keep before us the purpose of the revelation in the holy Word, we shall be unable to see the significance of this part of Genesis 25. By His mercy, the Lord has shown us the depth of this portion of the Word.

In both Genesis and Romans we are told clearly that Abraham was very old when he begat Isaac. Romans 4:19 says that Abraham considered his body as good as dead. Yet, forty years after Isaac's birth, Abraham married again (25:1), and when he became one hundred forty years of age, he still begat six sons (25:2). How can we explain this? If he was as old as a dead person when he was a hundred years of age, he certainly must have been more like a dead person when he remarried at the age of one hundred forty. In chapter twenty-three Sarah died and was buried, in chapter twenty-four Abraham obtained a wife for Isaac, and in chapter twenty-five he himself married again. What does this mean?

Genesis 25 also includes a record of the birth of Jacob and Esau. Why is such a wonderful record included in the same chapter which names the six sons of Abraham's concubine? The record of Abraham's six sons is negative, whereas the record of the birth of Jacob and Esau is positive. If you were composing this chapter, would you put these two records together? None of us would have written this chapter in such a way. Nevertheless, according to the inspiration of the Holy Spirit, it must be very significant.

HAVING NO MATURITY IN LIFE

If we consider all these matters, deep in our spirit we shall realize that the Holy Spirit's intention in this chapter is to show that Abraham was not a person matured in life. Although he was old in his physical life, he was not matured in his spiritual life.

As we have seen, God's purpose is to work Himself into a corporate person that He might have a corporate expression. In order to accomplish this, God created the heavens, the earth, and man with a spirit as his receiving organ (Zech. 12:1). This man was created in God's image to express Him and with His dominion to represent Him in His authority. In Genesis 3 we see that Satan injected himself into man, and man became fallen. In chapters three through eleven man had at least four falls. After the fourth fall, God came in to call Abraham out of the fallen race and establish him as the father of the called race. God's intention in making Abraham the father of the called race was to work Himself into that race for the fulfillment of His purpose. Although God did not have the opportunity to work Himself into the created race, the Adamic race, He now had an opportunity to work Himself into the called race, the Abrahamic race. The record from the last half of chapter eleven through the first part of chapter twenty-five shows how much God worked with this person. However, when we come to the end of the record of Abraham's life, do we see a person who was matured in life and who expressed God in every way? No. Abraham was not yet such a person.

Many Christians appreciate Abraham too much. Although I respect Abraham and I do not belittle him, I must point out that, as the record of Genesis indicates, he was not matured in the divine life. Chapter twenty-four is wonderful, but it is not wonderful with respect to Abraham's life but with respect to his activity. Abraham did a wonderful thing in choosing a proper wife for his son; yet, immediately after this, he remarried. Genesis 25 does not say, "After Abraham had found a good wife for Isaac, he lived with them in the presence of the Lord for more than thirty years. One day, he called Isaac and Rebekah to him, laid his hands upon them, blessed them, and then went to be with the Lord." If the record were like this, we would all appreciate it, saying, "Here is a saint who was matured in life." What is the proof of the maturity in life? It is blessing others. When we are young, we receive blessings from others. But when we are mature, we pass on blessings to others. Although Abraham was old, he did not bless anyone. This proves that he did not have the maturity in life.

MARRYING KETURAH AFTER SARAH DIED   ✦   The record in Genesis 25 is not a record of blessing; rather, it is a record of remarriage. Abraham married Keturah after Sarah died. Is remarriage a sign of the maturity in life? Certainly not!

BEGETTING ANOTHER SIX SONS AFTER ISAAC   ✦   Abraham's life may be divided into three sections: the section with Ishmael, the section with Isaac, and the section with the six sons. Ishmael was produced by Abraham's flesh, and Isaac was produced by God's grace.

What about the six sons? They were produced by even more flesh. After the birth of Ishmael, Abraham's flesh was dealt with, and grace came in to replace it. But after the birth and growth of Isaac, Abraham's flesh became active again. In the first section, the section with Ishmael, Abraham's flesh was onefold, but in the third section, the section with the six sons, his flesh was sixfold, having been intensified six times. While the younger flesh produced one Ishmael, the older flesh produced six sons.

The Bible is honest, telling us that Abraham married Keturah and begat six sons by her. But Abraham knew God's will. Verse 5 says, "Abraham gave all that he had unto Isaac." Isaac was the unique heir, the heir chosen, designated, and established by God. None of the other sons were reckoned as heirs (v. 6), for they were all sons of the concubine and, like Ishmael, were rejected by God. Abraham had two concubines. The first gave birth to Ishmael, and the second gave birth to six sons. But God did not want any of them. Both before and after the birth of Isaac, Abraham did something which God did not want. How can we say that such a life is mature?

DIED WITHOUT MATURITY IN LIFE   •   The intention of Genesis 25 is to show that Abraham did not have the maturity in life. He died without this, for as we have seen, he died without blessing anyone. Although Abraham was good, he was not mature in the divine life. It is right that we appreciate him, but we must realize that he had a great lack. He was called, had faith, and lived in fellowship with God, but, to use a New Testament term, he did not have sufficient transformation.

What is transformation? Once again I would like to use the example of petrified wood. As water flows through the wood, the element of wood is carried away and the elements of minerals are added in its place. As the mineral elements are wrought into the wood, the wood is transformed into stone. This is petrification. We are wood, and the flow of living water must carry away our natural element and bring into our being all the divine, heavenly, holy, and spiritual elements. In this way we are transformed.

If you read chapters twenty-three through twenty-five again, you will see that Abraham was not a fully transformed person. He was a man who lived in fellowship with God and who acted according to His leading, but he was not transformed in full. Rather, he remarried and exercised the flesh which had been dealt with by God to bring forth six more "Ishmaels." Although we must be like Abraham, we need to see that in himself he was not a complete pattern.

BURIED WITH SARAH IN THE CAVE OF MACHPELAH   ✦   Undoubtedly Abraham died in faith. His two sons Isaac and Ishmael buried him in the cave of Machpelah (vv. 9-10), which he had obtained for Sarah in chapter twenty-three. It must be that his sons buried him according to his desire.

NEEDING JACOB AND ISAAC FOR HIS COMPLETION

Although Abraham was good, he was not complete. He had to be completed and perfected by the lives of Jacob and Isaac. According to the implication of the divine record, Abraham, Isaac, and Jacob are not three separate individuals. In like manner, their God, the God of Abraham, the God of Isaac, and the God of Jacob, is not three gods but the one Triune God. In Abraham, we see God the Father; in Isaac, we see God the Son; and in Jacob, we see God the Spirit. The Father, the Son, and the Spirit, the three-in-one, are the unique Triune God. In the same principle, Abraham, Isaac, and Jacob are a triune person. Being three-in-one, they are a complete person in the experience of life.

JACOB'S BEING CHOSEN   ✦   In Abraham's record we see the matter of calling. According to the divine revelation, however, calling is not the first item. God's selection comes before God's calling. When Abraham was in Chaldea worshipping idols, that was the time of God's calling, not the time of His selection. The time of God's selection was before the foundation of the world. In eternity past Abraham was chosen, and in Chaldea he was called. But where is the record of Abraham's selection? It is in Genesis 25 in the record of Jacob's selection. In himself, Abraham had no selection; his selection was in Jacob's selection. Abraham's life had neither a full beginning nor a complete ending, for he had neither selection nor maturity in life, both of which are with Jacob. In other words, as far as the experience of life is concerned, by himself Abraham cannot stand as a complete person in the eyes of God. He needs Jacob and Isaac. These three persons, Abraham, Isaac, and Jacob, represent the spiritual experience of a complete man. In the record of Jacob's life, there is no mention of being called. Where and when was Jacob called? He was called with Abraham in Genesis 11, just as Abraham was selected in Jacob. In Abraham we clearly see God's calling, but we do not see selection nor the maturity in life.

In Genesis 25 we have three genealogies: the genealogy of the children of Keturah (vv. 2-4), the genealogy of the sons of Ishmael (vv. 13-16), and the genealogy of Isaac (vv. 19-26). In the first two genealogies no one is selected by God. None of the sons of Keturah' nor the sons of Ishmael were chosen by Him. Even Esau, one born of Isaac, was not chosen. Of all those named in this chapter, only one is chosen—Jacob. These three genealogies are put together in one chapter for a definite purpose—to show the kind of person God rejects and the kind of person He chooses. God chose the most naughty one, Jacob, whose name means a supplanter, a heel holder. If we were God, we would never have chosen such a naughty, supplanting one. Nevertheless, Jacob was God's choice. We see in this chapter that what Abraham produced was not what God wanted. None of his six sons was God's choice. In producing them, all he did was in vain. Likewise, none of Ishmael's descendants were chosen by God. After Isaac had been married for twenty years, he "entreated the Lord for his wife, because she was barren: and the Lord was entreated of him, and Rebekah his wife conceived" (v. 21). Rebekah gave birth to twins, the second of whom was God's choice. Of the more than twenty births recorded in this chapter, all were in vain except one. In this chapter God seemed to be saying to Abraham, "You have brought forth many children by your flesh, but all is in vain. Not one who is the result of your flesh is My choice."

This chapter reveals that the life which lacks maturity will always labor in vain. If we are not matured in life, although we may be quite active, doing many things, all our labor will be in vain. None of it is according to God's selection. Abraham was a dear saint with a very good life, but his life was not mature and he did much which was in vain. Nothing that came out of his flesh was God's choice. Do you want to have a life like this? By the record of Abraham's life we see that he was not complete. He needed Jacob and Isaac to complete and perfect him. As this chapter reveals, for his completion and perfection he needed Jacob's being chosen.

JACOB'S MATURITY IN LIFE ✦ Abraham also needed Jacob's maturity in life. According to the book of Genesis, the first person to bless others was Melchisedec (14:18-19). As the book of Hebrews reveals, Melchisedec was a type of Christ. But even when Abraham was very old, much older than Jacob lived to be, he never blessed anyone. Although he received the blessing, he never passed on blessings to others. After Melchisedec, the next person to bless others was Isaac. But Isaac blessed blindly; he was cheated and did not bless in a clear way. Rather, he blessed the wrong person, giving the birthright to Jacob instead of to Esau (ch. 27). However, as the record at the end of Genesis reveals, Jacob, although he could not see well, blessed in a very clear way. After Jacob became mature, he blessed whomever he met. Wherever he went, he did nothing except bless others. When Jacob was brought before Pharaoh, the first thing he did was bless him (47:7). After talking a while with Pharaoh, Jacob blessed him again (47:10). Jacob was not only a blessed person; he was also a blessing person.

While it is easy to receive a blessing, it is not easy to bless others. A grandson cannot bless his grandfather, because the grandson lacks the maturity in life. Because Jacob was mature, he blessed everyone he met, including Pharaoh, who was an unbeliever, a Gentile king. Jacob did not feel that he had to do anything for anyone. His burden was simply to bless others.

Consider the case of Jacob's blessing the two sons of Joseph (48:8-20). When Jacob laid his right hand upon Ephraim instead of upon Manasseh, the firstborn, Joseph was displeased and attempted to move his father's right hand to Manasseh's head, saying, "Not so, my father: for this is the firstborn; put thy right hand upon his head" (48:18). But Jacob refused and said, "I know it, my son, I know it" (48:19). Jacob seemed to be saying, "I may be blind physically, but I am very clear spiritually. You don't know what I am doing, but I know." Here we see that Jacob blessed Joseph's two sons with a clear, full, and rich blessing.

Jacob also blessed his twelve sons in a very clear way. These blessings are the foundation of the basic prophecies in the Bible. If we would know the prophecies in the Bible, we must go back to their foundation, to their basic elements, as seen in the blessings rendered by Jacob to his twelve sons. Jacob could bless his sons in a way that was full of divine revelation because he was fully matured in the divine life. He was born a Jacob, but he was transformed into Israel. He was born a supplanter, a heel-holder, but he was transformed into a prince of God. He had become so clear and full of life. When we are clear and full of life, we can do nothing but bless. This is a sign of maturity.

As we have seen, Abraham, Isaac, and Jacob form one complete person in the experience of life. Abraham did not bless, because he did not have the maturity in life. Isaac, having some maturity but lacking the richness of the maturity of life, blessed in a blind way. Jacob, who was mature in life, blessed in a full and clear way. Whatever he spoke was the divine word, and whatever he blessed was a prophecy concerning God's economy with all His children. Eventually, Jacob became Israel, the expression of God.

If we have the light from the Scriptures as a whole, we shall see that the book of Genesis is a miniature of the complete revelation of the entire Bible. At the end of Genesis we see a man called Israel, a transformed person who is transparent, clear, and full of life. The transformed Israel is a seed, a miniature, of the New Jerusalem. At the beginning of Genesis we have man created in God's image. At the end of Genesis we have a transformed person, a man not only outwardly in the image of God, but a man in whom God has wrought Himself, making him His expression. Although many Christians appreciate Abraham, his life was not high enough. Israel's life was much higher.

ISAAC'S ENJOYMENT OF THE INHERITANCE   ◆   For his completion, Abraham also needed Isaac's enjoyment of the inheritance (24:36; 25:5). From the day Abraham was called by God, God began to rob him of things. Firstly, God took away his brother and then his father. Later, God rejected Eliezer, commanded Abraham to cast out Ishmael, and told him to offer Isaac on the altar. After Isaac had been returned, Sarah died. Abraham's life was not a life of enjoyment; it was a life of being robbed. Isaac's life, on the contrary, was a life full of enjoyment. Isaac did not do anything; he simply inherited all his father had.

In our Christian life we have the experiences of both Abraham and Isaac. On one hand we are always being robbed. God rejects whatever we have. He seems to say, "You like it, but I don't like it. You want to give it, but I won't take it. You want to preserve it, but I reject it." In a very good sense, God always acts contrary to our wishes and intentions. Abraham wanted to take his father with him, but the father was taken away. He wanted to have Lot, but Lot separated from him. He wanted Eliezer to be his heir, but Eliezer was rejected. He wanted to keep Ishmael, but God commanded him to cast out the son of the bondwoman. Abraham loved his son Isaac, but God required that he be offered to Him upon the altar. A while later, Sarah, Abraham's dear wife, was taken. I doubt that Abraham had much time for enjoyment.

But there is another side to our Christian life. While we are suffering the robbing, we are enjoying our inheritance. This is why the records of Abraham and Isaac overlap, whereas the records of those who preceded them, such as Abel, Enoch, and Noah, do not. The record of Isaac is mixed together with that of Abraham. While Abraham was suffering, Isaac was enjoying. While Abraham was weeping, Isaac was rejoicing. This indicates that our Christian life is a life of night and morning. Night is at our left hand and morning is at our right hand. In the Christian life, night and morning go together. Many times I have been unable to determine whether I was in the night or in the morning. While I was in the morning I was in the night, and while I was in the night, I was in the morning. On the one hand, I was Abraham being robbed of everything, and on the other hand, I was Isaac enjoying the inheritance.

We all have been selected with Jacob and have been called and have believed with Abraham. As we have been robbed with Abraham and have been enjoying with Isaac, one day we all shall be matured with Jacob. We should not say that a certain brother is a Jacob or Abraham or Isaac. We should call him a Jacob-Abraham-Isaac. He is Jacob at the beginning and at the ending, and he is Abraham with Isaac in the middle. These three are one complete person. As we have seen, the maturity in life is neither with Abraham nor Isaac but with Jacob.

The sign of the maturity of life is blessing. I have seen thousands of Christians. Nearly every one has been either supplanting or complaining. Some saints complain about the elders, the brothers, and all the churches. It seems that the only church they like is the New Jerusalem. Complaining is a sign of immaturity. When you have matured, you will not complain; you will bless, saying, "O God, bless all the brothers and all the churches." For the one who is matured in life, the supplanting hand has become the blessing hand. The more mature you are, the more you will bless others. You will not only bless the good ones, but the bad ones and even the worst ones.

Abraham's life was wonderful and has been appreciated by Christians throughout the centuries. But, as we have seen, he was not mature in the divine life. Our God is not only God the Father, but also God the Son and God the Spirit. He is not only the God of Abraham, but also the God of Isaac and the God of Jacob. May we all see that we need all three aspects, the life of Abraham plus the lives of Isaac and Jacob. The Triune God is working within us as the Father, the Son, and the Spirit to make us the full expression of Himself. He is the Triune God, and we must be a person of three aspects in the spiritual experiences of the divine life. We need to be transformed in full. When we have been fully transformed, God will have the fulfillment of His purpose.   ✖

27

INHERITING GRACE

The grace of the Lord Jesus be with all the saints. Amen.
Revelation 22:21

Through whom also we have obtained access by faith into this grace in which we stand.
Romans 5:2

By the grace of God I am what I am;
and His grace unto me did not turn out to be in vain,
but, on the contrary, I labored more abundantly than all of them,
yet not I but the grace of God which is with me.
1 Corinthians 15:10

I am crucified with Christ; and it is no longer I who live,
but it is Christ who lives in me; and the life which I now live
in the flesh I live in faith, the faith of the Son of God,
who loved me and gave Himself up for me.
Galatians 2:20

The grace of the Lord Jesus Christ
and the love of God and
the fellowship of the Holy Spirit
be with you all.
2 Corinthians 13:14

We have pointed out in previous messages that, according to the experience of life, Abraham, Isaac, and Jacob are three parts of one complete person and that we should not consider them as three separate individuals. If we know the life in the book of Genesis, we shall see that, in the eyes of God, these three persons are one complete unit in the experience of life.

In this message we come to the second aspect of the experience of the called—the experience of Isaac (21:1—28:9; 35:28-29). It is not easy for Christians to understand the experience of Isaac. It is quite easy, on the contrary, to understand the three main aspects of Abraham's experience: being called by God, living by faith in God, and living in fellowship with God. But what shall we say about Isaac? As we read the record of his life in chapters twenty-one through twenty-eight, what do we see of the experience of life? We do not see that he was called, lived by faith in God, or lived in fellowship with God. According to Genesis, we see how Isaac was born, was married, and begat two sons. But it is difficult to say what experience of life we find in the record of Isaac.

In the record of Isaac's life the experience of grace is implied. What Isaac experienced was the inheriting of God's grace. The grace of God was not as fully revealed in the Old Testament as it is in the New Testament, because grace actually came through Jesus Christ (John 1:17). After Christ came, there is a full and thorough revelation of grace, and in the New Testament the word grace is used again and again. The New Testament even closes with the mention of grace: "The grace of the Lord Jesus be with all the saints. Amen" (Rev. 22:21). The Bible begins in the Old Testament with the word, "In the beginning God created the heaven and the earth," and it ends in the New Testament with the word, "The grace of the Lord Jesus be with all the saints." Although the record in Genesis concerning Isaac does not have the term grace, nevertheless such a thing is implied there. This is the reason that it is quite difficult for many to understand the Bible. In the Bible, there may be a certain thing but not the term to describe it. Although Isaac's experience is recorded in Genesis, it is difficult to designate the experience he had as the experience of grace.

According to the New Testament revelation, as far as the experience of life is concerned, Abraham, Isaac, and Jacob should not be considered as three separate individuals, but as aspects of one complete person's experience of life. Abraham represents the aspect of being called, of living by faith in God, and of living in fellowship with God. Isaac represents the aspect of inheriting grace and enjoying the inheritance of grace. Jacob represents the aspect of being chosen, being dealt with by the Lord, and being transformed into a prince of God. In the experience of life, there is the aspect of enjoyment, the enjoyment of grace. Most of us have heard messages saying that the Christian life should be a suffering life, a life of bearing the cross and groaning in prayer. Have you not heard messages telling you that today is not the time of enjoyment but the time of suffering and of bearing the cross, and that our enjoyment will begin at the time of the Lord's coming back? I do not say that this is wrong, but I do say that it is only one aspect of the Christian life. There is another aspect—the aspect of enjoyment.

In the biblical and experiential sense, grace means enjoyment. Grace is the enjoyment in our Christian life. Our Christian life has three aspects: the aspect of Abraham, the aspect of Isaac, and the aspect of Jacob. In the aspect of Abraham we cannot see much enjoyment. Although Abraham was blessed and was enlarged, he did not have very much enjoyment. He lost his father, and Lot became a grief to him. Eliezer, in whom he trusted, was rejected, and Ishmael, the son he begat by his own endeavor with his concubine, was cast out. After Isaac was born, God required that Abraham offer him up as a burnt offering. Not too long after Isaac was returned, Abraham lost his dear wife. Throughout his whole life we can see the aspect of loss. Although the Bible does not show that Abraham suffered very much, he lost almost everything. Is this all the Christian life is? If it is, then the Christian life is only a life of losses. The matter of loss is just one aspect of the Christian life. Romans 5:2 does not say, "We have access into this loss in which we stand." No, it says, "We have the access by faith into this grace in which we stand." God has no intention of keeping us in loss. His intention is to bring us into grace, into the enjoyment.

God wants to bring us into the enjoyment of grace, but there is a frustration to this grace—the self. We ourselves are the frustration. Although Christ has come and grace has come with Him, and although we have been brought into the grace in which we stand, the greatest frustration to this grace is you and I. Hence, before we can have the experience of Isaac, we need Abraham who represents the first aspect of the experience of life. Abraham's life reveals that if we would enjoy God's grace and have the full enjoyment of God's riches, we must be dealt with, circumcised, and cut off. If Abraham had not been circumcised, Isaac would never have been born. Isaac came after

Abraham's circumcision. After Abraham was circumcised in Genesis 17, God told him that Isaac would be born (17:19). Eventually, in chapter twenty-one, Isaac was born. Isaac came with God's visitation. He was born by God's visitation. God's visitation equals the birth of Isaac. God visited Sarah and that visitation became the birth of Isaac. This is grace.

God has come to be enjoyed by His called ones. But if we would have this enjoyment, the self must go. Once the self has gone, Isaac comes. This means that grace comes. It is not easy to lose the self. In order for the self to go, we must suffer loss. Are you willing to lose yourself? I do not believe that anyone is willing to lose himself. Nevertheless, we must lose ourselves before grace can come. To lose the self is to lose our face. When we keep our face we lose grace. If we want to receive grace, we must lose our face. Brothers, as you deal with your wife in your daily living, you must be prepared to lose yourself. If you do this, grace will come. After Abraham was circumcised, Isaac came. This is the principle. With us, the self must go and then grace will come. We must firstly be Abraham and then we become Isaac.

It was not easy for Abraham to lose himself. In a good sense, God forced him to lose himself. When God called Abraham, He did not say, "Abraham, you must lose yourself and then I will come in to be your grace and enjoyment." No, when God called him, He promised to bless him. The blessing in the Old Testament somewhat equals the grace in the New Testament. What is the difference between blessing and grace? When God gives us something free, that is a blessing. But when this blessing is wrought into our being, it becomes grace. God promised Abraham that He would bless him. When the blessing was wrought into Abraham, it became grace. Abraham's self and natural man were the strongest frustration to God's blessing and forced God to deal with him.

The same is true in our experience. We all have been called, and God has given us the blessings in Christ (Eph. 1:3). However, after being called, we are still in ourselves and exercise our self-effort to obtain God's blessing. When I was young, I realized that my flesh was not good. When I was told that the flesh had been crucified on the cross, I was very happy. Then I began to exercise my own effort to put the flesh on the cross. But in exercising my own effort, I frustrated God's grace. The crossing out of the flesh had already been accomplished; it did not need the exercise of my effort. Yet I, the self, was trying to put my flesh on the cross. That self was the greatest frustration to God's grace. It separated me from grace. If we consider our past experience, we shall see that after hearing the good news, we tried many times by ourselves to obtain the things we heard in the good news. Our self-effort has been a frustration to God's grace. Because of this, God has been forced to deal with us.

Being called by God, living by faith in God, and living in fellowship with God are all for the enjoyment of God. We have been called to the enjoyment of God, we must learn to live by faith in God that we may have the enjoyment of God, and we need to live in fellowship with God that we may participate in all His riches. All this is for one thing—the enjoyment of God. But we do not see this enjoyment with Abraham; we see it with Isaac. We all have had at least some experience of being called by God, living by faith in God, living in fellowship with God, and suffering loss. We are real Abrahams today. But we can also testify that, much to our surprise, in the midst of our loss there has been some enjoyment. While we were suffering a loss, unconsciously we were enjoying something. Whenever we suffered a dealing from God, we simultaneously had some enjoyment. While we were the suffering Abraham, we were also the enjoying Isaac. For this reason, the record of Isaac does not immediately follow the record of Abraham. Rather, it is mingled with the record of Abraham's life. While Abraham was still there, Isaac came in, for they were not two separate individuals in the experience of life, but two aspects of the experience of a complete person. We need the experiences of both Abraham and Isaac. Perhaps even today you had a certain experience and said, "I don't know why this has happened to me." But deep within you do know. In the midst of your loss, you gain and enjoy Christ. This is the experience of Isaac.

If we only had Abraham without Isaac, we would be very disappointed with Abraham's record. We would say, "What is the good of being the father of faith if it is only a matter of suffering loss?" But once we see the experience of Isaac, we shall say, "Now I understand why Abraham suffered the loss of so much. All the negative experiences of Abraham were for the positive enjoyment with Isaac." Abraham was for Isaac. Abraham acquired a great deal, having been blessed and having become enlarged, but he gave all that he had to Isaac (24:36; 25:5). Abraham suffered for Isaac's gain. The more

Abraham suffered, the more Isaac gained. I would say, "Poor Abraham, you are just a suffering person. All that you have gained through your suffering is not for you but for Isaac." We all must realize that today we are not only Abrahams but also Isaacs. If you say to me, "Brother, you are a poor Abraham always suffering," I would reply, "Don't you know that I'm also an Isaac? I have suffered loss that I might gain. I lose as Abraham and I gain as Isaac. I'm not just Abraham. My name is Abraham-Isaac. On the loss side, I am Abraham; on the gain side, I am Isaac."

We are both Abraham and Isaac. As Abraham, we have been called by God, have learned to live by faith in God, and have learned to live in fellowship with God. At the same time, as Isaac, we do nothing except enjoy all we have gained from Abraham's experience. Which kind of experience do you appreciate more—Abraham's or Isaac's? Without Abraham's experience we cannot have Isaac's. God is dealing with us as He dealt with Abraham that we might have the experience of Isaac.

The matter of grace has been hidden, concealed, and veiled throughout the years. What is grace? Grace is something of God which is wrought into our being and which works in us and does things for us. It is nothing outward. Grace is God in Christ wrought into our being to live, work, and do things for us. In 1 Corinthians 15:10 Paul says, "By the grace of God I am what I am; and His grace unto me was not in vain, but I labored more abundantly than all of them, yet not I, but the grace of God with me." This word is quite deep. Paul did not say, "By the grace of God I have what I have. I have a good car, a good job, and a good wife by the grace of God." He did not even say, "By the grace of God I do what I do." It is not a matter of doing, having, or working; it is absolutely a matter of being. Hence, Paul says, "By the grace of God I am what I am." This means that the very grace of God had been wrought into his being, making him that kind of person. In Galatians 2:20 Paul says, "No longer I who live, but Christ lives in me." If we put this verse together with 1 Corinthians 15:10, we see that grace is simply Christ living in us. It is "not I, but the grace of God," "no longer I, but Christ." Grace is not outside of us or beside us. It is a divine Person, God Himself in Christ, wrought into our being to be the constituent of our being. Because of the lack of revelation, Christians have misunderstood and misinterpreted grace, thinking of it as something outside of them. But grace is just the Triune God wrought into our being to be what we should be and to live, work, and do things for us so that we may say, "I am what I am by the grace of God. It is not I, but the grace of God."

We all have been taught to have good behavior and to love one another. As a result, we try to behave ourselves and to love others. But it does not matter whether we can love others or not, for God will never recognize our love. Abraham succeeded in bringing forth Ishmael, but God rejected him. God seemed to say, "No, Abraham, that is not what I want. I want something that has been wrought into you and worked out from you. You brought forth Ishmael without My visitation. I was in heaven and you were on earth bringing forth Ishmael. Because he was unrelated to Me and to My visitation, I will never recognize him. One day, I shall visit Sarah and My visitation will bring forth Isaac. I will recognize only him." If we love others in ourselves, God will never recognize that love, because it does not come from His visitation. God wants to visit us, get into us, live for us, and even love others for us. He will only recognize that kind of love. Your love is an Ishmael; the love by God's visitation is an Isaac. Whether you are humble or proud, crooked or straight, means nothing. God does not recognize anything which comes out of you apart from His visitation. Whatever is not of grace is not recognized, not counted, by God. We all must say, "O Lord, I will not do anything without Your visitation. Lord, if You will not visit me and work something through me and out of me, I will do nothing. I will neither hate nor love, be proud nor be humble. I want to be blank. Lord, without Your visitation, I am nothing." God's visitation is the practical grace. When I love others and am humble by God's visitation, not by my self-effort, that is the enjoyment of grace.

As we have seen, God's intention is to work Himself into a corporate man that He might have a corporate expression. This is the basic concept of the divine revelation in the Bible. This is God's eternal purpose. God called Abraham with the purpose of working Himself into him, but Abraham had a strong self. This natural self was the strongest frustration to God's purpose. The same is true with us today. God's purpose is to work Himself into us to be our life and even to be our living, but our natural self frustrates this. Therefore, God must cut us and deal with us that He may get into us to be everything to us. God does not need us to love others and to be humble that society might be improved. If God wants a better society, He only needs to say, "Better society," and it will come into being. He calls things not being as being (Rom. 4:17) and does not need our help. God wants to work Himself into us to be our humility and our everything. He wants us to say, "Lord, I am nothing and will not do anything. I just open up to You that You might come in, make Your home in me, live in me, and do everything for me. Lord, You live and I'll enjoy Your living. Whenever You do something in me, I'll say, 'Praise You, Lord. This is wonderful! I am not the doer; I am an enjoyer, appreciating all You are doing for me.'"

God's intention today is to deal with Abraham that Isaac may come. His intention is to deal with our natural being that we may have the full experience of Himself in Christ wrought into us as our enjoyment. I have been experiencing married life for close to fifty years, experiencing much enjoyment and much suffering. Before I was married, I truly loved the Lord, and I often told Him how much I loved Him. After I was married, I went to the Lord and assured Him, saying, "Lord because I love You, I want to be the best husband." Eventually, I failed. I went to the Lord and confessed all my failures. After experiencing the anointing, I was happy and I made up my mind to try again to be the best husband. But I failed once more, and this experience of ups and downs was repeated again and again. Later, I even gave a message in which I said, "The Christian life has many nights and mornings. Never be disappointed over your failures. Just wait for several hours and you will be in the morning." For years and years I went through days and nights, nights and days. One day, I received the revelation and said, "Stupid man, who told you to do so? Christ is here waiting to be your grace. You must say, 'Lord, I am nothing and I can do nothing. Even if I could do something, it would never be recognized by You. Come, Lord, and do Your job and be the best husband for me. This is Your job, not mine. You charge me, and I return the charge to You and ask You to fulfill it. Lord, You be the best husband and I will praise You for it.'" Whenever I prayed like this, the Lord always did the best job. This is grace.

Grace is God working Himself into our being as our enjoyment. The very God today is not only God the Father, but also God the Son and God the Spirit. Moreover, God the Spirit is the Spirit of grace (Heb. 10:29), and this grace is the grace of life (1 Pet. 3:7), which is "the varied grace" (1 Pet. 4:10), the "all grace" (1 Pet. 5:10), and the "sufficient grace" (2 Cor. 12:9). The Triune God is such a grace, and this grace is now with our spirit (Gal. 6:18). Grace is the divine Person of the Triune God as the Spirit indwelling our spirit. It is the Spirit of grace indwelling our spirit to be our enjoyment that we may enjoy God as our life and our everything, even as our living. This is why every one of Paul's Epistles ends with the words, "Grace be with you." For example, 2 Corinthians 13:14 says, "The grace of the Lord Jesus Christ, and the love of God, and the fellowship of the Holy Spirit be with you all." Grace is not outside of us; it is in us. Whatever we call it, the Spirit of grace or the grace of life, it is something living and divine in our spirit. We do have such a divine reality, the Triune God Himself, in our spirit as our grace and enjoyment. When He loves others through us, this love is our enjoyment. When He lives Himself out through us, this living is also our enjoyment. Day and night we may enjoy His living through us.

Why then do we suffer? Because the self, the ego, the natural man, is still here and must be dealt with. Praise Him that no dealing is in vain. Every dealing from God is a breaking of our natural man that we may enjoy more of Him as our grace. Thus, we have Abraham and Isaac; we have the suffering of the loss and the enjoyment of the gain. This gain is not the gain of outward things; it is the gain of the indwelling One, that is, the Spirit of grace and the grace of life. Again I say, whatever God gives as a gift outside of us is, at the most, a blessing. When this gift is wrought into our being, becoming the life element within us, it is grace. The blessing must become the grace. In the Old Testament, God gave many things to His people as blessings, but all those things were merely outward blessings. Before Christ came, none of those blessings had been wrought into God's people. Christ came not only to die on the cross for us, but, after His death, to become the life-giving Spirit to enter into our being. Thus, in the New Testament, we have the terms "in Christ" and "Christ in you." Now He is in us and we are in Him. Whatever God gives us in Christ has been wrought into our being and has become grace, our enjoyment. Now we are not merely under His blessing; we are in His grace and His grace is in us. What are you enjoying today—blessing or grace? The New Testament never says, "Blessing be with you." Rather, it says repeatedly, "Grace be with you."

BORN OF GRACE

After Abraham's natural strength and self-effort were dealt with by God, Isaac was born (17:15-19; 18:10-14; 21:1-7). This implies that Isaac was born of grace, which is represented by Sarah (Gal. 4:24-28, 31). The record of Genesis says this transpired at "the time of life" (18:10, 14). Whenever the effort of the natural life ceases, that is the time of life. At the time of life something is born in grace. Grace is related to life, and life goes with grace. Hence, grace is called "the grace of life" (1 Pet. 3:7).

GROWN IN GRACE

Isaac was grown up in grace (21:8). By his history we see that he did not do anything. He was born and he was grown up. I do not say that he grew up, but that he was grown up. Like a farmer who grows apples in his orchard, God grew Isaac like a tree in His orchard. Isaac was grown up by God in grace.

Second Peter 3:18 tells us to "grow in grace." This indicates that to grow is the feeding and watering as revealed by Peter in 1 Peter 2:2 and by Paul in 1 Corinthians 3:2 and 6. To grow in grace is to grow in the enjoyment of all that Christ is to us as our spiritual food and living water. All the riches of what Christ is to us are for our growth in life. The more we enjoy the riches of Christ (Eph. 3:8), the more we grow in life (Eph. 4:15).

BEING THE HEIR IN GRACE

Isaac also became the heir in grace (21:9-12). All that his father had was his, for Abraham gave all his riches to this unique heir. Likewise, we should have no enjoyment in ourselves. All the enjoyment of the inheritance must be in grace.

OBEYING IN GRACE

Isaac also obeyed in grace (22:5-10). In my reading of Genesis 22 in the past, I could not understand how Isaac, a young man, could have been so obedient. Eventually, I saw that he was obedient because he was saturated with grace. He was absolutely in grace, and his obedience was also in grace. That obedience brought in God's provision. It is the same with us today. Whenever we obey in grace, we shall meet the provision of God.

God's grace is powerful, enabling us to bear anything. Paul told Timothy to "be empowered in the grace" of Christ (2 Tim. 2:1). Grace can even reign over all things (Rom. 5:21). We should not fall from grace (Gal. 5:4) but rather be confirmed by it (Heb. 13:9). The more we bear in grace, the more provision of grace we meet and participate in.

INHERITING ALL FROM THE FATHER

Isaac inherited all things from his father (24:36; 25:5). It was by grace, not by his effort, that he became the heir of the father's riches. He was not required to do anything that he might inherit the father's riches and he did not do anything for the inheritance. It was absolutely and unconditionally of grace.

In the New Testament, all the called believers are heirs of God's absolute and unconditional grace. God has called us and has blessed us with all the spiritual blessings in Christ (Eph. 1:3). In Christ He has put us into grace that we might become the heirs of grace, inheriting all the riches of the divine fullness as our enjoyment. Our Christian life must be like Isaac's, doing nothing by himself, but inheriting and enjoying all that the father has. In the inheriting of grace, we must cease from the effort of our natural life that we may keep ourselves open and available for the enjoyment of grace.

INHERITING THE PROMISE GIVEN TO HIS FATHER

Isaac inherited not only all that his father had, but also the promise which God had given to his father concerning the good land and the unique seed, which is Christ in whom all the nations of the earth will be blessed (26:3-5). This promise was actually for the fulfillment of God's purpose that God might have a kingdom on the earth in which to express Himself through a corporate people. Both the good land and the seed are for the formation of a kingdom for God on the earth. In this kingdom God can be fully expressed in the seed, into which He will work Himself and which will be transformed into His image. This was a promise given to Abraham and inherited by Isaac.

But it is a fulfillment with us today. Today we are enjoying the Triune God as our grace. Through our enjoyment of grace the kingdom of God will be realized and God in Christ will be fully expressed for eternity.   ✖

28

RESTING AND ENJOYING

Isaac went out to meditate in the field at the eventide: and he lifted up his eyes, and saw, and, behold, the camels were coming. And Rebekah lifted up her eyes, and when she saw Isaac, she lighted off the camel.

Genesis 24:63-64

And it came to pass after the death of Abraham, that God blessed his son Isaac; and Isaac dwelt by the well Lahai-roi.

Genesis 25:11

Isaac was forty years old when he took Rebekah to wife....
And Isaac entreated the Lord for his wife, because she was barren: and the Lord was entreated of him, and Rebekah his wife conceived....
And when her days to be delivered were fulfilled,
behold, there were twins in her womb.

Genesis 25:20-21, 24

And the Lord appeared unto him the same night, and said,
I am the God of Abraham thy father: fear not, for I am with thee, and will bless thee, and multiply thy seed for my servant Abraham's sake.
And he builded an altar there, and called upon the name of the Lord, and pitched his tent there: and there Isaac's servants digged a well.

Genesis 26:24-25

We thank the Lord that in the Old Testament He has given us a wonderful and clear picture of the experience of life. In the New Testament we have the revelation of the experience of life, but we do not have as clear a picture of it as we have in the Old Testament. We are all familiar with the proverb which says that a picture is better than a thousand words. Although we have spent many years considering the experience of life as revealed in the New Testament, we cannot be certain about it only by the words in the New Testament. We also need the pictures in the Old Testament. By the Lord's mercy, we have seen through the years that all the stories in the Old Testament depict the various aspects of the experience of life. Deep within, I feel that the Lord has shown us the full picture and has enabled us to understand its real significance.

As we have already pointed out, there are three aspects to every Christian's experience of life—the aspect of Abraham, the aspect of Isaac, and the aspect of Jacob. If we did not have this clear view, we would only consider Abraham, Isaac, and Jacob as three separate individuals. But, after receiving the revelation and understanding it in the light of the New Testament, we realize that these three men are not three separate individuals, but three aspects of one complete person in the experience of life. Some, finding it difficult to believe that Abraham, Isaac, and Jacob represent three aspects of one complete person, may say, "How can you say that Abraham is not a complete person? Abraham is just Abraham, and the same is true for both Isaac and Jacob." If you do not believe that these three people are three aspects of the complete experience of one person, I would ask you this question: Can you see God's selection in Abraham? The first item in our experience of God is His selection, His choice, which was made before the foundation of the world. We see this clearly in the New Testament (Eph. 1:4), but we cannot see it in the experience of Abraham. Thus, as far as God's selection is concerned, Abraham needs someone else to perfect him. The selection which we cannot find in Abraham's life is revealed in Jacob's. In addition to being selected, we Christians are also called. In Isaac we see neither selection nor calling. Hence, in himself, Isaac is not complete. Isaac's calling is in Abraham just as Abraham's selection is in Jacob. By these two examples we should all be convinced that Abraham, Isaac, and Jacob depict three aspects of one complete person in the experience of life. In a sense, we are all Abrahams, for we have been called and have learned to live by faith in God and in fellowship with Him. Since we have also been put into the position of grace, we are also Isaacs. As we shall see in later messages, we are Jacobs as well.

The aspect of Isaac unfolds the matter of grace. We have not only been called and have learned to live by faith in God and in fellowship with Him, but we are daily enjoying something of God. If we do not have any enjoyment in our Christian life, we will not be able to live the Christian life. Rather, we would be very miserable. Praise the Lord that we not only have the aspect of Abraham but also the aspect of Isaac, which is the aspect of grace. Grace simply means the enjoyment of God. It is God Himself becoming our enjoyment in our spirit. Many times we have difficulties which trouble us mentally and emotionally. Nevertheless, while we are suffering in our mind and emotion, there is a sweet sense deep within our spirit. It seems that if we did not have this suffering, we would not have this enjoyment. The Christian suffering brings us the Christian enjoyment. From the moment we called on the name of the Lord Jesus and received Him as our Savior, we began to have these two aspects in our experience. Perhaps the very night you received the Lord Jesus your wife gave you a difficult time, disagreeing with your becoming a Christian and calling it silly. She immediately began to persecute you, and you suffered in your mind, emotion, and senses. But while you were suffering, deep within you sensed something sweet which caused you to be happy. Thus, even at the beginning of your Christian life you had both the aspect of suffering, which is the aspect of Abraham, and the aspect of enjoyment, which is the aspect of Isaac.

In the previous message we saw that Isaac inherited grace. With him, everything was a matter of grace. He was born in grace, was grown up in grace, and was made an heir of grace. In this message we need to see that with Isaac there was also the matter of enjoyment. His life was a resting and enjoying life. The record of Isaac's life does not indicate that he suffered much. Rather, it reveals that he was always resting. This is proved by his meditating in the field (24:63). Could Isaac have meditated if he had not been quiet and restful? No. In order to meditate we must be restful. Whenever we are troubled, we are unable to rest. Isaac was always resting. In Genesis 24, he had lost his mother, did not have a wife, and his servant had gone away from him. Yet, he was not troubled. He went to the field to meditate, not to cry out to the Lord. He did not say, "O Lord, what should I do? I have lost my mother, I do not have a wife, and my servant has gone away. Lord, have mercy upon me!" Isaac did not cry out in that way. Instead, he meditated.

Although we cannot find the word resting in the record of Isaac's life, the fact is there nonetheless. Isaac was a very restful person. In spite of the troubles he encountered with the Philistines over the wells, he was always at rest. Although Isaac faced some troubles, he himself was not troubled. While the Philistines were contending for the wells, he remained restful. Isaac seemed to be saying, "If you don't want me to stay here at this well, then I'll go elsewhere. When you come to bother me there, I'll go to still another place." By this we see that Isaac was truly a restful person. Are you always restful? Consider your experience during the past twenty-four hours. Did anything bother you and cause you to lose your rest? Most of us would have to admit that we have been troubled. This shows that although we are Isaacs, we are not always resting. Recently I was doing some difficult and exhausting work on the book of Revelation. But I can praise the Lord that as I was working, I was very restful and I could say, "I have nothing and I can do nothing. There is no need for me to do anything, because the Lord is doing it all." We all need to be restful people.

Isaac was not only resting; he was also enjoying. His entire life was a life of enjoyment. When he was old, he still had the taste for "savoury meat" and asked Esau to go out to the field and prepare him the meat which he loved (27:1-4). When Rebekah heard this, she called Jacob to fetch her two kids of the goats that she might prepare the meat for Isaac (27:5-10). Eventually, after both Jacob and Esau had come with meat for their father, Isaac got a double portion. Esau, Rebekah, and Jacob were busy, but Isaac just sat there enjoying the meat. By this we see that Isaac was an enjoying person, always enjoying the provision of grace. This enjoyment was his destiny.

Enjoyment is also our destiny. Young brothers, do not worry about finding a wife. If you remain restful and full of enjoyment, the best wife will come to you. In our Christian life there is the aspect of enjoyment. I have been striving since I was twelve years of age. Now, after almost sixty years, I can testify that many times my striving has frustrated the coming of the enjoyment. If I had not striven, the enjoyment would have come much earlier and in a richer way. Why does striving frustrate the enjoyment? Because enjoyment is our destiny. We all have been predestinated for it. Young brothers, forget about your striving. Simply go home, pray, praise, and sleep. The next morning rise up, have a good morning watch, and eat a hearty breakfast. Do not worry about finding a wife. Rebekah will come to you. This is the enjoyment which is our destiny. Are we not the sons of God? How can the sons of God be pitiful people? We must declare, "Praise the Lord that I am a son of God! The almighty, all-sufficient God is my Father!" The word father denotes a rich provision. As long as we have a rich father, we have the provision and have no need to worry. We should simply enjoy this bountiful provision. This is our destiny.

LIVING IN BEER-LAHAI-ROI

Although enjoyment is our destiny, we must still take care of the place where we have the enjoyment. Let us consider the names of the places where Isaac had enjoyment. Firstly, we have Beer-lahai-roi, which means "the well of the living One who sees me" or "the One who reveals Himself" (24:62; 25:11). At Beer-lahai-roi God visits us and reveals Himself to us. Secondly, Isaac had some enjoyment at the well named Esek, which means contention. Esek was a place of contention, fighting, and quarreling. The third place was Sitnah (26:21). Sitnah means enmity, hatred, or opposition. The fourth place was called Rehoboth. Rehoboth has a positive meaning—"broad places" or "broad ways." The last place was called Sheba, which means an oath (26:22-33). Hence, Beer-sheba means the well of an oath. Isaac enjoyed grace at each of these five places.

Before we consider the significance of these places, we must see where Isaac was grown up. He was grown up in Beer-sheba beside the well and the tamarisk tree. Before he was married, he left Beer-sheba and went to the south country (24:62). As we have seen, in the Bible to go southward means to go downward. I do not believe that Abraham left Beer-sheba or Hebron when Isaac did. He remained either in Beer-sheba or in Hebron. After his mother had died and his servant had left, Isaac went downward to the south country. Then he returned. The King James Version says, he "came from the way of Lahai-roi." In Hebrew, it says he "came from going to Lahai-roi," meaning that he returned from Lahai-roi. As he returned from going to Lahai-roi, he gained a wife. If he had stayed in Lahai-roi, not returning to Beer-sheba or Hebron, he would have missed that meeting with Rebekah. When he came back from going to Lahai-roi,

Rebekah came. Abraham's servant did not know that Isaac had left the place where Abraham was. It was of the Lord that Isaac return from his downward way. He returned because he was destined for the enjoyment.

We all have had similar experiences. After going downward, we suddenly said, "Oh, I must go back." The time of our return was the exact time that Rebekah came. I have experienced this a number of times. I have gone downward and then suddenly said to myself, "I must go back." As soon as I returned, the enjoyment came.

As soon as Isaac had returned from going away, the enjoyment came. By coming back to the proper standing, he obtained a wife. However, after his marriage, he and his wife journeyed southward again. Genesis 25:11 says that after the death of Abraham, Isaac dwelt by the well Lahai-roi. As a result of going downward, he found himself at enmity with the Philistines.

We need to see a clear picture of Isaac's record. He did not go downward as far as Egypt. He went southward to Philistia, to the land of the Philistines. According to the record in Genesis, God's people have difficulties whenever they go southward. Abraham had trouble in Egypt and in the land of the Philistines. His son Isaac also had trouble when he went to Philistia, for he had contention and enmity with the Philistines. Although he enjoyed the broad ways, the widening, at Rehoboth, he did not have the Lord's appearing there. In Lahai-roi, Esek, Sitnah, and Rehoboth there was no appearing of the Lord. The Lord did not appear to Isaac until he went up to Beer-sheba. The very night that Isaac went up from Rehoboth to Beer-sheba the Lord appeared unto him (26:23-24).

Here we must see a crucial point, a point about which many Christians are not clear. As Christians, we are destined for some enjoyment. Wherever we are and whether or not we are right or wrong, we have been destined for enjoyment. Even when Isaac went downward to Lahai-roi, he still enjoyed a well, the well of the living One who sees us and reveals Himself to us. Some might say, "This is wonderful. As long as I have the living One and He sees me and reveals Himself to me, that is good enough." In reading the Bible, however, we must keep the principle of the first mention. Lahai-roi, which is first mentioned in 16:14, was the place where Hagar went after fleeing from Sarah. Since Sarah represents grace, Hagar's fleeing from her meant that she had left the standing of grace. In the wilderness, in a place of suffering, God visited her. Hence, Lahai-roi was a place where one who had left the standing of grace could still have some enjoyment of God's visitation.

In the past we might have questioned whether our standing was right, feeling that we were somewhat removed from the standing of grace. Although we had this doubt within us, we still had some enjoyment and we comforted ourselves, saying, "If I were wrong, I would not have this enjoyment. But here I have the well of the living One who visits me. Since I have such an enjoyment, this place must be all right." But it is not all right. On the one hand, we are destined for enjoyment, and wherever we are we shall have some measure of it. On the other hand, we may have this enjoyment on the wrong standing, not in the place where Abraham planted the tamarisk tree, but in the place where Hagar escaped from grace. Lahai-roi was the place of one who had escaped from grace but who still enjoyed something of God's visitation. Nearly all of us have had this experience. We doubted our position, but we still had some enjoyment and felt confirmed by it. Do not take this enjoyment as a confirmation. Although the enjoyment is our destiny, we may have it on an improper ground, at Beer-lahai-roi, not at Beer-sheba.

A well signifies enjoyment and satisfaction. Throughout his entire life, Isaac never suffered thirst. Wherever he went, to a wrong place or to a right one, there was a well. His life was marked with a well. Some may argue with us, saying, "You say that I am wrong in my position, in my standing. Why then do I have a well here?" Your enjoyment of a well does not justify your standing, for the enjoyment is your destiny. In the past, many of us held the religious concept that if we are wrong, God will give us up and we shall not have any more enjoyment. But however wrong we may be, we are still children of our Father, and He will never give us up. I may be the most naughty child, but each day I continue to enjoy my father's provision. This enjoyment is our destiny, our portion.

When some hear that Isaac had a well wherever he went, they may think that, since this enjoyment is also their destiny, they may go wherever they want. Do not think like this. You may have a well for your enjoyment, but you will miss the Lord's appearing and be unable to fulfill God's eternal purpose. Later we shall see that God's purpose can never be fulfilled in Lahai-roi, Esek, Sitnah, or even in Rehoboth. It can only be fulfilled in Beer-sheba, and we must remain there. If we do, we shall experience the Lord's appearing and have the ground to inherit the promises to fulfill God's eternal purpose. Although we may have wells, even "a well of living water" (26:19, Heb.), in other places, those wells cannot enable us to fulfill God's eternal purpose. His purpose can only be fulfilled at the well near the tamarisk tree in Beer-sheba.

Although Isaac had some enjoyment at every place where there was a well, God was not satisfied and used the environment to force Isaac to return to Beer-sheba. God seemed to say, "Isaac, you are settled, but you are not settled in the right place. I shall stir up contention that will force you to go back to Beer-sheba." Isaac had been going down, but God used the circumstances to force him to come up from Beer-lahai-roi to Beer-sheba. Since Isaac did not have the heart to return, God had to force him to return to His place.

Some Christian teachers have encouraged the believers to follow the example of Isaac and not to strive with others. According to this teaching, when we dig a well and others take it, we should simply tolerate it and give it to them. If we go to another place and dig another well and others take it over, we should not fight for it but go to still another place. Eventually, we shall come to the third place, the place of broad ways. But this teaching does not see God's purpose, which was to bring Isaac back to Beer-sheba, the place where God appeared to him. At Beer-sheba, after the Lord's appearing, Isaac built an altar, called upon the name of the Lord, and pitched his tent (26:24, 25). Isaac did not build an altar in any other place. The Lord's appearing with His promise and the testimony were all at Beer-sheba. Only at this place did Isaac receive the promise for the fulfillment of God's eternal purpose. He did not receive it at Beer-lahai-roi, the place of the living One who sees and reveals Himself; nor at Esek, the well of contention; nor at Sitnah, the well of enmity; nor even at Rehoboth, the well of the broad ways. Although Isaac had the enjoyment everywhere, he only had the Lord's appearing (which is different from God's mere visitation) in Beer-sheba. Only in the unique place, in Beer-sheba, could he inherit the promise and have a life of testimony for the fulfillment of God's purpose. It is only at Beer-sheba, the well of the oath, that we can have the Lord's appearing, inherit the promise, build an altar, call upon the name of the Lord, and pitch a tent as a testimony. Here and only here can we fulfill God's eternal purpose.

The enjoyment which we may have everywhere because it is our destiny is not a confirmation or a justification of our standing. The correctness of our standing can only be determined by the Lord's appearing, not merely by the enjoyment. In many places we have had the enjoyment, but when we were there, we had the deep sense that we did not have the Lord's appearing. Moreover, in those places we did not have an altar or a tent, and we did not call upon the Lord's name from deep within our spirit. Although we may have some enjoyment elsewhere, only in Beer-sheba can we fulfill God's purpose.

SECURING A CHOICE BRIDE

We have seen that Isaac enjoyed all the wells. Wherever he went there was a well for his enjoyment. This reveals that whether we are right or wrong in our standing there is a well for our satisfaction. In addition to enjoying the wells, Isaac secured a choice bride (24:61-67). He gained her without doing anything. As he was meditating in the field, she came to him. Isaac was not a doing person; he was an enjoying person. His father and his servant did everything to secure a bride for him. Isaac did not even go to Rebekah; Rebekah came to him. In all of history I have never heard of another case in which the bride came to the groom. All Christian natural doings are just a type of supplanting, a type of heel holding. Never supplant or hold the heel of others. Rebekah is your portion and she will come. Before the foundation of the world, it was destined that Rebekah would be yours. Do you believe this? Do you dare to claim it? Isaac received his Rebekah simply by meditating in the field, not by doing anything. This is enjoyment.

GAINING TWIN SONS

After twenty years without having a child, Isaac gained twin sons (25:20-21, 26b). Did God not say in His promise that Isaac, the only seed of Abraham, would be the one in whom all the nations of the earth would be blessed? Suppose Isaac never had a son. How then could this promise be fulfilled? And if this promise were not fulfilled, how could God's purpose be accomplished? Thus, it was not only Isaac who needed a son, but also God who needed a seed out of Isaac. Because Isaac did not realize this for twenty years, God did not do anything. God had a need and intended to do something about it, but He required the cooperation from the human side. For twenty years Isaac was only enjoying, not caring about his need for a son. But after twenty years, he realized that he had such a need and that his need corresponded to God's need. Once he realized this, he prayed and God answered his prayer.

The same is true with us today. When we realize that our need corresponds to God's need and then pray accordingly, God will answer our prayer. Actually, His answer to our prayer is the fulfillment of His purpose. Our need must be God's need, and the prayer for our need should also be the prayer for God's need. When our need corresponds with God's and when we then pray for our need, God's need will be met also. When Isaac prayed for a child, whose need was greater—Isaac's or God's? Surely God's need was greater. Nevertheless, the greater need of God could only be fulfilled in the smaller need of Isaac. Only when man realizes his need and prays for it does God have the way to come in to fulfill His need. God has a purpose, and we have a need which corresponds to God's purpose. But God cannot do anything until we realize our need and pray about it. Then God will answer our prayer to meet our need for the fulfillment of His purpose. Eventually, Isaac had a son, Jacob, who not only fulfilled Isaac's need but also fulfilled God's eternal purpose. Out of Jacob came Christ, who brings in the church, the kingdom, and the New Jerusalem. All these eternal things came about through the meeting of Isaac's need, a need which corresponded with God's need.

Enjoyment is our destiny, and wherever we go there will be a well. But in the enjoyment of God's grace, we must render Him our human coordination that He may fulfill His eternal purpose through us. This means that our enjoyment of grace will never be in vain, for the enjoyment of grace on our side eventually becomes the fulfillment of God's purpose on His side.

RECEIVING A HUNDREDFOLD HARVEST
AND BECOMING GREAT

Isaac received a hundredfold harvest and became great (26:12-14). The word great in 26:13 means rich. Isaac "became great and continued to grow great until he became very great" (Heb.). He became rich by fulfilling the regular duty of sowing and through the Lord's blessing. This also was a matter of enjoyment, but this enjoyment was not on the proper standing. Isaac might have said to himself, "My standing must be right. If it were not right, how could the Lord have blessed me with all these riches?" But God might have said, "Isaac, you are settled here and have gained great riches, but I do not agree with your standing. I shall raise up the circumstances to force you to leave this place." May the Holy Spirit show us such a vivid picture here. On the one hand, there is the proper enjoyment; on the other hand, there is the improper standing. Even if we lack the proper standing, we may continue to have the enjoyment. But do not think that this enjoyment justifies your standing. As long as we have the enjoyment, our need is met. But for the fulfillment of God's eternal purpose, we need to get on the proper standing. Nevertheless, even if we are not on the proper standing, God still grants us His rich provision. This is wonderful. What a wonderful God! What a wonderful provision! We have been destined for the enjoyment. Even when we are wrong in our standing, we may still have the rich enjoyment. But God will not let us go. He will use our circumstances to bring us back to the proper standing that the fulfillment of His purpose might be realized.

FINDING THE "WELL OF LIVING WATER"

Before Isaac came back to Beer-sheba, he had enjoyment after enjoyment, grace upon grace. After receiving the hundredfold harvest, he found the "well of living water" and came into the "broad places," the "broad ways" (Rehoboth, 26:15-22). Although he had enjoyment in such a rich way, his standing was not right and he was forced to leave the broad ways and to come back to Beer-sheba.

COMING BACK TO BEER-SHEBA

When Isaac returned to Beer-sheba (26:23-33), the Lord immediately appeared to him, speaking to him and confirming His promise, saying, "I am the God of Abraham thy father: fear not, for I am with thee, and will bless thee, and multiply thy seed for my servant Abraham's sake" (26:24). Then, here in Beer-sheba Isaac began to have the proper testimony. He built an altar, called upon the name of the Lord, and pitched his tent (26:25). Here in Beer-sheba he had a life for the fulfillment of God's eternal purpose. Eventually, here in Beer-sheba the opposers were subdued (26:26-31). Beer-sheba is the right place, the place where we can have the proper standing, and the proper standing means a great deal both to God and to us. ▧

29

HAVING NATURAL WEAKNESS AS ABRAHAM AND LIVING IN THE NATURAL LIFE AS JACOB

Abraham journeyed from there toward the south country, and dwelt between Kadesh and Shur, and sojourned in Gerar. And Abraham said of Sarah his wife, She is my sister....

Genesis 20:1-2

And Isaac dwelt in Gerar. And the men of the place asked him of his wife; and he said, She is my sister...

Genesis 26:6-7

And the boys grew: and Esau was a cunning hunter, a man of the field; and Jacob was a plain man, dwelling in tents. And Isaac loved Esau, because he did eat of his venison: but Rebekah loved Jacob.

Genesis 25:27-28

Now Israel loved Joseph more than all his children....
And when his brethren saw that their father loved him more than all his brethren, they hated him.

Genesis 37:3-4

In the past two messages concerning Isaac, we have seen that he was the heir of grace and that he rested and enjoyed throughout his entire life. Now we must see that with this grace-enjoying person there were still the natural weakness and the natural life. It is difficult for us to understand this point. According to our natural, religious concept, we always think that if we are natural, we cannot have the enjoyment of grace. According to our religious concept, the enjoyment of grace depends upon how spiritual we are. In our teachings and exhortations, especially to our relatives and children, we say that in order to enjoy the grace of God we must be good, and that if we are not good, we are through with God's grace. Probably none of us has ever thought that participating in the grace of God does not depend upon our being spiritual. On the contrary, we all have thought that we must be spiritual in order to enjoy the grace of God.

Isaac was a model, a pattern, of the enjoyment of God's grace. In the whole Bible there is hardly another person who enjoyed grace as much as Isaac did. Throughout his entire life Isaac did nothing except enjoy the grace of God. His life was a grace-enjoying life. Nevertheless, in Isaac we see exactly the same natural weakness as we saw in Abraham. Furthermore, in Isaac we also see the natural life of Jacob. Like Jacob, Isaac lived in a natural way. Jacob loved his son Joseph according to his natural taste (37:3-4), and this caused trouble in the family. Joseph's brothers hated him because of his father's partial love for him. Isaac also loved Esau partially, loving him because he was a skillful hunter and could obtain the venison which Isaac loved (25:27-28). Thus, Esau was a father's boy. By this we see that Isaac and Jacob were the same as far as the natural life is concerned.

If you say that Isaac did not cheat anyone, I would point out that his wife Rebekah was his cheating helper. In a sense, Isaac differed from Jacob in the matter of supplanting, but this gap was filled by Rebekah. Every wife is a part of her husband; she is her husband's completion and perfection. Without Rebekah, Isaac probably would not have been an expert at cheating. But with Rebekah, he certainly became the same as Jacob. Jacob learned how to supplant from his supplanting mother, and his supplanting mother was the supplanting completion to his father Isaac. Therefore, in Isaac we see the natural life of Jacob.

Isaac was a grace-enjoying person. According to our natural concept, a person who has a natural weakness and who lives in the natural life can never enjoy the grace of God. This is our concept; it is not God's word. In the Bible, we cannot see that Isaac was very spiritual. He was a man who still had a natural weakness and who still lived in the natural life. Why then did he have such an enjoyment of God's grace? Simply because God had ordained it that way. With us Christians, there is the aspect of God's ordination. As we have already pointed out, it is our destiny to enjoy the grace of God. This destiny was preordained before the foundation of the world. Do not think that if you are spiritual, you are privileged to enjoy God's grace and that if you are not spiritual, you cannot enjoy His grace. This is a religious concept, and the Bible does not teach this. After hearing that enjoying grace does not depend upon our being spiritual, some may say, "If we don't need to be spiritual to enjoy God's grace, then let us be unspiritual." Do not say this. Neither being spiritual nor being unspiritual will help us to enjoy God's grace. It is entirely a matter of God's ordination, and it does not depend on what we are nor on what we can do. With us, there is the aspect of Isaac. We have been ordained by God to the enjoyment of grace. If we are spiritual, we shall not enjoy grace more, and if we are unspiritual we shall not miss the grace of God. But we should not say, "Let us do evil that good may come." Do not waste your time trying to be spiritual or trying to be unspiritual. Simply say, "O Lord, I worship You for Your ordination. You have ordained me to the enjoyment of grace." At the least, we all are a part of Isaac. In our being there is the aspect of having been ordained by God to the enjoyment of His grace.

When do you enjoy grace more—when you feel that you are spiritual and good in the eyes of God, or when you are down and feel that you are absolutely unworthy? I have enjoyed grace the most when I have been down. But we should not say, "Let us be down that we may enjoy grace the most." If you try to do this, it will not work. Again I say that it does not depend upon us but upon God's ordination. I hope that my word will encourage you neither to be spiritual nor to be unspiritual. Rather, I hope that it will encourage you to be nothing. But do not try to be nothing, for your trying is still something. If you could say, "I'll go home and forget everything," that would be wonderful.

In the record of Isaac's life we see a person who enjoyed God's grace in every way. Do you believe that a man who had such an enjoyment of God's grace could still have the natural weakness of lying in a substantial way? He lied in the way of sacrificing his wife. Perhaps we would say, "If I were such a person, I would never lie in that way." Do not say this. We may enjoy even more grace and then lie more substantially than Isaac did.

Consider your experience. Although you have never lied in sacrificing your wife, you have lied substantially to your wife. In my early years, I was much affected by religious concepts, believing that Christians, especially the so-called spiritual Christians, would never lie. Eventually, I discovered that Christians, including the so-called spiritual ones, also lie. Not only the worldly people lie; the Christians and the spiritual people also lie. This is the condition of the fallen race. What then shall we do? We should not do anything. God has selected us out of this fallen race, and His ordination has come to us. This does not mean that when we behave ourselves or become spiritual in the eyes of God, we shall then receive more grace. Although Isaac never tried to behave himself or to be spiritual, he continually enjoyed grace. I do not encourage you to be religious or to be unrelig- ious. I do not encourage you to be anything, for the enjoyment of God's grace does not depend upon our being spiritual.

Isaac wanted to bless his son Esau. However, he mixed the blessing with his natural taste. In 27:3 and 4, Isaac said to Esau, "Now there- fore take, I pray thee, thy weapons, thy quiver and thy bow, and go out to the field, and take me some venison; and make me savoury meat, such as I love, and bring it to me, that I may eat; that my soul may bless thee before I die." Isaac seemed to be saying, "Esau, before I die, I would like to eat venison one more time. If you get some veni- son for me, then I shall bless you." Here we see that Isaac mixed up God's blessing with his natural taste. Although we may wonder how such a person could bless others, Isaac did bless.

Isaac, who was not religious like we are, was not conscious of being unspiritual. Suppose you are a father who wants to give a bless- ing to one of his sons. I believe that you would be very cautious and alert, praying, fasting, and daring not to speak in the flesh nor according to your natural taste. If you were a Chinese brother, you certainly would not say to the son whom you are about to bless, "Son, go to Chinatown and get some Chinese food for me and then I'll bless you." No Chinese brother would dare to do this, because we are all so religiously conscious of being spiritual. We all would say, "Now that I am about to bless my son I must be with the Lord and not have my natural taste." Isaac, however, was bold, telling Esau, "Before I die I would like to eat venison once more. Get me the venison that I love and I'll bless you." Isaac was honest, saying, "My soul may bless thee" (27:4). What a mixture! Isaac, who continually enjoyed the grace of God, blessed blindly. But he blessed in faith, and his blessing was honored by God (Heb. 11:20).

When I read this portion of the Word as a young man, I was unable to understand how there could be so much mixture here. I said, "Isaac, what are you doing? If you want to eat venison, then don't talk about blessing. You shouldn't mix your natural taste with God's blessing. How can God honor a blessing that is mixed with your natural taste?" When Isaac plainly told Esau that if he would prepare venison for him he would bless him, he was not conscious of being religious. He was altogether outside of religion. There was no religion in his concept. If we had been there, we would have said, "Isaac, don't talk this way. If you want to have your natural taste, don't talk about God's blessing. God will never honor your blessing. Isaac, you are absolutely wrong." But Isaac would have said, "What are you talking about? I have never heard such religious talk. I don't have this concept. I have no religious consciousness whatsoever. I only know two things—that I want to satisfy my taste and that I want to bless my son. After I eat some meat, I shall bless my son. I don't know what it means to be spiritual or religious. I only know that I am the father, that he is my son, and that the greater always blesses the lesser." When I was young, I was much troubled about this, being unable to understand how Isaac, who enjoyed so much of God's grace, could still have the same natural weakness as Abraham and the same natural life as Jacob.

We need to see two points very clearly. Firstly, grace is not based upon what we are. Whether we are good or bad, spiritual or unspiritual, means nothing. Because God has ordained us to be the object of His grace, grace comes to us, and we cannot reject it. Secondly, as we have mentioned several times, Abraham, Isaac, and Jacob are not three separate persons in the experience of life but represent three aspects of the experience of one complete person. This is why in Isaac we can see both Abraham and Jacob. Isaac had the natural weakness of Abraham and the natural life of Jacob.

HAVING NATURAL WEAKNESS AS ABRAHAM

As we have seen, Isaac had the same natural weakness as Abraham (cf. 20:1-2, 11-13). Do you not have a natural weakness? Even the most spiritually conscious person has some natural weakness. What kind of weakness do you have? Although we all have some natural weakness, none of us can designate it. We know that we have such a weakness, but we do not know what it is. If you are certain that a particular matter is your natural weakness, that is not your weakness. Before Isaac was exposed in chapter twenty-six, he probably never realized that his natural weakness was the same as Abraham's. He might have thought that his weakness was one of many other things. But one day he went southward and his natural weakness was exposed.

By ourselves we can never know our natural weakness; it must be exposed. None of us is able to understand his own weakness. You yourself may not know your own natural weakness, but it is clear to everyone else because it has been exposed to them. Whoever would stay with you for a time would see your natural weakness. According to your religious concept, if you have some natural weakness, you should be through with grace. But God's grace is still with you. In the early days I also had this thought. But I have learned that grace does not depend upon what we are. Every object of divine grace has a weak point. Do not think that the Apostle Paul had no weakness. Peter, John, and Paul all had their weaknesses, but their weak points did not frustrate them from enjoying God's grace. Every one of us has his natural weakness. There has been only one person in history who had no natural weakness—Jesus Christ.

I am not encouraging you to be either spiritual or unspiritual, but I am encouraging you to be bold in the enjoyment of grace. Do not be deprived of the enjoyment of grace by your religious concept. Drop your concept and praise the Lord that you are the object of divine grace. Although we are unable to designate our natural weakness, we do know that we have some. Others, such as our wife, husband, or roommates, know what our weakness is. While others know, it is difficult for us to know. Some of us may not know our natural weakness until we see the Lord face to face. Praise the Lord that we are blind to our natural weakness. If we were not blind to our weakness, we would be frustrated from enjoying grace. While I am not encouraging you to keep your natural weakness, I am saying that it is good that we are unaware of it. When we are conscious of a certain weakness, our religious concepts frustrate us from the enjoyment of grace. But when we do not know our weakness, we only know to enjoy the grace of the Lord. In Genesis 26, Isaac's natural weakness was suddenly exposed. That exposure, however, did not frustrate him from the enjoyment of God's grace. In other words, the exposure of Isaac's natural weakness did not hinder him from trusting in God.

Isaac, leaving Beer-sheba, journeyed downward, southward, not to Egypt but to a place close to Egypt (26:1-2). God's intention was that His chosen people stay in the good land. Whenever the natural weakness of His people arose, they always went downward. We cannot find one instance in which God's people went upward, northward, when they were weak. The worst thing to do was to go downward to Egypt. This is what Abraham did (12:10). The second time Abraham went southward he only went as far as Philistia, the land of the Philistines (20:1). As Isaac, who was repeating Abraham's downward story, was going southward, God intervened and warned him, saying, "Go not down into Egypt; dwell in the land which I shall tell thee of" (26:2). Isaac's intention might have been to go down into Egypt, but God commanded him to dwell in the land of which He would tell him. Although Isaac did not stay in exactly the right place, he still had peace in enjoying God's grace. He was absolutely unconscious of being religious. How good it is to have no sense of being religious! However, once the enemy has injected something into our knowledge, it is very difficult to extract it. My burden in this message is to tell you that the enjoyment of God's grace does not depend upon our being religious. In Isaac we see a person who was not at all religious; yet he enjoyed the grace of God all the time.

Isaac not only did not stay in the right place; he also lied at the sacrifice of his wife (26:6-7) just as Abraham did. However, he and his wife were preserved by God's sovereign care (26:8-11). It was God's grace that kept him from the sacrifice of his wife.

LIVING IN THE NATURAL LIFE AS JACOB

In Isaac there was not only the natural weakness but also the natural life. He still lived in the natural life. He did not live a so-called spiritual life all the time. After Isaac prayed, God gave him two sons, Esau and Jacob. Isaac loved Esau because he was a skillful hunter and Isaac "did eat of his venison" (25:27-28). Isaac's love for his firstborn son was altogether in the natural life according to his natural taste, as was Jacob's love for Joseph (37:3-4). Since the husband took the lead to have a partial love, the wife followed. Esau, a "skillful hunter" (Heb.), was a father's boy, and Jacob, a "quiet man" who dwelt in tents (Heb.), was a mother's boy. Every mother loves a child who quietly stays around her. No mother would love a wild child who enjoys sports all day long. In Isaac's family, the father had a partial love for Esau, and the mother had a partial love for Jacob. What kind of life was this? Was it a spiritual life, a resurrection life? No, although it was not a sinful life, it was a natural life. We should not think that we are different, for every parent has some partial love. If you have several children, you will love one of them more than the others according to your taste, and all your children will know who is the object of your partial love. This partial love is not according to our spirit; it is according to our natural taste. We love a particular boy or girl because he or she suits our natural taste. This is the natural life.

The natural life always causes trouble. Out of this partial love in Isaac's family came the need of supplanting. Rebekah wanted her beloved son to receive the blessing. In chapter twenty-seven we see that she was very capable of supplanting (vv. 5-7). She taught Jacob how to supplant. In chapter thirty Jacob tricked his uncle Laban in the matter of the cattle (vv. 31-43). The principle is the same in chapter twenty-seven. Rebekah prepared savory meat and put goat skins on Jacob's hands and neck. When Isaac felt him, this caused him to say, "The voice is Jacob's voice, but the hands are the hands of Esau" (27:22). Here we see that Jacob was taught the supplanting skill by his mother, who was a part of his father. In a sense, the mother cheated the father, meaning that the second part of a person cheated the first part of the same person. All such family cheating is self-cheating. Eventually, everyone in the family was cheated. When I was reading this chapter, I said, "Rebekah, you thought you were smart. Actually you were stupid. Didn't you know that God had ordained Jacob to be the first? There was no need for you to help." Rebekah, who tried to help her son, lost him. Genesis does not tell us how long Rebekah lived. She might have died before Jacob returned from Laban's home. This means that Rebekah lost her son by cheating. Rebekah probably did not live to see her son Jacob again. She thought that she was helping him; actually, because of her supplanting, she lost him.

It is difficult to believe that a person like Isaac could still have such a natural weakness and still live in such a natural life. Isaac suffered because of his natural life (26:34-35; 27:41-46; 28:6-9). Although Isaac was always enjoying grace, there was an aspect of suffering in his life. Both Isaac and Rebekah suffered because they lived in a natural way, for Esau's wives were "a bitterness of spirit" to them (26:34-35, Heb.).

Because of the partial love in this family, Esau hated Jacob and wanted to kill him. When Rebekah heard of this, she told Jacob to flee to her brother Laban and to stay with him until Esau's anger had turned away. But Rebekah told Isaac another story (27:46). She seemed to be saying, "The wives of Esau have caused us so much bitterness of spirit that I could not bear to live if Jacob took such a wife. We should send him away to get a wife." Rebekah told the same thing in two different ways. Every wise wife does this, telling one story in two ways. Like many wives today, Rebekah lied to Isaac by telling the truth. Her intention was to send Jacob away, protecting him from Esau, but she did not tell Isaac of this. Rather, she said that she was tired of her Gentile daughters-in-law and that she did not want Jacob to have such a wife, suggesting to Isaac that they send Jacob away to take a wife from their own race. According to her intention, this was a lie; according to her speaking, however, it was the truth. This caused suffering.

While Isaac was enjoying grace, he was also suffering because of his living in the natural life. The natural life will not frustrate grace, but it will cause us to suffer. It will not decrease the amount of our grace, but it will increase our measure of suffering. As long as you have one aspect of your natural life, it will cause you to suffer. If you do not want to suffer, you should not live in the natural life. Do not practice your cleverness, exercise your wisdom to help God, or do anything in your natural life. This will only add to your suffering. It is better for us not to live in our natural life.

Although Isaac lived in his natural life, God was sovereign over all. In a sense, the natural life helped God's sovereignty. God had predestinated Jacob to have the birthright and to participate in the blessing of the firstborn. While Rebekah's supplanting caused her to suffer, it was sovereignly used by God to fulfill His purpose. Everything was under God's sovereignty for the accomplishment of His purpose. Therefore, we all can say, "Praise the Lord, whether I am good or bad, spiritual or unspiritual, God's purpose is being fulfilled. No matter what happens, I am under grace and in the enjoyment of grace." Nothing should frustrate us from the enjoyment of grace. Nevertheless, if we would avoid suffering, we should not live in the natural life.

NOT HAVING MUCH MATURITY IN LIFE

Isaac had some maturity in life, but not very much. Although he blessed, he blessed blindly (27:21-29). His blessing was according to his natural taste (27:1-4). He blessed blindly, not only physically but also spiritually, because he had been blinded by his natural taste. However, he did bless by faith (Heb. 11:20). He had said that his soul would bless, but eventually it was not his soul that blessed; it was his spirit that bestowed the blessing, and his blessing became a prophecy. No one can prophesy in the soul. If we would prophesy, we must be in our spirit. Thus, Isaac did bless in the spirit by faith.

Faith does not depend upon what we are; it depends upon what we see. Whenever you want to exercise faith, you should not look at yourself, at what you are, nor at your environment. You must look at what God is and to what He says. Then you will be able to exercise your faith in God and in His word. Isaac blessed by faith in this way. According to his situation, he was not qualified to have faith. But he did not consider what he was; he looked away to God and to God's promise, blessing his son by faith and in the spirit. If we would have faith, we must look away from ourselves, for if we look at ourselves, faith will disappear. Look unto God and see what He has spoken in His word. Then simply utter what God has already spoken. This is faith. Isaac blessed his son in this way.

DIED IN FAITH AT THE FULLNESS OF DAYS

Although there is no hint in the Bible that Isaac was very spiritual, he did not die in a miserable condition. He died in faith at the fullness of days (35:28-29). This is proved by the fact that his sons buried him, along with his wife Rebekah, in the cave of Machpelah (49:30-32). Before he died, he must have charged his sons to bury him in the cave of Machpelah, where Abraham and Sarah were buried. This proves that Isaac had the faith of Abraham.